Programming Windows® Services with Microsoft® Visual Basic® 2008

Michael Gernaey

PUBLISHED BY
Microsoft Press
A Division of Microsoft Corporation
One Microsoft Way
Redmond, Washington 98052-6399

Library of Congress Control Number: 2007939312

Printed and bound in the United States of America.

1 2 3 4 5 6 7 8 9   QWT   3 2 1 0 9 8

Distributed in Canada by H.B. Fenn and Company Ltd.

A CIP catalogue record for this book is available from the British Library.

Microsoft Press books are available through booksellers and distributors worldwide. For further information about international editions, contact your local Microsoft Corporation office or contact Microsoft Press International directly at fax (425) 936-7329. Visit our Web site at www.microsoft.com/mspress. Send comments to mspinput@microsoft.com.

Microsoft, Active Directory, MSDN, SQL Server, Visual Basic, Visual Studio, Win32, and Windows are either registered trademarks or trademarks of Microsoft Corporation in the United States and/or other countries. Other product and company names mentioned herein may be the trademarks of their respective owners.

The example companies, organizations, products, domain names, e-mail addresses, logos, people, places, and events depicted herein are fictitious. No association with any real company, organization, product, domain name, e-mail address, logo, person, place, or event is intended or should be inferred.

This book expresses the author's views and opinions. The information contained in this book is provided without any express, statutory, or implied warranties. Neither the authors, Microsoft Corporation, nor its resellers, or distributors will be held liable for any damages caused or alleged to be caused either directly or indirectly by this book.

Acquisitions Editor: Ben Ryan
Developmental Editor: Devon Musgrave
Project Editor: Valerie Woolley
Editorial Production: ICC Macmillan Inc.
Technical Reviewer: Anne Hills; Technical Review services provided by Content Master, a member of CM Group, Ltd.

Body Part No. X14-19032

To my loving wife, Brianne, who grants me the strength to do the impossible, the wisdom to realize it, the love to ensure its success, and the knowledge that I am never alone.

Contents at a Glance

Table of Contents

What do you think of this book? We want to hear from you!

Microsoft is interested in hearing your feedback so we can continually improve our books and learning resources for you. To participate in a brief online survey, please visit:

www.microsoft.com/learning/booksurvey/

Part IV Advanced Windows Services Topics

Introduction

Windows services are applications designed to run in the background on client or server systems on Microsoft platforms Windows XP, Windows Server 2003, and Windows Vista. Windows services are instrumental to the backbone of any infrastructure that runs Microsoft operating systems.

Each time you start your computer, dozens of individual services start to support the applications, hardware, kernel, and network communications that make Microsoft Windows the robust and scalable software platform that it is. Windows services can range from simple data managers to complex enterprise communication servers, allowing for a nearly unlimited number of concurrent users and systems. The Windows service architecture is a stable and viable solution for any small, medium, or large-scale business that requires customization in the business or IT department.

Microsoft provides a large number of operational and enterprise services covering printing, Web services, FTP services, mail services, network services, and streaming media with their server platform of operating systems.

Microsoft Visual Studio 2008 provides templates and wizards that allow developers to easily and effectively develop customized Windows services that can extend existing services or create enterprise solutions that can provide cross-domain, cross-network, and even worldwide solutions for the most complex situations. Microsoft Visual Studio 2008 offers you the ability to create these services, providing classes to easily add security and customization to your services.

Who This Book Is For

This book is recommended for any developer or IT professional who wants to create secure and customizable solutions for client server, data manipulation, and monitoring of network resources, both locally and remotely. Whether you are looking to produce a simple monitoring solution or a large number of data exchanges and want to understand how to create multi-threaded secured solutions, this book can help. Understanding how to create secure code and secure communications is a must for anyone looking to develop Windows services, and this book uses a variety of development, security, and notification techniques to show you how.

How This Book Is Organized

This book is divided into four sections. The first section provides an overview of creating basic single-threaded and multi-threaded Windows services. The second section describes how to interact with your service and create monitoring solutions that support administrative notifications.

The third section demonstrates how to communicate with multiple Internet protocols and create a server service allowing for client connections. The fourth section covers the advanced topics of scheduling, configuring, debugging, and securing your Windows service from the ground up.

System Requirements

You'll need the following hardware and software to run the code within the book:

- Windows Vista, Windows XP with Service Pack 2, or Windows Server 2003 with Service Pack 1
- Microsoft Visual Studio 2008 Beta 1 or later
- Microsoft SQL Server 2000 or later
- 600-MHz Pentium or compatible processor (1-GHz Pentium recommended)
- 192 MB of RAM (256 MB or more recommended)
- Video Monitor (800 x 600 or higher resolution) with at least 256 colors (1024 x 768 High Color 16-bit recommended)
- Microsoft mouse or compatible pointing device
- Microsoft Internet Information Services 6.0 or later
- Microsoft FTP Services (For SSL examples you will require an SSL-supported FTP service.)
- Microsoft SMTP Services

Find Additional Content Online

As new or updated material becomes available that complements your book, it will be posted online on the Microsoft Press Online Developer Tools Web site. The type of material you might find includes updates to book content, articles, links to companion content, errata, sample chapters, and more. This Web site will be available soon at *http://www.microsoft.com/learning/books/online/developer*, and will be updated periodically.

The Companion Web Site

This book features a companion Web site that makes available to you all the code used in the book. This code is organized by chapter, and you can download it from the companion site at this address: *http://www.microsoft.com/mspress/companion/9780735624337*

Support for This Book

Every effort has been made to ensure the accuracy of this book and the companion content. As corrections or changes are collected, they will be added to a Microsoft Knowledge Base article.

Microsoft Press provides support for books and companion content at the following Web site:

http://www.microsoft.com/learning/support/books

Questions and Comments

If you have comments, questions, or ideas regarding the book or the companion content, or questions that are not answered by visiting the site just mentioned, please send them to Microsoft Press via e-mail to

mspinput@microsoft.com
Or via postal mail to
Microsoft Press
Attn: Programming Windows Services with Microsoft Visual Basic 2008 Editor
One Microsoft Way
Redmond, WA 98052-6399

Please note that Microsoft software product support is not offered through the address above.

Part I
Defining Windows Services

Chapter 1
Writing Your First Service in Visual Basic 2008

Note Those of you who have already written services in previous versions of Visual Studio, such as Visual Studio 2005, can skip this chapter.

At some point, every developer faces the dilemma of how to implement a solution, or more important, how to architect a solution based on a given problem. To help resolve some of these factors, a developer has to be able to identify not only the issue or problem statement, but also the situational factors that make one solution better than another.

In many cases, Windows Services—which has existed on most of the Microsoft operating system platforms for more than 10 years—is used in a vast number of these solutions. Microsoft implement a large number of services inherent to any operating system, from Windows 98—which has long been unsupported—to the latest release, Windows Vista.

The allure of Windows Services for many is that it allows the developer to create anything from a simple data mining application to an extremely complicated, multi-user, multi-tier enterprise solution. You have no direct limitation on what you can do with services; however, determining whether a service is right for you still requires some diligence. Just because you *can* write a service does not mean you *should* write a service.

This chapter focuses on the steps required to create a simple Windows Service using the Visual Basic 2008 Windows Service Template in Microsoft Visual Studio 2008. Future chapters will extend this service to accomplish much more complex business solutions.

Generating the Project

With the Visual Studio 2008 Visual Basic templates, you can quickly and easily get started with the first service. Begin by opening Visual Studio 2008. If you are launching Visual Studio for the first time, you can select the Visual Basic Settings in the Settings dialog box that appears automatically if you want to set help filters and keyboard shortcuts to Visual Basic.

From the File menu, select New Project. For the Project Type, expand Visual Basic and then select Windows. In the Templates pane, select Windows Service. In the Name text box, type **Tutorials**. Verify that you have the .NET 3.5 SDK selected in the drop-down box above the Templates pane, and then click OK.

> **Note**   If you are using the Express version of Visual Studio Basic, the Windows Service template may not be available to you. You can look on Microsoft's MSDN site for templates or download the Professional version.

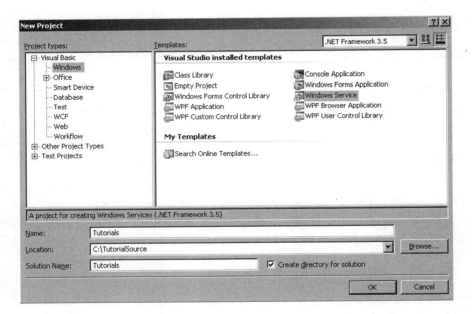

In the Solution Explorer, you will see Tutorials, under which you will then see My Project and then Service1.vb. Service1.vb holds the wizard-generated code that holds the required components, methods, and entry points to create and compile your service. Currently it is empty except for stubs for the *<OnStart>* and *<OnStop>* methods.

Renaming Our Project Files

Now that we have wizard-generated code ready, we want to properly identify the service and rename the wizard-generated labels. Service1.vb represents the service. For this reason, rename the Service1.vb file **Tutorials.vb**. At this point, the solution, the project, and the service should all be named Tutorials.

 Note   If the solution is not visible, go to Tools, Options, Projects, and then Solutions. Select the check box labeled Always Show Solution.

Understanding the Wizard Code

Let's start by reviewing the code generated by the wizard. Right-click the Tutorials.vb file and select View Code. You will see the class definition along with two methods, <*OnStart*> and <*OnStop*>. They are both blank, but they are both required for your service to run properly.

```
Service1                                             (Declarations)

Public Class Service1

    Protected Overrides Sub OnStart(ByVal args() As String)
        ' Add code here to start your service. This method should set things
        ' in motion so your service can do its work.
    End Sub

    Protected Overrides Sub OnStop()
        ' Add code here to perform any tear-down necessary to stop your service.
    End Sub

End Class
```

The <*OnStart*> Method

The <*OnStart*> method represents the entry point into your service. This is what the underlying Service Control Manager (SCM) will call when the user clicks Start on the Control Panel Services screen. You will notice that <*OnStart*> has one argument. This argument contains the parameters defined in the Administrative Tools, Services, Service Properties. This is where the application is started and also where we will later add functionality that will make the service useful.

 Note   The Service Control Manager is the centralized administrative authority over how services are installed, configured, and ultimately run.

The <*OnStop*> Method

The <*OnStop*> method represents the exit point of your service. This is where we want to add cleanup code. It will be called when the user clicks Stop on the Services tab under Administrative Tools.

Other Events

Services support more than just the *<OnStart>* and *<OnStop>* events. Two other very important events are *<OnPause>* and *<OnContinue>*.

<OnPause> allows a user to temporarily suspend operation of your service without shutting it down. At times you might want to debug your service or you might need to perform an action on a server that your service relies on. Allowing it to run while you perform your maintenance could be detrimental. If your service supports *<OnPause>*, you should implement the method to react to the pause event.

To use the *OnPause* and *OnContinue* methods, you must first enable these features in your service by following these steps:

1. Double-click Tutorials.vb in the Solution Explorer to open the Tutorials.vb Design window.

2. Left-click in the Design window to view the Tutorials.vb Design Properties tab.

3. Set the CanPauseAndContinue property to True.

> **Note**   If you do not see the Properties tab you can select View from the menu bar and then select the Properties Window.

Adding *<OnPause>*

In the Solution Explorer, right-click the Tutorials.vb and select View Code.

Below the current *<OnStop>* method, type **Protected Overrides Sub *<OnPause>*** and select Enter. As you type this, you should notice that the options for different methods to override appear in the IntelliSense.

You will notice that a single piece of code, `<MyBase.OnPause()>`,will appear in your method definition. This allows your service to call the base class just in case you have implemented some general code in it. Since we have not, you can remove this code by highlighting it and deleting it. We will not be adding any code to this method at this time.

Adding *<OnContinue>*

<OnContinue> is the counterpart to *<OnPause>*. Once a service is paused it will need to be resumed. This is where *<OnContinue>* comes in. As we did with *<OnPause>*, we will add this method by typing in the following code below the *<OnPause>* method: **Protected Overrides Sub OnContinue.** Now click Enter. Once again you will see its implementation appear with the `<Mybase.OnContinue()>` code. Again, merely highlight this and delete it.

Now we will create the code to make the service useful.

Writing Our First Code

Now we need to modify the service so that it does something useful. Initially this will not be a major change, but later on we will be expanding the service.

In Visual Studio, click the Tutorials.vb tab and you will again see the *<OnStart>* and *<OnStop>* code. We will modify both methods to write an entry into the Application log.

This simple application demonstrates the process of creating a service in Visual Basic 2008; modifying the design template provided by Visual Studio 2008; and creating, building, and then installing the service.

Click the *<OnStart>* method. Under the comments section, we'll first add an error handler:

```
Try
Catch ex As Exception
End Try
```

You should never leave your code unprotected from exceptions, especially in a service where the message box that appears when an unhandled exception occurs cannot be processed without special implementation.

You use a Try/Catch block to capture exceptions that are thrown by your code if it generates custom exceptions, or to catch exceptions thrown by internal .NET classes. The important thing to notice here is that we are capturing an exception called Exception. In Visual Basic terms, this means any exception—or in other words, a catchall. Although using a catchall here is fine, you should always code your applications to catch only the specific exceptions that you can expect and then do what you need to based on that specific exception. We will deal more with this as we progress.

Modifying the *<OnStart>* Method

In the *<OnStart>* method we are going to write an event to the Application log when the service is told to start the "Hello, World" of beginner services. We plan to implement other code in this method in the future, so this will help you understand how to standardize code in your services.

Note   A service should not perform a large amount of work in the *<OnStart>* method. It must return within 30 seconds or the Service Control Manager will time out. In this example, the work is minimal, but in the future, as the service extends, we will avoid adding too much overhead to this method.

In Listing 1-1 we will modify the *<OnStart>* method to log an event as the user starts the service. If there is an error, we will do nothing for now. If the attempt to write the startup message fails, most likely an attempt to write a failure message to the Application log would also fail.

Listing 1-1   Modifications to *<OnStart>* to write to the Application log.

```
Try
    Dim StartLog As EventLog = New EventLog ("Application")
    StartLog.Source = "Tutorials"
    StartLog.WriteEntry("Tutorials Starting", EventLogEntryType.Information, 1000)
    StartLog.Dispose()
    Catch ex As Exception
    'We Catch the Exception
    'to avoid any unhandled errors
    'and we will stop the service if any occur here
    Me.Stop()
End Try
```

> **Note**   In this book, bolded lines within listings show new functionality added to code already shown or created. Listings without bolded lines contain all new functionality.

The preceding code creates an instance of the *EventLog* class, sets the source to Tutorials, writes an Entry, and then disposes of the EventLog instance. When this happens, the method returns and the Service Control Manager assumes the service is running.

You will note that in Catch we aren't actually doing anything. For now this is okay. However, in the future—and for real services—you may well want to shut down the service if this method fails, thereby limiting the work load of the *<OnStart>*.

Modifying the *<OnStop>* Method

In the *<OnStop>* method, shown in Listing 1-2, we are going to modify the method to write a single event to the Application log when the user stops the service. As with the *<OnStart>* method, we won't try to log a failure of the service to write the stop message.

Listing 1-2   Modifications to *<OnStop>* to write to the Application log.

```
Try
    Dim StopLog As EventLog = New EventLog ("Application")
    StopLog.Source = "Tutorials"
    StopLog.WriteEntry("Tutorials Stopping", EventLogEntryType.Information, 1001)
    StopLog.Dispose()
Catch ex As Exception

    'We Catch the Exception
    'to avoid any unhandled errors
    'since we are stopping and
    'logging an event is what failed
    'we will merely write the output
    'to the debug window
    Debug.WriteLine("Error stopping service: " + ex.ToString())
End Try
```

You will notice that the only real difference here between *<OnStart>* and *<OnStop>* is that we are sending a different message with a different EventID so that we can easily distinguish what the service is doing and validate that the code is working properly.

Modifying the *<OnPause>* Method

Once again in the *<OnPause>* method (shown in Listing 1-3) we are going to modify the method to write a single event to the Application log when the user pauses the service. As with *<OnStart>* we won't try to log a failure of the service to write the pause message.

Listing 1-3   Modifications to *<OnPause>* to write to the Application log.

```vb
Try
    Dim PauseLog As EventLog = New EventLog ("Application")
    PauseLog.Source = "Tutorials"
    PauseLog.WriteEntry("Tutorials Pausing", EventLogEntryType.Information, 1002)
    StopLog.Dispose()
Catch ex As Exception

    'We Catch the Exception
    'to avoid any unhandled errors
    'since we are pausing and
    'logging an event is what failed
    'we will merely write the output
    'to the debug window
    Debug.WriteLine("Error pausing service: " + ex.ToString())
    Me.Stop()
End Try
```

Modifying the *<OnContinue>* Method

Finally, in the *<OnContinue>* method (shown in Listing 1-4) we are going to modify the method to write a single event to the Application log when the user continues the service after it has been paused. As with *<OnStart>* we won't try to log a failure of the service to write the continue message.

Listing 1-4   Modifications to *<OnContinue>* to write to the Application log.

```vb
Try
    Dim ContinueLog As EventLog = New EventLog ("Application")
    ContinueLog.Source = "Tutorials"
    ContinueLog.WriteEntry("Tutorials Continuing", EventLogEntryType.Information, 1003)
    StopLog.Dispose()
Catch ex As Exception

    'We Catch the Exception
    'to avoid any unhandled errors
    'since we are resuming and
    'logging an event is what failed
    'we will merely write the output
    'to the debug window
    Debug.WriteLine("Error resuming service: " + ex.ToString())
    Me.Stop()
End Try
```

Making the Service Installable

Currently the service is not in an installable state. We have to add the proper components to allow the .NET Framework to install the service and make it compatible with the Win32 subsystem. In the Solution Explorer, right-click Tutorials.vb and select View Designer.

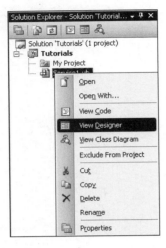

In the Toolbox, expand the Components section and then drag a ServiceController onto the Tutorials.vb design surface.

 Note   If you do not see the Toolbox, click Toolbox on the View menu.

After you add the control, you will see it on the designer surface as ServiceController1.

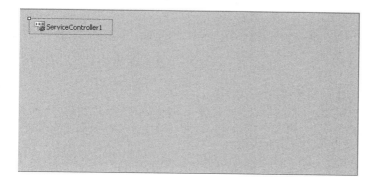

Setting the Service Properties

Right-click ServiceController1 and select Properties. In the properties window, click Service Name and type **Tutorials.** This name will be listed on the Administrative Tools, Services page. Save the project.

Double-click Tutorials.vb to open the Design window. Right-click anywhere in the gray window and select Add Installer. You should now see the ServiceInstaller1 control.

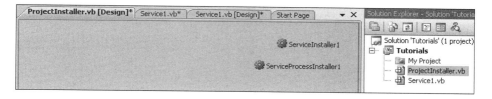

Right-click ServiceInstaller1 and select Properties. In the Properties window, type **Tutorials** for the Service Name.

Note   The service name is used when issuing net start and net stop commands from the Command Prompt command line.

For the Description property type **Tutorials Chapter 1**. For the DisplayName property type **Tutorials Chapter 1.** This is the name you will see in the service list.

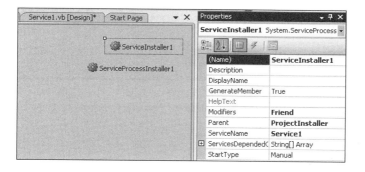

You will see the Description property listed in the Description column of the Control Panel\Services administrator console. You will see the DisplayName property in the Name column of the Control Panel\Services administrator console. You will not see the short name or the service name.

Setting the Startup Options

Right-click the ServiceProcessInstaller1 object and select Properties. For the Account property select LocalSystem. In Chapter 3, "Services and Security," I will cover the different options for the service startup account and the security impact on your service.

Additional Configuration Options

To better secure the service, we will set some of the optional security settings available to us in Visual Studio.

Adding a Signature Key File

It is important to protect your application as well as make it safe for others to use. Select Tutorial Properties from the project menu, and then click the Signing tab. Click Sign The Assembly. Select the drop-down box and choose New. Type in **Tutorials** as the key file.snk name and type in **Tutorials** for the password.

Adding Security-Specific Settings

After you set up the signature file, click the Security tab. Enable the default security settings by selecting the Enabled ClickOnce Security Settings check box. Save your settings and close the Properties window.

Building, Installing, and Deploying

Now that we have written the code and created installer components that will allow us to use the .NET Framework to install the service, we need to save and build the project.

Select the Save All option. Visual Studio displays the Save Project dialog box. In the Name text box, type **Tutorials**. Click Save.

You have multiple ways to build the project. You can right-click the project and choose Build. Or you can choose Build from the menu and click Build Solution. You will be able to determine whether your project's build was successful by looking at the status bar in the bottom left corner of the IDE. If the build failed, review the error list and correct the errors in the build.

After you build the project successfully, it is time to deploy it.

Creating Your Service Storage Location

Open Windows Explorer, and navigate to the Tutorials\Bin\Release directory. Copy the pdb and exe files to c:\temp. If this path does not exist, you can create it, or you can use whatever path you prefer. However, c:\temp is the path I will use in this example. After you copy the files, open the Visual Studio 2008 Command Window by selecting Start, selecting Run, typing **cmd** at the prompt, and clicking Enter. Type **cd c:\temp** to switch to the c:\temp directory. Type **installutil tutorials.exe** to install the service. If this does not work, read the next section to ensure that you have the proper configuration for the installation utilities.

Verifying That You Have .NET 2.0 Installed

At the command prompt you opened in the previous section, type **installutil Tutorials.exe**. This will run the .NET installutil utility, which will register your service. If you happen to have any other version of the framework installed, the incorrect installutil might be in the current path environment variables. Therefore, when you attempt to register the new service you get an error. You can easily figure out which version of the Framework is installed by typing **installutil** at the command prompt, and reading the version from the top of the output in the Command Prompt window. At the very top of the output you will see which version of installutil was executed.

If the incorrect version is in the path, your installation will fail. To remedy this, you can either run installutil from the Framework\2.0V directory or you can add the proper path for the 2.0V Framework into your environment variables. After you do this you will need to close the command prompt. When you reopen a new Command Prompt window, you will utilize the proper installutil.

 Note   In Windows Vista, you will need administrative privileges to install the service using the installutil.exe framework utility.

If you do not have the Framework 2.0 installed at all, you can download the different framework versions from the Microsoft Update Web site.

Verifying That Your Service Is Installed

After your service is installed, you can go to the Administrative Tools | Services screen and see the service Tutorials Display Name, with a description of Tutorials. In Windows Vista and Windows XP, click Start, click Control Panel, click Administrative Tools, and then click Services. In Windows Server 2003, click Start, click All Programs, click Administrative Tools, and then click Services.

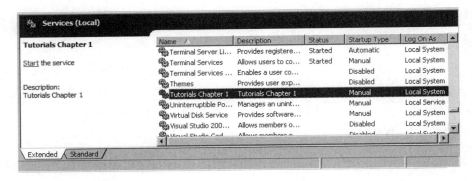

Right-click the service and select Properties.

<OnStart> Message

Click Start, click Control Panel, click Administrative Tools, and then click Event Viewer.I In the Application log, you should see the EventID 1000 with a Source of Tutorials. Double-click the event and you will see Tutorials Starting. This, of course, is the information we typed in the *<OnStart>* code.

Now let's test the rest of the events.

<OnPause> Message

On the Services Control Panel, right-click the service and select Pause. In the Application log, you should see your EventID 1002 event with the *<OnPause>* message. The actual code does not pause the service. We are merely demonstrating the ability to implement and use this event, which we will use in future chapters.

<OnContinue> Message

After you have validated the *<OnPause>* event, right-click the service again and choose Resume. You will notice that the only options you have are Stop, Resume, and Restart. At this point you should see your EventID 1003 event with the *<OnContinue>* message in the Application log.

<OnStop> Message

Click the service and select Stop. The Service Control Manager will call your *<OnStop>* method. In the event viewer you will see the EventID 1001, which is the Tutorials Stopping event.

This concludes the creation of the first service. Although it is a simple service, it gives you a basic idea of how to create and release a service developed in Visual Basic 2008.

Summary

- Microsoft Visual Basic 2008 has templates and wizards to help create services that run under Microsoft XP, Windows 2000, Windows Server 2003, and Windows Vista.

- Microsoft Visual Basic 2008 is a powerful and robust development language used to create scaleable enterprise solutions and services.

- Microsoft Visual Basic 2008 comes in several versions and licensing options. To find out more, please visit the following Microsoft product links:

  - *http://msdn.microsoft.com/vstudio/*
  - *http://msdn.microsoft.com/vbasic/*

Chapter 2
Expanding Your Service with Threads

In the previous chapter we created a simple project using the Microsoft Visual Basic Wizard and templates for Windows Services. Although we were able to install and run the service, it was not very useful—except for demonstration purposes.

You may remember that I said we wanted to avoid doing a large amount of work in the *<OnStart>* method. But if we aren't going to do the work there, where do we do it? This is where *threads* come in. Threads are like mini-processes within the service. Threads allow you to perform multiple actions at the same time within the same application or service.

To determine whether your service requires threads—or how many threads it requires—you have to understand threads a little better. Those of you who already understand how threads work—not just the concept—can skip this section.

Cleaning Up the Service from the Previous Chapter

Before we continue much farther, it is important to note that in many cases we will be continuing the code from the previous chapter. To do this successfully, you should remove the service instance from the previous chapter when you start the next chapter. To uninstall the Tutorials service, open a Visual Studio Command Prompt window and switch to the c:\temp directory. Type **installutil tutorials.exe /u** and press Enter. If the service is still installed, you will see that it has successfully been stopped and uninstalled. If it was not installed, a failure occurs. If you are in the wrong directory, you will receive an error. If you inadvertently deleted the service from the temp directory before you removed it, don't worry. Just rebuild your Chapter 1 code and then remove it.

Understanding Threads

Every application or service has at least one thread. Although the service will usually have much more than just one thread, it has to have at least one thread to perform any work. When an application (or in this case, a service) starts, its primary thread is fired up and begins processing messages from the system. These messages can be mouse clicks, keyboard input, custom events, operating system alerts, and more.

The service we are working with in this book has a primary thread called by the Service Control Manager (SCM). Remember that the SCM states that your service is running only if your <OnStart> method returns within 30 seconds of the start request. Imagine, however, if you only used the primary thread to do work. When <OnStart> is called, you have potentially a lot of code running that would prevent the <OnStart> method from completing in 30 seconds. Therefore the SCM reports back to the user that the service did not start successfully.

With threads, not only can we perform work within the service, but we can also allow the service's primary thread to perform its primary function—coordinating with the SCM through exposed methods such as <OnStart> and <OnStop>.

For example, suppose you write a game. The game won't perform very well if you expect to draw a large number of graphical aspects at the same time. Like your service, these games require separate threads to perform much of this work.

Determining How Many Threads to Create

You have already been exposed to the minimal integration thread between the SCM and the service, which is the primary SCM thread. For any decent service or real-world application, you will need at least one more thread, which will perform the work while your main thread waits for events triggered by the user.

> **Note**   You can trigger a <ServiceMethod> that is exposed to the SCM, within your service, but this kind of method is normally triggered by the user through the Administrative Tools, Control Panel, Services panel utility.

The question of how many threads to use is a tricky one. Creating too many threads is dangerous and cumbersome—not only from a coding perspective, but also from an administrative and support perspective. You have to understand that when you add threads, you add complexity to your service or application because of threads' effects on memory, CPU, and other resources.

Thread Synchronization

Many applications and services are written to access data or resources. The developer might want to write code that has multiple threads that can access or share this data at the same time.

Microsoft SQL Server 2005 is a great example, allowing multiple users while sharing data among them. Imagine only allowing one connection and one thread to the entire database system at a time. Ouch!

But what if you were sharing data with dozens of users and all of them tried to update the same record at the same time? This is just not possible—the system has no way to determine how to resolve this situation. Developers must synchronize the order of access to shared data and resources and thereby protect the system from catastrophic anomalies.

Before you determine exactly how many threads you may need or if you need to synchronize your threads (which takes much more effort), you must determine the actions and results you expect to accomplish as well as the data and/or resources required to produce the desired result. If you access other .NET classes or components, it is very important to read up on those components to determine their thread-safe capabilities, which will be defined in the Microsoft Developer Network documentation for Visual Studio 2008. Many are only thread-safe when created as static or shared, depending on the language you create your service in, which will also be specified in MSDN.

Creating Threads

In this chapter we will continue to use code from Chapter 1. The first thing we must do is tell the project that we will be using threads. Visual Basic 2008 supports native threads, which were not supported in earlier versions of Visual Basic.

At the top of the Tutorials.vb file we need to add another import for the .NET *Threading* class, shown in Listing 2-1.

Listing 2-1   Threading Namespace import statement.
```
Imports System.Threading
```

This allows the service to use the classes within the Threading namespace directly, without having to define the namespace for each type declaration. Initially we will only create one thread. Remember, however, that by default the service already has a primary thread. We will use the new thread as a worker thread. Remember also that services are not required to have any specific number of threads—or any extra threads at all. However, to make a service robust we need to use threads that allow us greater control over the tasks required by the service.

Thread Methods

First we must create a thread method, which is used as the starting point of a thread. When you create a thread, it is assigned to a thread method. This method will be used by the thread when it starts. This code can be used by any number of threads. However, the thread itself is isolated, and does not have direct access to other methods or class data members unless they are shared.

The New Code

For this example we will be adding some very simple threading code. The code will write an event into the event log database similar to the way we did in Chapter 1. However, we will use the new thread method to perform the work and we will use the current *<OnStop>* code to clean up the thread and specify that the service is shutting down.

Thread Funtion Code

The first thing we must do is create the thread function or method. In the Tutorials.vb code file, create the method shown in Listing 2-2.

Listing 2-2   Simple thread function.

```
Private Sub ThreadFunc()
    Try
    Catch tab as ThreadAbortException
    Catch ex as Exception
    Finally
    End try
End Sub
```

In this example, I am creating a method called *<ThreadFunc>*. As I mentioned, threads can only access shared data members in a class or must be passed the information directly. In this example, I intentionally do not use what is called an overloaded *parameterized* thread method. I will be using the parameterized method in future chapters. We are going to make a change to the existing code, by adding a log event method that will allow us to write information to the event log but can also be called from the thread.

One important thing to note in the *<ThreadFunc>* method's Try/Catch block is that there are two exception handlers. The second handler catches an exception called Exception. This is a catchall: It will catch any unhandled or thrown exceptions not caught by a previous handler.

The first handler catches an exception called ThreadAbortException. When you want to clean up a thread, your only option is to abort the thread. (I'll discuss this further later in the chapter.) When you abort the thread, it will throw this exception, which allows you to catch the error and perform cleanup before the thread is exited.

The last handler you will see is Finally, which is always called in a Try/Catch scenario, whether an exception occurs or not. Finally allows you to clean up anything you want to clean up before you exit the thread—or potentially before you reach this code again if it is in a loop.

Note   To ensure garbage collection of objects created in this thread, you have to understand scope. If you create an object after the Try definition, you cannot clean it up in the Catch or Finally blocks. You must define them outside this scope first.

Event-Logging Code

To properly use event-logging code, we must add an Imports statement under the threading import, as shown in Listing 2-3.

Listing 2-3   Import to interact with event log database and debug .NET classes.
```
Imports System.Diagnostics
```

Now we can create an event logging procedure, shown in Listing 2-4.

Listing 2-4   Shared method for event log database entry creation.
```
Private Shared Sub WriteLogEvent(ByVal pszMessage As String, _
ByVal dwID As Long, ByVal iType As EventLogEntryType, _
ByVal pszSource As String)
  Try
    Dim eLog As EventLog = New EventLog("Application")
    eLog.Source = pszSource
    Dim eInstance As EventInstance = New EventInstance(dwID, 0, iType)
    Dim strArray() As String
    ReDim strArray(1)
    strArray(0) = pszMessage
    eLog.WriteEvent(eInstance, strArray)
    eLog.Dispose()
  Catch ex As Exception
    'We cannot log an event above
    'So we will skip attempting
    'to write this error in the log
    Debug.WriteLine(ex.ToString())
  End Try
End Sub
```

The preceding method is defined as being shared, which means that we can access this method from any instance of or reference to this class, even from a non-shared or static thread method. The <WriteLogEvent> will write an event to the Application log. If an exception is generated, we will ignore it for now, because if we can't write to the event log, we can't do much else, except maybe log to a flat file or a database.

The code in Listing 2-4 uses the *WriteEvent* method, which uses the more up-to-date version of the .NET *EventLog* method. You will notice that I am using the *EventInstance* class. This is the more accurate approach to writing events that support the InstanceId property (compared to the older EventID property).

Now that we have an event logging function, let's update the <OnStop> and <OnStart> methods.

Updating the <*OnStart*> Method

As shown in Listing 2-5, we want to change the current <*OnStart*> method code to use the new <*WriteLogEvent*> method

Listing 2-5   Modifications to <*OnStart*> method to use the <*WriteLogEvent*> method.

```
Dim StartLog As EventLog = New EventLog("Application")
StartLog.Source = "Tutorials"
StartLog.WriteEntry("Tutorials Starting", EventLogEntryType.Information,
 1000)
StartLog.Dispose()
```

Replace the code in Listing 2-5 with the following:

```
WriteLogEvent("Tutorials Starting", 1000, EventLogEntryType.Information,
 "Tutorials")
```

This code allows the <*OnStart*> method to call the newly created shared method and to write to the event log. This makes the <*OnStart*> code cleaner. Next we must update the <*OnStop*> method.

Updating the <*OnStop*> Method

Listing 2-6 shows the current <*OnStop*> method.

Listing 2-6   Modifications to the <*OnStop*> method to use the <*WriteLogEvent*> method.

```
Dim StopLog As EventLog = New EventLog("Application")
StopLog.Source = "Tutorials"
StopLog.WriteEntry("Tutorials Stopping", EventLogEntryType.Information,
 1001)
StopLog.Dispose()
```

Replace the code in Listing 2-6 with the following code:

```
WriteLogEvent("Tutorials Stopping", 1001,
EventLogEntryType.Information, "Tutorials")
```

Updating the <*OnPause*> Method

Listing 2-7 shows the current <*OnPause*> method.

Listing 2-7   Modifications to the <*OnPause*> method to use the <*WriteLogEvent*> method.

```
Dim StopLog As Event log database = New EventLog("Application")
StopLog.Source = "Tutorials"
StopLog.WriteEntry("Tutorials Pausing", EventLogEntryType.Information,
 1001)
StopLog.Dispose()
```

Replace the code in Listing 2-7 with the following code:

```
WriteLogEvent("Tutorials Pausing", 1002, EventLogEntryType.Information,
 "Tutorials")
```

Updating the *<OnContinue>* Method

Listing 2-8 shows the current *<OnContinue>* method.

Listing 2-8 Modifications to the *<OnContinue>* method to use the *<WriteLogEvent>* method.

```
Dim StopLog As Event log database = New EventLog("Application")
StopLog.Source = "Tutorials"
StopLog.WriteEntry("Tutorials Continuing",
EventLogEntryType.Information, 1003)
StopLog.Dispose()
```

Replace the code in Listing 2-8 with the following code:

```
WriteLogEvent("Tutorials Continuing", 1003, _
 EventLogEntryType.Information, "Tutorials")
```

Updating the Thread Method

Now we can add code to the *<ThreadFunc>* method, which will make the thread useful and demonstrate its ability to communicate with the shared *<WriteLogEvent>* method.

Listing 2-9 shows what the entire method code will look like.

Listing 2-9 *Thread* method code with event-logging support.

```
Private Sub ThreadFunc()
Try
  WriteLogEvent("Thread Function Information - " + Now.ToString, 1005, _
 EventLogEntryType.Information, "Tutorials")
Catch tab As ThreadAbortException '
Catch ex As Exception
  WriteLogEvent("Thread Function Error - " + Now.ToString, 1005, _
 EventLogEntryType.Error, "Tutorials")
End Try

End Sub
```

The code shown in Listing 2-9 will attempt to write an event to the Application log. In the event of an exception, the code again tries to write an event to the Application log. I have added this code only for demonstration purposes so that you can see how TheadAbortException is raised. However, here we are using another method to make the call and that method has its own error handlers, so no unhandled exceptions should occur here.

Executing the Thread

Once all the code is in place, we have to create a thread, assign it to use the thread method, and then start the thread. Threads have several properties, which I will describe in this section.

Note Remember that we are not using a parameterized thread for this example. Therefore the event log entry contains a static message.

Because the desired functionality of the service is to have the *<OnStart>* method do minimal work and then return back to the SCM, we will modify the *<OnStart>* method to create an instance of a thread, assign it to the thread method, set the priority, and then execute or start the thread. Once these steps have been completed, the thread will write to the Application log its standard started message and return control back to the SCM. Because we create the thread in its own space, the *<OnStart>* method is not blocked by its creation or the work it performs. Therefore, minimal time is required to set up and execute a thread.

Updating *<OnStart>*

We need to update the *<OnStart>* method to create and run a thread that will execute the new *<ThreadFunc>* code. Listing 2-10 shows what the finished method should look like.

Listing 2-10 Updated *<OnStart>* method with thread support.

```
Protected Overrides Sub OnStart(ByVal args() As String)
'Add code here to start your service. This method should set things
'in motion so your service can do its work.
  Try
    Dim tmpThread As New Thread(AddressOf ThreadFunc)
    tmpThread.Name = "Tutorials Worker Thread"
    tmpThread.Priority = ThreadPriority.Normal
    tmpThread.Start()
    WriteLogEvent("Tutorials Starting", 1000, _
EventLogEntryType.Information, "Tutorials")
  Catch ex As Exception
    'We Catch the Exception
    'to avoid any unhandled errors
    'and we will stop the service if any occur here
    Me.Stop()
  End Try
End Sub
```

Once you have completed implementing the changes to the *<OnStart>*, save and build the project.

Install and Test Your Service

Copy the tutorials.exe from the bin\Release directory to the c:\temp directory, replacing the Tutorials.exe we created in Chapter 1. Open a Visual Studio Command Prompt window and switch to the c:\temp directory. Type **installutil tutorials.exe** and press Enter. After the service installs correctly, open the Services control panel utility by clicking Start, clicking Administrative Tools, clicking Control Panel, and then clicking Services. Then start the Tutorials service by right-clicking it and selecting Start. Using the Event Viewer, you will see the events from the *<OnStart>* and *<ThreadFunc> methods*. Stop the service and you will now see the event from the *<OnStop>* method.

Note In subsequent chapters, I won't explain how to install and remove your service—I will simply indicate when you need to do so.

What Is Thread Cleanup?

We have now expanded the code so that we can call methods on the class and/or code within thread functions. However, we have not yet made it possible to clean up the threads if the user were to stop the service while the threads were actively processing. We need to have control over the cleanup of the threads because unlike applications that run on the client, services are required to either shut down quickly or update the Service Control Manager with an estimate of how much longer the services need to shut down. If the Services does not request more time, the SCM will consider the service to be in a hung or unresponsive state, which will most likely require a reboot of the system. In some cases you can look in Task Manager or use the Windows Resource Kit to terminate the rogue service. Over time, however, attempting to forcibly terminate a process can cause operating system or application instability.

Thread Cleanup Availability

We need to make the threads that we create accessible to the rest of the service methods, not just the one that starts or creates the thread. You can do this in many ways—by creating a pool of threads or a class of thread-exposing objects, for example—but for now we're going to use the simplest way possible. We will be adding a list, or collection of threads, that is available privately to the service but is not available to external processes.

Threads and Accessibility

By default, threads have limited access to other members or data in your service. Each thread only has access to either shared data members or methods and—if you are using a parameterized thread method—the object that is passed to it. Threads—which run in different scopes to be able to share data—must be coded in a way that protects your data. (For more information, see "Thread Synchronization" earlier in this chapter.) From a UI perspective, it is possible to create delegates which can be used to participate with other threads. In this case you do not need synchronization to use the delegates themselves, but you may need synchronization within the method executed on the delegate, to protect the actions being performed on the delegate's behalf.

A Problem with the Current *<OnStart>* Thread

If you look back at the previous *<OnStart>* method, you'll notice that we are creating a thread. The problem is that we are creating the thread with a local variable instance, which makes it local-scope only. Once the thread has started, it will continue to run. However, the thread variable, or pointer to the thread, goes out of scope, and we .now have no way to directly access the thread and stop it from doing its work—or clean it up. This lack of access would be a huge problem if a thread became unstable, or worse if it exhibited rogue behavior such as accessing off-limits data or causing a memory leak, CPU spike, or other resource issue.

Fixing the Thread-Scope Issue

To resolve the thread-scope issue we have to make the thread available to either the global scope of the application or to some part of the service that allows us to clean up threads. In this example—because we are only using a single thread—we are going to create a private data member of type *Thread* that is global to the service class, which we are calling *Tutorials*.

Directly after the class definition code, add the code shown in Listing 2-11.

Listing 2-11 Code to add a private thread member variable to the service.

```
Public Class Tutorials
    Private m_WorkerThread As Thread = Nothing
```

The code in Listing 2-11 will create a variable that will store a thread pointer after we create it. This variable doesn't store anything yet. We have to assign it something before we can use it. When we add the code shown in Listing 2-12, the class definition allows this variable to be available to any method in the service, except directly by the threads we create because those threads require differently scoped variables. Again this variable is intended to be available to the service, not just by the threads we create, so that we can clean it up later. The variable is not required to be available to the threads themselves because a thread can clean itself up.

Creating the Thread in *<OnStart>*

We need to change the current *<OnStart>* method so that it no longer uses a local variable for the thread. In the *<OnStart>* method we will change the code shown in the first part of Listing 2-12 with the bolded code that follows it.

Listing 2-12 Modifications to *<OnStart>* to fix the thread-scope issue.

```
Dim tmpThread As New Thread(AddressOf ThreadFunc)
tmpThread.Name = "Tutorials Worker Thread"
tmpThread.Priority = ThreadPriority.Normal
tmpThread.Start()
m_WorkerThread = New Thread(AddressOf ThreadFunc)
m_WorkerThread.Name = "Tutorials Worker Thread"
m_WorkerThread.Priority = ThreadPriority.Normal
m_WorkerThread.Start()
```

Now that we are creating a thread using the private class variable, we have to worry about cleaning it up.

Thread Cleanup

Before we get into the code itself, you have to understand that like other .NET variables, thread variables have a scope. Global variables are just that—global—and can be accessed by other methods. Originally the thread variable was only local to the *<OnStart>* method. Now it is not.

Why is this distinction so important? You should never just create threads that your application can't clean up. When an application exits, the threads and resources the application allocated should be released, even if those resources are no longer visible to the application itself

However, a service works a little differently. When a service shuts down, it expects you to have cleaned up any existing threads. If you didn't, and the service recognizes this fact—and you haven't told the service to wait for you to complete cleanup—the service will cause the Service Control Manager to throw back an error to the user. You will often need to use Task Manager to terminate the now rogue and abandoned application service.

Cleaning Up the *<OnStop>* Method

In the *<OnStop>* method, we will not only write an event to the Application log, but also shut down the thread. It's important to note that *<OnStop>* is similar to *<OnStart>* in that it can only take so much time before returning. However, in the *<OnStop>* method you can request more time from the SCM to continue cleaning up. We won't need to do this because we only have two actions and both are extremely simple.

The top part of Listing 2-13 shows the current code, which we will replace with the bolded code that follows it. This is the new cleanup code.

Listing 2-13 Modifications to *<OnStop>* to support new thread scope.

```
Try
WriteLogEvent("Tutorials Stopping", 1001, EventLogEntryType.Information,
 "Tutorials")
Catch ex As Exception
WriteLogEvent(ex.ToString, 1001, EventLogEntryType.Error, "Tutorials")
End Try
Try
  If Not m_WorkerThread Is Nothing Then
    Try
      m_WorkerThread.Abort()
      m_WorkerThread = Nothing
    Catch ex As Exception
      m_WorkerThread = Nothing
    End Try
  End If
  WriteLogEvent("Tutorials Stopping", 1001, _
EventLogEntryType.Information, "Tutorials")
Catch ex As Exception
  WriteLogEvent(ex.ToString, 1001, EventLogEntryType.Error, "Tutorials")
End Try
```

Now we are able to control how the thread is terminated and when, because the thread is a data member of the service class. This means that any method that is part of the service class can terminate that thread at any time. You should always ensure that the thread still exists before attempting to abort it.

About Thread Abort

When you call Abort on an active thread, inside that thread's instance of the thread method it will throw a ThreadAbortException. So we will add a handler for this exception. Currently the service thread function completes its task so quickly that we will not see the abort exception. The thread exits normally before we could call the *<OnStop>* method.

> **Note** When you abort a thread, there is no guarantee that the thread will terminate or even throw the ThreadAbortException immediately.

Making Thread Cleanup Useful

Although we have added in thread cleanup code, we still have a problem. The current thread method implementation actually performs only a single action and then exits. Although this doesn't make the cleanup code totally useless, its value is questionable because the thread has already exited and cleaned itself up.

To remedy this, we will modify the thread method to do two things:

- Add a handler for the ThreadAbortException
- Add code to keep the thread alive so that the cleanup code will execute

Adding Code to ThreadAbortException

Listing 2-14 shows the code we add to ensure that the ThreadAbortException handler is being used properly.

Listing 2-14 Modifications to *<ThreadFunc>* to handle ThreadAbortException.

```
Try
    WriteLogEvent("Thread Function Information - " + Now.ToString, 1005, _
EventLogEntryType.Information, "Tutorials")
Catch tab As ThreadAbortException 'this must be listed first as
Catch ex As Exception
    WriteLogEvent("Thread Function Error - " + Now.ToString, 1005, _
EventLogEntryType.Error, "Tutorials")
End Try
Try
  WriteLogEvent("Thread Function Information - " + Now.ToString, 1005, _
  EventLogEntryType.Information, "Tutorials")
'this must be listed first as Exception is the master catch
Catch tab As ThreadAbortException
'Clean up the thread here
WriteLogEvent("Thread Function Abort Error - " + Now.ToString, 1006, _
  EventLogEntryType.Error, "Tutorials") Catch ex As Exception
  WriteLogEvent("Thread Function Error - " + Now.ToString, 1005, _
  EventLogEntryType.Error, "Tutorials")
End Try
```

In Listing 2-14 we added ThreadAbortException, which will attempt to write an event to the Application log, alerting us about a request to abort the thread. The only problem is that this can't happen because the code runs only once and then exits. By the time you do start the service it has probably run this code and exited. To fix this we need to make sure that the thread continues to run long enough for the cleanup code and this new exception to be executed.

Keeping the Thread Alive

To resolve the issue of the thread exiting too quickly, we will add in a loop that will run the code to write an event over and over. In many cases threads will do the same work repeatedly. However, this doesn't mean that the thread will be active all the time—instead, it will have a sleep interval before it continues its work or starts over again.

We will define a constant called THREAD_WAIT, shown in Listing 2-15. This constant is just below m_WorkerThread at the top of Tutorials.vb.

Listing 2-15   Creating the thread loop wait variable.
```
Public Class Tutorials

    Private m_WorkerThread As Thread = Nothing
    Private Const THREAD_WAIT As Integer = 5000
```

We will wrap the current code in a Do/Loop and use a *Thread* class's *Sleep* method to pause the thread.

> **Tip**   The *Thread* class's *Sleep* method uses milliseconds to represent its sleep time. You must convert seconds, minutes, or your *TimeSpan* into milliseconds.

Listing 2-16 shows the new thread method code.

Listing 2-16   New thread method code implementing keep-alive logic.
```
Do
  Try
    WriteLogEvent("Thread Function Information - " + Now.ToString, 1005, _
EventLogEntryType.Information, "Tutorials")
'this must be listed first as Exception is the master catch
  Catch tab As ThreadAbortException
'Clean up the thread here
    WriteLogEvent("Thread Function Abort Error - " + Now.ToString, 1006, _
EventLogEntryType.Error, "Tutorials")
  Catch ex As Exception
    WriteLogEvent("Thread Function Error - " + Now.ToString, 1005, _
EventLogEntryType.Error, "Tutorials")
  End Try
  Thread.Sleep(THREAD_WAIT)
Loop
```

The thread will run the code, sleep for five seconds, and then run the code again. When the thread is aborting in the *<OnStop>* method, it will cause the ThreadAbortException to be called, in which case it will log another event, letting us know that the thread was aborted. We could perform any necessary cleanup there. However, do not make a habit of spending long amounts of time in the *<OnStop>* method or you could possibly lock up the service.

Install and Verify

Before you compile and install your new service version, make sure to remove the old one. When you run the service, you will see the information event logging the time every five seconds until you stop the service.

Now you have an understanding of how to use threads in your services. There is no real limit to how many you can use. However, you should use threads and resources wisely. Threads that run out of control can hang your systems, lock up your processors or your data, block users from retrieving information and, even worse, crash your system.

Extending *<OnPause>* and *<OnContinue>*

Remember that we created a way to indirectly control the flow of service. Using *<OnPause>* and *<OnContinue>*, we can write code that will allow us to either block threads from doing work or make them intuitive enough to know whether they should exit or merely delay their processing responsibilities.

Ways to Control Thread Processing

We will implement a couple of different ways to control what the threads do.

Thread Suspension

Our first attempt at thread control will be to use the built-in *Thread* class method called *Suspend*. This method will allow us to stop a thread in its tracks, or at least attempt to. A thread suspension can fail, in which case we would end up in a situation that we must code for—a rogue thread. However, for the purposes of this example, we will implement the Thread Suspension and Thread Resume features of the *Thread* class.

Updating *<OnPause>*

We will use the *<OnPause>* method to suspend the thread; we will use *<OnContinue>* to resume the thread. Listing 2-17 shows the updated code for *<OnPause>*.

Listing 2-17   Modifications to *<OnPause>* to support thread suspension.

```
Protected Overrides Sub OnPause()
    Try
        If (Not m_WorkerThread Is Nothing) Then
            Try
                m_WorkerThread.Abort()
            Catch ex As Exception
                'we do not care about this
                'exception as we are shutting it down
                'anyway
                m_WorkerThread = Nothing
            End Try
```

```
        End If

        WriteLogEvent("Tutorials Pausing", 1002,
    EventLogEntryType.Information, "Tutorials")
      Catch ex As Exception
        'We Catch the Exception
        'to avoid any unhandled errors
        'since we are pausing and
        'logging an event is what failed
        'we will merely write the output
        'to the debug window
        Debug.WriteLine("Error pausing service: " + ex.ToString())
        Me.Stop()
      End Try
    End Sub
```

Updating *<OnContinue>*

We now have to update the *<OnContinue>* method to allow us to resume the thread. Listing 2-18 shows the updated code.

Listing 2-18   Modifications to *<OnContinue>* to support continuing the thread.

```
Protected Overrides Sub OnContinue()
    Try
      Try
          'Create a new thread
          'and start it just like
          'in the OnStart
          m_WorkerThread = New Thread(AddressOf ThreadFunc)
          m_WorkerThread.Name = "Tutorials Worker Thread"
          m_WorkerThread.Priority = ThreadPriority.Normal
          m_WorkerThread.Start()
      Catch ex As Exception
          WriteLogEvent("Tutorials Unable to Continue:" + vbCrLf +
    ex.ToString(), 1010, EventLogEntryType.Information, "Tutorials")
          m_WorkerThread = Nothing
      End Try

        WriteLogEvent("Tutorials Continuing", 1003,
    EventLogEntryType.Information, "Tutorials")
      Catch ex As Exception
        'We Catch the Exception
        'to avoid any unhandled errors
        'since we are resuming and
        'logging an event is what failed
        'we will merely write the output
        'to the debug window
        Debug.WriteLine("Error resuming service: " + ex.ToString())
        Me.Stop()
      End Try
    End Sub
```

In Listing 2-18, we use the *Resume* method to start the thread back where it was suspended. You have to be careful about how your code handles being suspended. While the thread is suspended, you will receive no processing notifications. Therefore, thread suspension is not always the best solution. Let's look at another scenario.

Using Thread State Control

Another way to control thread processing is through state variables. You can use individual variables for each state, or—as in the following example—you can use a type that will affect each thread.

Listing 2-19 shows the code we will add to the thread definition at the top of the class definition.

Listing 2-19   Code to create a thread state capability.

```
Private Const THIRTY_SECONDS As Long = 30000
Private Const TIME_OUT As Long = 15000
Private Structure Thread_Action_State
    Private m_Pause As Boolean
    Private m_Stop As Boolean
    Public Property Pause() As Boolean
      Get
        Return m_Pause
      End Get
      Set(ByVal value As Boolean)
        m_Pause = value
      End Set
    End Property
    Public Property StopThread() As Boolean
      Get
        Return m_Stop
      End Get
      Set(ByVal value As Boolean)
        m_Stop = value
      End Set
    End Property
End Structure
Private Shared m_ThreadAction As New Thread_Action_State
```

This code adds the following features to the service:

First we are adding a constant called THIRTY_SECONDS. I mentioned earlier the service can request additional shutdown time from the SCM. In this case we are going to request an additional 30 seconds to complete processing and cleanup before we exit.

Next we add the TIME_OUT constant. Because we are now using multiple threads, we need to make sure that the processing threads are completed before the primary thread says we are done by exiting the *<OnStop>* method. To do this, we will use the processing thread's *Join* method, which will allow us to either block indefinitely for that thread to complete or wait for a specified period of time. In this case we will wait 15 seconds for the thread to complete its task or shut itself down.

Next we add the Thread_Action_State structure. This structure has two properties: one states whether the service is paused, telling the processing threads to pause, and the other tells the threads that the service is shutting down and they need to exit.

Last we add the m_ThreadAction variable. This variable is shared, or static, meaning that all threads can see these values and there is no need to pass it around to each thread. This also means that the variable can be accessed directly without creating an instance of the class itself. The thread class instance is created automatically when you start the service so you don't need to instantiate it by any other means. The default values are false, so the threads will neither be stopped nor paused when the service starts up.

Updating *<OnPause>*

Now that we have added new state controls, we need to modify *<OnPause>*, *<OnStop>*, and *<OnContinue>* to reflect the state changes. In the previous *<OnPause>* we suspended the thread. We need to remove or comment that code out and add in the new state change code. *<OnPause>* should now look like the code shown in Listing 2-20.

Listing 2-20   Modifications to *<OnPause>* to use thread state management.

```
Protected Overrides Sub OnPause()
  Try
    m_ThreadAction.Pause = True
    WriteLogEvent("Tutorials Pausing", 1002, EventLogEntryType.Information, _
"Tutorials")
  Catch ex As Exception
    'We Catch the Exception
    'to avoid any unhandled errors
    'since we are pausing and
    'logging an event is what failed
    'we will merely write the output
    'to the debug window
    Debug.WriteLine("Error pausing service: " + ex.ToString())
    Me.Stop()
  End Try
End Sub
```

This code will merely change the state of the threads to Paused. Although we have more work to do, controlling the thread's state is much simpler here than suspending the threads—and safer, too.

Updating *<OnContinue>*

As with *<OnPause>*, *<OnContinue>* must reflect a similar change, shown in Listing 2-21.

Listing 2-21   Modifications to *<OnContinue>* to support thread state management.

```
Protected Overrides Sub OnContinue()
  Try
     m_ThreadAction.Pause = False
     WriteLogEvent("Tutorials Continuing", 1003, EventLogEntryType.Information,
Tutorials")
  Catch ex As Exception
     'We Catch the Exception
     'to avoid any unhandled errors
     'since we are resuming and
     'logging an event is what failed
     'we will merely write the output
     'to the debug window
     Debug.WriteLine("Error resuming service: " + ex.ToString())
     Me.Stop()
  End Try
End Sub
```

You will notice that just as *<OnPause>* set the state to True, we now set it to False so that the threads can continue their work.

Updating *<OnStop>*

Last we will update *<OnStop>*, which requires a bit more work than updating the previous two methods. Not only do we need to tell the threads to stop, but we also want to attempt to wait for them so that we know they are completed and cleaned up before exiting. Listing 2-22 shows the updated code.

Listing 2-22   Modifications to *<OnStop>* to support thread state management.

```
Protected Overrides Sub OnStop()
    ' Add code here to perform any tear-down
    'necessary to stop your service.
   Try
      If (Not m_WorkerThread Is Nothing) Then
         Try
             Me.RequestAdditionalTime(THIRTY_SECONDS)
             m_WorkerThread.Join(TIME_OUT)
             m_ThreadAction.StopThread = True
         Catch ex As Exception
             'Do Nothing
         End Try
      End If

      WriteLogEvent("Tutorials Stopping", 1001,
EventLogEntryType.Information, "Tutorials")
   Catch ex As Exception
      'We Catch the Exception
      'to avoid any unhandled errors
      'since we are stopping and
      'logging an event is what failed
```

```
        'we will merely write the output
        'to the debug window
        m_WorkerThread = Nothing
        Debug.WriteLine("Error stopping service: " + ex.ToString())
    End Try
End Sub
```

First, I replaced the Abort and Nothing lines of code. Because we aren't going to directly clean up the thread, instead telling it when to clean itself up, we have to remove these.

As mentioned when I described the new *<OnStop>* code, I will first request an additional 30 seconds from the SCM so that it doesn't believe we are being unresponsive.

Next I will add the *Join* method to the worker thread. This is like saying to the thread, "I am waiting for you to exit. Let me know when you are done." However, although I could wait forever for the service to exit, I have asked for only 30 extra seconds from the SCM. Therefore I have set a 15-second time-out for the thread to exit before I move on, so that I don't cause the SCM to consider the service unresponsive to the stop request.

Next I set the state of the threads to stopped. You may wonder why I didn't do this first. I could have but then, by time I got to the *Join* method, the thread could be invalidated and cause an exception. I'm prepared for that possibility, but I prefer to avoid it.

The last step is to write the original event, exit, and return control to the SCM.

> **Note**   If for some reason the thread I join with is not cleaned up in the allotted time, it will get cleaned up when the process exits. However, if this doesn't happen we may need to reboot or terminate the service in Task Manager.

Updating *<ThreadFunc>*

At this point all the code I added is useless unless I first modify the *<ThreadFunc>* method to handle these state changes. I usually don't directly add state change checks to my threads without wrapping them in a call that returns a bool. I find that sometimes I want to do more than just exit or pause a thread when the state changes. Because I want to have multiple state change checks in my thread—which could make it quite large or complex—I wouldn't want to copy and paste this excessive code all over. I don't need to add a wrapper method for every state change possible because I already defined these state changes in the the StopThread and Pause properties of the Thread.

Listing 2-23 shows the new *<ThreadFunc>* code.

Listing 2-23   Modifications to thread method to support thread state management.
```
Private Sub ThreadFunc()
  While Not m_ThreadAction.StopThread
    If Not m_ThreadAction.Pause Then
      Try
        WriteLogEvent("Thread Function Information - " + Now.ToString, _
```

```
1005, EventLogEntryType.Information, "Tutorials")
        Catch tab As ThreadAbortException _
'this must be listed first as Exceptionis the master catch
        'Clean up the thread here
        WriteLogEvent("Thread Function Abort Error - " + Now.ToString, _
1006, EventLogEntryType.Error, "Tutorials")
      Catch ex As Exception
        WriteLogEvent("Thread Function Error - " + Now.ToString, 1005, _
EventLogEntryType.Error, "Tutorials")
      End Try
    End If
    Thread.Sleep(THREAD_WAIT)
  End While
End Sub
```

This function has changed quite a bit. First, I changed from a Do Loop to a While End While loop. I am using an outer loop to validate that the thread is not in a stopped State. If I hit this state, I will exit the While loop and exit the thread, hence shutting it down.

I am validating that the service is not in a Paused state. If the service is in a Paused state, none of the code is executed and it will merely hit Thread.Sleep. This causes the service thread to sleep for five seconds. Then it attempts to do the While loop and If check again. This process will continue until someone stops the service, in which case it will exit. Pausing will not exit— it will just stop it from doing any active processing.

When this thread exits the *Join* that the main thread attached to in the *<OnStop>* method, the event is released and *<OnStop>* method processing continues, causing the service itself to finally exit and the SCM to report it has stopped.

Importance of the THREAD_WAIT Value

Because we are only doing a 15-second join with this thread to validate that it has shut down, if we set the THREAD_WAIT beyond 10 or 12 seconds, the thread could very likely still be asleep before it validates that it was supposed to shut down. Therefore you should check before you go to sleep whether you were supposed to stop. Pausing is not a big deal, but if you were to have a process internal to the thread that took more than 5 to 10 seconds to complete, and it had just started, and then you went to sleep for 5 or more seconds, you could easily exceed this 15-second join. For this reason, update your *<ThreadFunc>* by wrapping your Sleep call as shown in Listing 2-24.

Listing 2-24   Update to thread method thread sleep call code.

```
If Not m_ThreadAction.StopThread Then
  Thread.Sleep(THREAD_WAIT)
End If
```

You may think this is merely adding extra code, but it isn't. It is saving us from missing our required deadline of 15 seconds.

Summary

We have successfully created a fairly extensive multi-threaded service. At this point you might not see its value because we only have one worker thread. However, the abilities we have included in this version can be easily extended in upcoming chapters, where we will use more than just one worker thread. Controlling thread states is of key importance to services for stability and usability.

- Threads are a way to allow applications to perform multiple actions in a concurrent manner.

- Microsoft Visual Basic 2008 supports threads natively with the *System.Threading* class.

- Microsoft Visual Basic 2008 makes the creation of threads simple, but you must also be careful when using this powerful programming technique.

- Use caution when creating threads. Overuse or improper use can cause severe side effects and instability.

Chapter 3
Services and Security

Whether you are writing a stand-alone application, a server application, or a service, you need to take security into account. Security comes in many different levels and applies to many different facets of an application, user, computer, network even a company's enterprise architecture. No matter what you are writing—a simple data gathering service, an application monitor, a batch job processor, or a complex data mining service—you need to understand the role that security plays in your development and support model.

Understanding what to look for to ensure that your service, data, server, and network are secured is the key to avoiding security risks and potential loss of customer or personal information.

Security Privileges and Services

You have to think about a number of things when it comes to services and security. Services themselves have to run in a security context that has permissions to do what you program the service to do. Imagine that you are programing the service to read a file from the hard disk, read a setting from the registry, or even log on to a Windows Authentication–only SQL Server. If the account that your services runs under does not have the appropriate privileges, your service will fail to perform the tasks you assigned it, and although the service itself may actually run, it will be useless.

Running a service in a higher privileged context than is required can cause security holes, which provide opportunities for unapproved network access, application access, and data loss. Never grant more authority than your service requires to perform the tasks required of it.

You should always determine what your service needs to do before you begin to code it. Then, based on these needs, you determine the required security rights. To help determine what options you have in terms of security, let's look at the default settings you have to choose from when building a service.

Service Account Security

When you build a service, you have to select an account that the service will run under. This is considered the *security context*, because the account (context) that your service runs under is not necessarily the same as the user who may be logged on at the time.

For example, if you open up the Services Control Panel and look at the Log On As column, you will see many different listings. Let's look at what the choices are when we install a service.

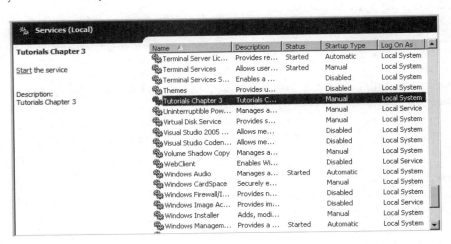

Let's open up the Services Control Panel and right-click the Tutorials service. Select Properties and then click the Log On tab.

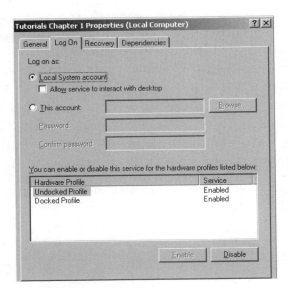

Local System

You have two options: to run as a Local System Account or to run as a specific user account. For the moment ignore the option Allow Service To Interact With Desktop—I'll cover that in a moment. Most services use some predefined system accounts that are created when the operating system is installed. Although these accounts are technically user accounts, they are predefined with specific security attributes, privileges, and default security response types when queried by remote computers. In most cases you should use one of the predefined NetworkService or LocalService accounts.

The Local System account itself has access to most resources on the local computer that it exists on. It has no password and is not considered a real user. It is an account created for use by the service control manager (SCM) under whose context many services run. However, this account has quite extensive privileges, and any service running under this account has those privileges. For this reason it is important to avoid using this account unless necessary. You can and should create an account with the minimum privileges required to perform the service's duties.

Note one important thing about the Local System account: Although it has a large amount of privileges when running on the local computer, it has almost no privileges when attempting to access network resources. For this reason, the Local System requires *null sessions*—sessions with only anonymous authentication (in other words, no authentication).

You can restrict null sessions on computers throughout your network, protecting them from services running on remote computers. If you plan to access remote resources, it's better in many situations to use the local computer's Machine Account and then grant that account access to the remote resources.

User Accounts

You can create, define, and give any user account the required specific privileges and security rights—such as if you wanted the service to query data from a database on a computer running Microsoft SQL Server that requires a valid Windows account. You can set the service to run as a user who has Windows Authentication to Microsoft SQL Server—whether a local account or a domain account—and then when the service queries SQL Server, it will send the credentials as if it were that. Let's look at the options:

- **User** This option causes the system to prompt for a valid user name and password when the service is installed and runs in the context of an account specified by a single user on the network. This is the most powerful of all security contexts because you define what access the account has when the account is created. If you run the service as a domain enterprise administrator, the service will have the privileges of that domain administrator. You need to define the exact privileges that are required by a service to determine whether this is a viable and reasonable option. You'd be hard-pressed to find a situation that would require such extreme privileges. Under Windows 2000, Windows Server 2003, and Windows Vista, you are best off assigning your service as a Network

Service account or a Machine account. After doing so, you can grant privileges to other computers, or services such as Microsoft MSMQ, by adding the machine account that the service runs under to the remote resource.

- **Local Service**   A service running as a Local Service runs in the context of a reduced-privilege user on the local computer and presents anonymous credentials to any remote server. This option is appropriate for situations that require very limited security and that do not require access to remote network resources. Because the service would only access remote resources using null sessions with anonymous access, it is not recommended that you use it for network resource access.

    Null sessions (anonymous logons) pass no user name and no password to the local or remote resource for authentication. If the remote system has blocked null sessions or anonymous logon, you won't be able to access the required resource. In this case you should consider using the Network Service account.

- **Local System**   This option runs in the context of an account that provides extensive local privileges and presents the computer's credentials to any remote server. This is a very powerful account to use and will allow you to perform almost any action. You must be careful when using Local System as your security context because allowing a service to run as Local System grants more privileges than most services require. Consider this option only when requiring privileges equivalent to those of an administrator. In most cases, you should consider the more restrictive options and then extend the default privileges of those accounts, instead of granting the service more privileges under a Local System. If the service does not require elevated or interactive privileges, consider using Local Service or Network Service accounts instead.

- **Network Service**   A service running as a Network Service runs in the context of a non-privileged user on the local computer and presents the computer's credentials to any remote server. This account is much more powerful than Local Service, but is still much more secure than Local System, especially when it comes to remote computers who query this service. External services running in the context of the Everyone and Authenticated Users groups merely receive anonymous credentials that they would not be able to use to spoof the computer credentials given by Local System.

What is spoofing? When services run in a security context higher than is required, they run the risk of external users attempting to mimic, or *spoof*, the credentials of the service itself. In this case, a malicious user may intend to use executables, batch command files, or other executable processes by exploiting the capabilities of your services. Once these processes are running, they have the same privileges as your service and therefore can spoof the service credentials and force the service to perform tasks it was not intended to perform—against other services or resources it was not granted explicit access to.

You may not always be clear about what you initially need, and sometimes you may need to rely on trial and error. If you are unsure, talk with your network administrator and work out how to create a user account that can be managed by your administrator so that it can be limited to doing only what it needs to do. In instances in which a service may need to run on a large number of computers and does not require special privileges or network access, consider using the LocalService or NetworkService accounts. If the service requires a lot of network access or privileges, a secured domain account is often the best option.

When deciding on the service account you want to use, the level of of security should be paramount. The choices can be considered in the following order, from most to least secure:

- Local Service account
- Network Service account
- A local user account
- A domain user account
- Local System account
- The local administrator account (not recommended)
- A domain administrator account (not recommended)

Securing the Service

It is very important to think about not just what your service will do, or what security context it needs to run in, but how to protect your service and your business from unauthorized usage of your service and its functionality.

Imagine that you have a service that can download important customer information or internal employee information, sales figures, or other confidential information. In these cases you probably want to keep access to this service and its functionality secure. You want to limit the access that the service has.

Protecting Data

Let's say you design a service that has the ability to download all customer and credit card information from one data store and then process the data to store into another data store. What do you need to secure?

- Access to the data store that holds the customer information
- Access to the directory to which the service downloads the information before processing
- Access to the secondary data store that will hold the customer information
- Access to temporary data and data connections

Each type of access has particular issues that must be addressed. However, as with all applications or services, each type of access has different types of functionality. Therefore you should always look at your service and determine what actions it takes, how you will perform them, and which of those actions need to be secured. That last step—determining how to secure them—is important. Local development resources at your company, on the Internet, and from local administrators can often help you with any of these steps.

Access to the Data Store That Holds the Customer Information

Normally this type of data is stored in a back-end database. Database servers that run on the Windows platform usually support NTLM and Kerberos-type authentication, as well as SQL Server authentication, using built-in logons. In this situation we have to figure out how to allow the service access to the data without providing too much access or access that can be abused by someone with malicious intent.

As I'll explain in the following sections, you can have the service run in the context of a user who has access to the database, or you can supply the service with the security context or logon information with which it can impersonate the user's security access. You can also specify security logon information in the connection string used to connect to the database.

As a User   If you decide to run the service as a user with security rights, make sure that the user account has only the privileges required to retrieve the data and to process it locally, especially if you plan to store the data temporarily on the local disk.

Impersonation   If you decide to supply the service with the security credentials for either a Windows account or a SQL Server logon, you have to decide how to get this information to the service while keeping it safe. It does no good to secure the use of your service if you make it easy to obtain the logon credentials that provide access to the confidential information.

You can place the user name and password in an encrypted file or encrypted registry key, or you can use a secondary Web Service or COM+ application that has permission to access the database on behalf of the service. Both are good ways to provide access to the data while securing logon information.

Access to the Directory to Which the Service Downloads the Information Before Processing

It is possible to process the data in two formats. The first format is memory only, where you might query the information and then store it in local memory resident ADO.NET datasets, or other memory-mapped data objects that are then processed directly to the secondary data store. The second option is to save the data temporarily to the file system, where it is either processed by the same service—possibly on a separate thread—or by another service.

Although not a direct concern for the developer, from an operational support and security point of view, if the data is stored in memory, your operations team should keep track of access to the server where the data is being processed. Depending on the data itself, you might not be able to encrypt the memory used to store the data while it is being processed. This means you must be diligent about local server access.

When determining whether you should store data in temporary local files, you should look at some possible solutions for helping to ensure the safety of your data:

- Encrypt the data as it is saved to disk.

- Store temporary files in encrypted folders accessible only by the service account.

- Process the file in memory and not create an unencrypted version on disk.

Access to the Secondary Data Store That Will Hold the Customer Information

At times you will be pulling data from one database or data store and you might want to migrate it, or convert it to another format and then store it in a secondary database or data store. In this case you will need to review the security model and approach that you use.

Imagine that you are running the service as a local user account or even as a domain account or machine account. The service itself might have access to the data store that you retrieve from, but not have access to the back end. This could be due to trust issues in the domain, multi-homed servers, or any other security or configuration requirement on your network or business. If this is the case, your service could be sharing the data between two components, instantiated by the service but running under two different security contexts. In this case the service is running under one account and so is child process 1 (or thread 1) and the second thread needs to run as a secondary account. In this case you are passing data through the service itself between two threads or two components created by the service, but running under different security contexts. This following list, while not exhaustive, gives you some options for possible solutions to this problem:

- Create matching SQL logons on both servers and then share this data between both connections.

- Use Windows authentication by running the service under an account that has access to both data stores. Use a SQL logon for one data store and use the security context of the service for the other.

- Use multiple user security contexts on a per-thread basis and share the data between the threads. This option requires that you inherent from existing security contexts, create new secuirty contexts that you then pass onto a new thread, or that you have the thread impersonate a security context that has the required access. Although there aren't many situations in which you would run a service in such a model, threading and services are not limited to a single security context. Microsoft provides APIs and .NET methods for creating such threads.

- Use COM+ services or Web Services to perform the data retrieval and storage.

You can perform data retrieval from different data sources in many different ways. What's important is to make sure that you don't give the service too much authorization, while at the same time protecting the logon information so that data on both servers is protected.

Access to the Temporary Data and Data Connections

Not only do you need to make sure the data is protected while you are processing it, but you also need to make sure that the data is secured once it has been processed. Make sure that you clear any data and memory buffers, close any unused connections and recordsets, and most important, make sure to destroy any locally stored data.

Summary

- Security for any application, especially in any workplace environment, must be a paramount consideration. Microsoft provides many mechanisms to protect the software written using Microsoft technologies. These protection mechanisms need to be clearly understood, helping to make your service, your network, and your data as safe as possible.

- Windows Services has different levels of security that provide for a wide range of protection, based on the security context of the service when running.

- Security comes in many forms, and you must consider all of them when writing any application—especially Windows Services.

Part II
Creating Interactive Windows Services

Chapter 4
Services and Polling

Even in this event-driven world of Microsoft .NET, you'll have to write a solution that will poll to gather the information or perform the tasks that you intend your service to do. Whether you are polling Microsoft SQL Server, Microsoft MSMQ, Microsoft Exchange, or even the file system, services can play a key role in integrating the functionality you are exposing and the solution that you have designed to solve whatever problem you are facing. Services have the capability to encapsulate large, scaleable application requirements.

Polling the File System

Services are great for acting as a polling mechanism. In this example we will be monitoring for files that are being added to a specified directory. Whether these files come from another computer, a specific user, MSMQ, an SQL job, or an FTP site with the appropriate privileges, we can monitor for files that arrive and then perform some predefined task. In this first section we will monitor a specific directory for new text files. We will log an event for each new text file that we find.

Adding a Module File

We will continue this chapter by extending the already-existent code from Chapter 2, "Expanding Your Service with Threads." We will modify the existing code to help us resolve the addition of the new module.

The service is going to continue to grow, so to help to keep things cleaner and more readable, let's add a module file to the project. In the Solution Explorer, click the Tutorials project icon and select Add Module. Name the file **modService.vb** and click Add.

As shown in Listing 4-1, cut and paste the THREAD_WAIT definition from the Tutorials.vb file into the modService.vb and change the definition from Private to Public.

Listing 4-1   Move the THREAD_WAIT definition to the modService file.

```
Module modService
  Public Const THREAD_WAIT As Integer = 5000
```

Adding Event Log InstanceIds

I want to define some custom *InstanceId*s that we can use specifically when we log an event to the event log. Currently we are just hard-coding them, but adding definitions for them would be cleaner. So add the code shown in Listing 4-2 to your modService file.

Listing 4-2   New program constants.

```
Public Const ONSTART_ERROR As Integer = 1000
Public Const ONSTOP_ERROR As Integer = 1001
Public Const THREAD_ERROR As Integer = 1002
Public Const THREAD_ABORT_ERROR As Integer = 1003
Public Const ONSTART_INFO As Integer = 2000
Public Const ONSTOP_INFO As Integer = 2001
Public Const THREAD_INFO As Integer = 2002
Public Const ONPAUSE_INFO As Integer = 2003
Public Const ONCONTINUE_INFO As Integer = 2004
```

> **Note**   An *InstanceId* is a kind of ID used in the EventViewer Log files, such as Application, System, and Security. The IDs that I am defining in each chapter are here to help you make sure you are logging the proper event in the specific event log for any error or information we need to log.

Adding New Polling Code

The next step is to create the code that will look for these files and then add an event into the Application log. To do this we must modify the current *<ThreadFunc>* method. Before we modify *<ThreadFunc>*, we need to add another import statement to the top of tutorials.vb that will be used interact with the file system. Although the import is not required, it makes it easier to create class instances of the IO namespace without having to declare the entire namespace for each variable declared.

Add the code shown in Listing 4-3 to the top of the Tutorials.vb file.

Listing 4-3   Add a new Imports statement.
```
Imports System.IO
```

We can now directly access the file system classes used to check for any text files, without using the entire namespace. We will also need a directory to monitor. You can create this directory anywhere you want. I have created a directory called "incoming" and placed it in my c:\temp directory.

Introduction to Instrumenting a Resource File

An important factor in programming is *localization*–displaying information to a user based on the geographic locale or local language used. You use a resource file and the .NET built-in localization management methods to help make this happen.

We will implement a resource file to keep track of any strings or text that we have previously coded into the service as well as any new resource strings that we will add later on as we build on the service.

Creating the Resource File

In addition to allowing us to handle localization issues better, a resource file gives us the ability to avoid issues such as passing literal strings to method calls, which Microsoft discourages. To create the resource file, select the Tutorials project name, right-click, and select Properties. Click the Resources tab. If a resource file is not available, you will be prompted to create one. After you have created the resource file you will see a grid structure where you can enter string literals, names, and descriptions.

Not only will we add new strings, but also previously coded literals. Then I will demonstrate how to access these resources in your application.

First let's add a string called IncomingPath and give it a value of *c:\temp\incoming*, or wherever you created your incoming folder. Leave the value for Description empty.

Adding Previous Literals to the Resource File

I have added the string literals shown in Table 4-1; we will use them to replace the currently hard-coded values in the service.

Table 4-1   List of Resources Created for This Service

Name	Value YYY
IncomingPath	c:\temp\incoming
Source	Tutorials
ServiceStarting	Tutorials Starting
ServicePausing	Tutorials Pausing
ServiceStopping	Tutorials Stopping
ServiceContinuing	Tutorials Continuing
ThreadMessage	Thread Function Information
ThreadAbortMessage	Thread Function Abort Error
ThreadErrorMessage	Thread Function Error
ThreadName	Tutorials Worker Thread
ThreadIOError	Thread Function IO Error -
OutgoingPath	c:\temp\outgoing

Microsoft Visual Basic makes it very easy to access resources through the Visual Basic My Object.

Using the My Object, you can access a resource by typing **My.Resources.*ResourceName***. For instance, using the resource file you just created, My.Resources.IncomingPath returns the string c:\temp\incoming.

Updating the Service Events

We want to use the new service events properly by modifying the current events. This will allow us to reuse these structured literals quickly.

Modifying Our *<OnStart>*

We will be modifying our current tutorials.vb thread function code to reflect both the changes in using our resource file and to use our new InstanceId constants.

Listing 4-4   Modifications to *<OnStart>* to support the new resource file.

```
Protected Overrides Sub OnStart(ByVal args() As String)
  ' Add code here to start your service. This method should set things
  ' in motion so your service can do its work.
  Try
    m_WorkerThread = New Thread(AddressOf ThreadFunc)
    m_WorkerThread.Name = My.Resources.ThreadName
    m_WorkerThread.Priority = ThreadPriority.Normal
    m_WorkerThread.Start()
    WriteLogEvent(My.Resources.ServiceStarting, ONSTART_INFO, _
    EventLogEntryType.Information, My.Resources.Source)
  Catch ex As Exception
    'We Catch the Exception
```

```
        'to avoid any unhandled errors
        'and we will stop the service if any occur here
        Me.Stop()
    End Try
End Sub
```

The listing shows that I am now using the My Object to read from the localization resource file.

I am also using the ONSTART_INFO constant instead of the hardcoded values from previous chapters. This will be the model from now on.

Modifying *<OnStop>*

Now let's update the *<OnStop>* method to reflect the use of Resources and WriteEventLog call changes. Listing 4-5 shows the changes.

Listing 4-5   Modifications to *<OnStop>* to support the new resource file.

```
Protected Overrides Sub OnStop()
' Add code here to perform any tear-down necessary to stop your service.
    Try
        If (Not m_WorkerThread Is Nothing) Then
            Try
                Me.RequestAdditionalTime(THIRTY_SECONDS)
                m_WorkerThread.Join(TIME_OUT)
                m_ThreadAction.StopThread = True
            Catch ex As Exception
            m_ThreadAction = Nothing
            End Try
        End If
        WriteLogEvent(My.Resources.ServiceStopping, ONSTOP_INFO, _
        EventLogEntryType.Information, My.Resources.Source)
    Catch ex As Exception
    End Try
End Sub
```

Modifying *<OnPause>*

As shown in Listing 4-6, you must once again update *<OnPause>*.

Listing 4-6   Modifications to *<OnPause>* to support the new resource file.

```
Protected Overrides Sub OnPause()
    Try
        m_ThreadAction.Pause = True
        WriteLogEvent(My.Resources.ServicePausing, ONPAUSE_INFO, _
        EventLogEntryType.Information, My.Resources.Source)
    Catch ex As Exception
        'We Catch the Exception
        'to avoid any unhandled errors
        'since we are pausing and
        'logging an event is what failed
        'we will merely write the output
```

```
        'to the debug window
        Debug.WriteLine("Error pausing service: " + ex.ToString())
        Me.Stop()
            'do nothing
    End Try
End Sub
```

Modifying *<OnContinue>*

Listing 4-7 shows how to update the *<OnContinue>* method.

Listing 4-7   Modifications to *<OnContinue>* to support the new resource file.

```
Protected Overrides Sub OnContinue()
    Try
        m_ThreadAction.Pause = False
        WriteLogEvent(My.Resources.ServiceContinuing, ONCONTINUE_INFO, _
        EventLogEntryType.Information, My.Resources.Source)
    Catch ex As Exception
     'We Catch the Exception
     'to avoid any unhandled errors
     'since we are resuming and
     'logging an event is what failed
     'we will merely write the output
     'to the debug window
     Debug.WriteLine("Error resuming service: " + ex.ToString())
     Me.Stop()
    End Try
End Sub
```

> **Note**   Remember to enable Pause and Continue for your service if you did not continue from the code in the previous chapter.

Writing a New Thread Method

This chapter requires us to extend the capabilities of the current thread function. In the next section, we will extend the usage of the threads.

Modify your existing *ThreadFunc* to match the code shown in Listing 4-8.

Listing 4-8   Updates to the current thread method.

```
Private Sub ThreadFunc()
  While Not m_ThreadAction.StopThread
    If Not m_ThreadAction.Pause Then
      Try
          For Each TextFile As String In
              My.Computer.FileSystem.GetFiles( _
              My.Resources.IncomingPath, _
              FileIO.SearchOption.SearchTopLevelOnly, "*.txt")
              If m_ThreadAction.Pause Or m_ThreadAction.StopThread Then
```

```
            Exit For
        End If
        Try
           WriteLogEvent(My.Resources.ThreadMessage + TextFile, _
           THREAD_INFO, EventLogEntryType.Information, My.Resources.Source)
        Catch ex As Exception
           WriteLogEvent(My.Resources.ThreadErrorMessage +
                Now.ToString, _
           THREAD_ERROR, EventLogEntryType.Error, My.Resources.Source)
        End Try
      Next
    Catch fio As IOException
      WriteLogEvent(My.Resources.ThreadIOError + Now.ToString, _
      THREAD_ABORT_ERROR, EventLogEntryType.Error, My.Resources.Source)
    Catch tab As ThreadAbortException
      'this must be listed first as Exception is the master catch
    'Clean up thread here
      WriteLogEvent(My.Resources.ThreadAbortMessage + Now.ToString, _
      THREAD_ABORT_ERROR, EventLogEntryType.Error, My.Resources.Source)
    Catch ex As Exception
      WriteLogEvent(My.Resources.ThreadErrorMessage + Now.ToString, _
      THREAD_ERROR, EventLogEntryType.Error, My.Resources.Source)
    End Try
   End If
  If Not m_ThreadAction.StopThread Then
    Thread.Sleep(THREAD_WAIT)
  End If
 End While
End Sub
```

The code in Listing 4-8 searches for any text files in the IncomingPath without looking in any subdirectories. After it finds a file it attempts to log an event using the text name and the standard message.

Note   You must remember to set the constant IncomingPath to the directory you created, otherwise the path will not exist and your query will always fail with an IOException.

Install and Verify

Now you need to recompile the new code, remove the old service, and install the new tutorials.exe.

Start the service. If that directory has no .txt files, you won't see any entries in the Application log. However, if you were to create or copy .txt files into the directory while the service was still running, not only would you see entries in the Application log, but you would also see them duplicated every five seconds, which is the sleep time. As you remove, delete, add, and create .txt files in your temp file directory, you will see new entries about every five seconds in the Application log.

> **Note**   Remember to stop the current service before continuing so that you do not fill the Application log with unwanted events.

Monitoring with Multiple Threads

We have successfully created a multithreaded polling service, which can be very useful, if you had to monitor more than one directory; for example, you could either have one thread monitor all the directories, or you could create multiple threads, using one per directory. You could also create a pool of threads, monitoring not only file system directories but also FTP folders and MSMQ queues so you could make sure that the proper thread handles the correct source and processing occurs correctly.

Expanding Processing

For this example, we will expand the service. We will monitor the incoming directory for files and then move these files to a newly created output directory. Although we don't process these files directly, the local service might be able to move files and then have another application process them after they are moved to the output directory. We are merely emulating the creation and pre-processing move to another application's processing folder.

Creating the Code

Create the code by following these steps:

1. Start by creating another folder, which we will call "outgoing." I create mine in the c:\temp directory, which is where the incoming folder is.

2. Add another resource entry called **OutgoingPath** and set its value to **c:\temp\outgoing**.

3. Add another set of InstanceId values in the modTutorial file.

4. In the modService.vb module file, add the following constant directly below the THREAD_INFO constant:

   ```
   Public Const FILE_WRITE_INFO As Integer = 3000
   ```

5. We also want to add a new error const under the existing definitions, as shown in the following code:

   ```
   Public Const FILE_WRITE_ERROR As Integer = 3001
   ```

Modifying the *<ThreadFunc>* Method

We need to modify the current *<ThreadFunc>* method so that instead of only logging an event-log entry, it will move the file to the new output folder. We will modify the code as shown in Listing 4-9.

Listing 4-9   Modifications to the *Thread* method.

```
Private Sub ThreadFunc()
  While Not m_ThreadAction.StopThread
    If Not m_ThreadAction.Pause Then
      Try
          For Each TextFile As String In _
              My.Computer.FileSystem.GetFiles( _
              My.Resources.IncomingPath, _
              FileIO.SearchOption.SearchTopLevelOnly, "*.txt")
              If m_ThreadAction.Pause Or m_ThreadAction.StopThread Then
                  Exit For
              End If
              Try
                  Dim FileOutput As String = My.Resources.OutgoingPath
                  + "\" + My.Computer.FileSystem.GetName(TextFile)
                  My.Computer.FileSystem.MoveFile(TextFile, FileOutput)
                  WriteLogEvent(My.Resources.ThreadMessage + TextFile,
                  THREAD_INFO, EventLogEntryType.Information,
                  My.Resources.Source)
              Catch ex As Exception
                  WriteLogEvent(My.Resources.ThreadErrorMessage +
                  Now.ToString, THREAD_ERROR, EventLogEntryType.Error,
                  My.Resources.Source)
              End Try
          Next
      Catch fio As IOException
          WriteLogEvent(My.Resources.ThreadIOError + Now.ToString,
              THREAD_ABORT_ERROR, EventLogEntryType.Error,
              My.Resources.Source)
      Catch tab As ThreadAbortException
          'this must be listed first as Exception s the master catch
          'Clean up thread here
          WriteLogEvent(My.Resources.ThreadAbortMessage + Now.ToString,
              THREAD_ABORT_ERROR, EventLogEntryType.Error,
              My.Resources.Source)
      Catch ex As Exception
          WriteLogEvent(My.Resources.ThreadErrorMessage + Now.ToString,
              THREAD_ERROR, EventLogEntryType.Error, My.Resources.Source)
      End Try
    End If

    If Not m_ThreadAction.StopThread Then
        Thread.Sleep(THREAD_WAIT)
    End If

  End While
End Sub
End Try
```

We are going to continue to use My Object to move the file from its current location to the OutgoingPath resource setting.

After the file is written to the output folder we log an event to the eventlog as we did in the previous version. If an exception occurs, we write an event that covers the error.

Installation and Verification

Before we compile and install the new service, we need to make one more change. The Local Service account (which we've been using for the service) doesn't by default have the proper authority to write to the Outgoing directory, and we must fix this.

Changing the StartUp Account

In Solution Explorer, double-click ProjectInstaller.vb. Select the ServiceProcessInstaller1 control, right-click, and select Properties. Change the Account property from LocalService to LocalSystem. Save and then build the project.

> **Note**   You could grant the Local Service account Modify permissions to both the incoming and outgoing folders instead of using the Local System account.

Install the newly created service and start it. Open Windows Explorer and click the c:\temp\incoming directory. In the right-hand pane, right-click, and choose New Text Document—or you could copy one or more existing text files into this folder from another location. Click in the white space to save the file. Within five seconds the file should disappear. The file will appear in your outgoing directory, and you should see a 2003 event in the Application log for each file that you created.

Extending the Threading Model

At this point, we have created a multithreaded service by adding a worker thread. However, we are currently limited to one worker thread. We're going to change that now.

We have a few ways to resolve the fact that we're using only one worker thread. A couple of factors affect what we decide to do. First, we need to consider the requirements of the problem we are trying to solve. Currently we're polling a file location to determine whether any .txt files exist and, if they do, reacting to that information.

To determine the threading model we need, we have to ask several questions:

- Can we monitor more than one file folder?
- Can we monitor more than one file type per folder?
- Can we move files of diffent types to different output folders?
- Do we want to move more than one file at a time, per type, per folder?

Monitoring More Than One Folder

If we were going to monitor the same type of files but have more than one folder, monitoring them all by using one thread wouldn't make much sense. The framework that we have designed allows our service to have multiple threads, all of which process one file type each.

Currently we have one folder and one file type: .txt. We also have one worker thread. However, we could easily create an array, a collection of threads, all of which read from a separate folder simultaneously. However, we need to fix a few things to make this work:

- We need to add string resources for each folder being monitored.

- We need to modify <ThreadFunc> to accept a parameter that would specify the folder location so that each thread monitors the proper folder.

- We need to modify the class to create a collection of threads instead of a single worker thread.

- <OnPause>, <OnContinue>, and <OnStop> stay the same because each thread already knows how to pause, continue, and stop based on the code already available.

Monitoring More Than One File Type Per Folder

You may decide that not only do you have multiple file folders, but that you also have multiple file types. Each file type can be processed differently, even though they come frome the same initial incoming folder.

For this scenario we need to make some more changes to the code:

- We need to update the data passed to the thread so that both the Incoming folder and file type are monitored for, or a list of file types is monitored for. This most likely means passing in a structure or class with the information we need.

- We need also need to update the <ThreadFunc> method to pass a new array of file type wild cards to the <GetFiles> call—which is only looking for .txt at this point.

Outputting to More Than One Folder

You could decide that you want each file type to be processed or sent to a different output folder. This has the following requirements:

- Again we need to update the resource strings to have a list of possible output paths.

- We need to update the <ThreadFunc> method to take a parameter indicating where to move the file to instead of the current parameter setting which is the OutgoingPath resource.

Processing More Than One File Type Per Folder

In the final modification, we are going to create multiple threads per incoming folder. This means that not only can we read from the same folder with multiple threads, but we can output to multiple folders. Each thread has to be configured with the incoming folder. Multiple threads can share the same file type to monitor for. If the threads are pointing to the same file type, we want to avoid having multiple threads monitor the same folder, because of issues with synchronization. However, when it comes to an output folder, we can share a single output folder among multiple threads, each thread writes differently named files, with different file types, so there is no need for synchronization.

When Complexity Steps In

One scenario is complex: multiple threads per file type, per folder. This means that more than one thread would be told to monitor a given folder. The problem is that there is no way for one thread to know that another thread is actively processing a given file. This might cause the service to have a large number of errors, which would waste CPU cycles—or you would spend more time with thread contention and failures than you would processing anything useful.

How do we get around this? In reality we don't have many options. Any option that allows more than one thread at a time to process (or in this case, move) files will inadvertently end up fighting with another thread. This means that we either accept having a single thread per file type, per folder, or we create a master worker thread that looks for all files on the disk and then places the files into a queue shared between the producer thread and the consumer threads.

Although this is definitely possible, you always want to ensure that you don't add too much complexity to your service just to be able to have more than one thread. If you only have a very low volume of files, this solution might not be worth the complexity or the processing overhead.

In the scenario we're working with in this chapter, we will try both methods. First, however, we have to resolve the fact that the current service implementation makes these solutions more difficult to accomplish than should be required. We are going to remedy this in the following sections.

Adding a FileWorker Class

The threads need access to the parameters and properties of file locations and file types. To simplify this process, we'll create a class that we'll use to create an instance of the worker thread. This class will contain all the functionality and properties we need, and we won't have to add all the direct functionality to the service. You will also be able to reuse this functionality in other applications that you design.

Designing a New Class File

Add a new class file to the Tutorials project and call it *FileWorker*. Then add the following imports to the top of the class definition, as shown in Listing 4-10.

Listing 4-10   Add the file require imports.

```
Imports System.Resources
Imports System.IO
Imports System.Text
Imports System.Threading
```

Adding a Constructor

Next we want to add a constructor. The constructor can be blank for now, as shown in Listing 4-11.

Listing 4-11   Add a blank constructor to the new class.
```
Public Sub New()
End Sub
```

Adding a Worker Thread

Now we want to add a single worker thread to the class, as shown in Listing 4-12. Later on we will have more than one worker thread.

Listing 4-12   Add the following thread to the new class.
```
Private m_WorkerThread As Thread = Nothing
```

Now we need to add a property that grants access to the worker thread so that we can join the thread from outside the class, as shown in Listing 4-13.

Listing 4-13   Expose the thread by adding a property.
```
Public ReadOnly Property WorkerThread() as Thread
  Get
    Return m_WorkerThread
  End Get
End Property
```

We use the *ReadOnly* accessor because we don't want users to be able to set this value; we only want them to be able read it.

Adding the Worker Thread Function

Because we will be replicating most of the functionality of the current service *<ThreadFunc>*, you can copy and paste it from the Tutorials.vb file into the FileWorker class file. We will not modify the function.

Adding the Thread Action State

Similar to the service class, we need to be able to tell the worker class when to pause, continue, or stop. Add a class file and call it **threadactionstate.vb**. Copy the ThreadActionState structure from the tutorials.vb and paste it into the new threadactionstate.vb class file.

We are going to change the Thread Action State from a structure to a class. We need to do this because we will be passing a reference to our Thread Action State shared variable to the *FileWorker* class instances. Remember to comment out the version that currently exists in the Tutorials service class, unless you have already removed it.

As shown in Listing 4-14, create a local reference in the *FileWorker* class.

Listing 4-14   Define the following thread state variable.
```
Private m_ThreadAction As ThreadActionState
```

Adding a WriteLogEvent

Copy the *WriteLogEvent* method from the *Service* class to the *FileWorker* class. Although we could copy the event to our modService file and make it publicly accessible, we are going to create a self-contained reusable class.

Adding Our *<Start>* Method

The last thing we need to do now is to add our *<Start>* method. This method will be used to start the worker process *<ThreadFunc>* in each instance of our *FileWorker* class.

Listing 4-15   Create the following *Start* method.

```
Public Sub Start()
  m_WorkerThread = New Thread(AddressOf ThreadFunc)
  m_WorkerThread.Priority = ThreadPriority.Normal
  m_WorkerThread.IsBackground = True
  m_WorkerThread.Start()
End Sub
```

Implementing the Worker Class

Before continuing, we need to make adjustments external to this class.

Adding a FileWorker Collection

We need to add a collection to the service that can hold the number of worker class instances we plan to create. As shown in Listing 4-16, we will create five worker threads. This number is simply for example purposes and could easily change on a dynamic basis, which I will demonstrate shortly.

Listing 4-16   Declaration for the worker collection in the Tutorials service class.

```
Private m_WorkerThreads As New Collection
```

Adding New File Type and Input Locations

With this implementation, we need to be able to supply five specific file locations or a combination of file locations and file types. These should be implemented as resource strings For a total of five input locations, I have to add four more. Table 4-2 lists the locations.

Table 4-2   New File Type Location

Name	Value
IncomingPath2	C:\temp\incoming2
IncomingPath3	c:\temp\incoming3
IncomingPath4	c:\temp\incoming4
IncomingPath5	c:\temp\incoming5

For the service to work properly, I need to add five unique file types. In this implementation we want to create the additional four folders listed previously. You can create them anywhere you wish, but make sure that the service resources are updated to reflect their location.

Creating the *FileWorkerOptions* Class

Each instance of the *FileWorker* class needs to know three things:

- The file input location
- The file output location
- The file type to process

Therefore we will add another class called *FileWorkerOptions*. Instead of creating another class file, we simply add the code shown in Listing 4-17 to the *FileWorker* class .vb file.

Listing 4-17   Adding a new property class to FileWorker.vb.

```
Public Class FileWorkerOptions
  Private m_Output As String
  Private m_Input As String
  Private m_FileType As String
  Public Property Output() As String
    Get
        Return m_Output
    End Get
    Set(ByVal value As String)
      m_Output = value
    End Set
  End Property
  Public Property Input() As String
    Get
        Return m_Input
    End Get
    Set(ByVal value As String)
      m_Input = value
    End Set
  End Property
  Public Property FileType() As String
    Get
        Return m_FileType
    End Get
    Set(ByVal value As String)
      m_FileType = value
    End Set
  End Property
End Class
```

As shown in Listing 4-18, we now create an instance of *FileWorkerOptions* in the *FileWorker* class.

Listing 4-18   Create an instance of *FileWorkerOptions*.

```
Private m_FileWorkerOptions As New FileWorkerOptions
```

Updating the FileWorker Constructor

We need to modify the constructor to reflect the required parameters that need to be passed into the class instance when it is created. Because these are required parameters, we must remove the parameterless constructor. First, as shown in Listing 4-19, we need to pass in a reference of the *ThreadActionState* from the Tutorials service class as well as the *FileWorkerOptions* settings for each specific *FileWorker* class instance.

Listing 4-19 Update the FileWorker constructor.

```
Public Sub New(ByRef threadaction As ThreadActionState, ByVal _
              fileworkeroptions As FileWorkerOptions)
    m_ThreadAction = threadaction
    m_FileWorkerOptions.Input = fileworkeroptions.Input
    m_FileWorkerOptions.Output = fileworkeroptions.Output
    m_FileWorkerOptions.FileType = fileworkeroptions.FileType
End Sub
```

We use a reference to *ThreadActionState* because it is a shared instance from the Tutorials service class. When the values of the *ThreadActionState* are updated, we want them reflected in each *FileWorker* class instance so that the threads will properly react to state changes.

Because each *FileWorker* has its own options, we need to have these options passed into the *FileWorker* class, then stored locally. We may want to expose these properties so that we can update them on the fly. For example, pause the service, update the options, and then continue.

Updating Our *<FileWorker.ThreadFunc>*

To reflect the changes to our processing based on a per *FileWorker* instance we have to update the *<ThreadFunc>* method to allow for the options we are passing into the class instance.

Listing 4-20 Updated *FileWorker* thread function.

```
For Each TextFile As String In My.Computer.FileSystem.GetFiles( _
  m_FileWorkerOptions.Input, _
  FileIO.SearchOption.SearchTopLevelOnly, _
  m_FileWorkerOptions.FileType)
  If m_ThreadAction.Pause Or m_ThreadAction.StopThread Then
    Exit For
  End If
  Try
    Dim FileOutput As String = My.Resources.OutgoingPath + "\" + _
                      My.Computer.FileSystem.GetName(TextFile)
    My.Computer.FileSystem.MoveFile(TextFile, FileOutput)
    WriteLogEvent(My.Resources.ThreadMessage + TextFile, THREAD_INFO, _
              EventLogEntryType.Information, My.Resources.Source)
  Catch ex As Exception
    WriteLogEvent(My.Resources.ThreadErrorMessage + Now.ToString, THREAD_ERROR, _
              EventLogEntryType.Error, My.Resources.Source)

  End Try
Next
```

Notice that now we are using the passed-in options for Output, FileType, and Input locations. This allows each instance of the class to monitor different locations and different file types. In this example we are using five different locations, one file type, and one file output path. We could easily use one location, five file types, and five output paths.

Before we continue to update the code we need to create the five file type entries in our resource file to reflect those we will monitor in our incoming paths. I have created the following entries listed in Table 4-3 in my Tutorials Resource file.

Table 4-3   New File Type Resource Entries

Name	Value
FileType1	*.txt
FileType2	*.bat
FileType3	*.dat
FileType4	*.inf
FileType5	*.ico

Once you have created these entries you can continue to make the modifications for this chapter.

Updating *<Tutorials.ThreadFunc>*

We are no longer performing the processing in the class *ThreadFunc*. However, we will still use it to create the instances of the *FileWorker* class, set the options, and start the processing. If we don't, we could cause <OnStart> to take too long to complete and return control to the service control manager (SCM). Again, it is never a good idea to tie up the <OnStart> method. Listing 4-21 shows the modifications required to our <ThreadFunc> method to support the new multi-file processing capabilities.

Listing 4-21   Updated Tutorials.ThreadFunc.

```
Private Sub ThreadFunc()
    Try
        Dim tmpOptions(5) As FileWorkerOptions
        Dim iLoop As Short
        Dim tmpWorker As FileWorker
        For iLoop = 0 To 4
            tmpOptions(iLoop) = New FileWorkerOptions
            tmpOptions(iLoop).Output = My.Resources.OutgoingPath
        Next
        tmpOptions(0).FileType = My.Resources.FileType1
        tmpOptions(0).Input = My.Resources.IncomingPath
        tmpOptions(1).FileType = My.Resources.FileType2
        tmpOptions(1).Input = My.Resources.IncomingPath2
        tmpOptions(2).FileType = My.Resources.FileType3
        tmpOptions(2).Input = My.Resources.IncomingPath3
        tmpOptions(3).FileType = My.Resources.FileType4
        tmpOptions(3).Input = My.Resources.IncomingPath4
        tmpOptions(4).FileType = My.Resources.FileType5
```

```
        tmpOptions(4).Input = My.Resources.IncomingPath5
        For iLoop = 0 To 4
          m_WorkerThreads.Add(New FileWorker(m_ThreadAction,
                tmpOptions(iLoop)))
          tmpWorker = m_WorkerThreads(iLoop + 1)
          tmpWorker.Start()
        Next
      Catch fio As IOException
        WriteLogEvent(My.Resources.ThreadIOError + Now.ToString,
          THREAD_ABORT_ERROR, EventLogEntryType.Error,
          My.Resources.Source)
        Me.Stop()
      Catch tab As ThreadAbortException
        'this must be listed first as Exception s the master catch
        'Clean up thread here
        WriteLogEvent(My.Resources.ThreadAbortMessage + Now.ToString,
          THREAD_ABORT_ERROR, EventLogEntryType.Error,
          My.Resources.Source)
      Catch ex As Exception
        WriteLogEvent(My.Resources.ThreadErrorMessage + Now.ToString,
          THREAD_ERROR, EventLogEntryType.Error, My.Resources.Source)
        Me.Stop()
      End Try
    End If
  End Sub
```

The previous code listing creates five instances of the *FileWorkerOptions* class—one instance for each instance of *FileWorker* that we plan to create. Then it instantiates and sets the option properties. Finally, it creates five instances of the *FileWorker* class, passing each instance a reference to the *ThreadActionState* shared variable and the instance-specific *FileWorkerOptions* settings, and then starts that instance's thread function.

I never recommend that you hard-code options into your application. Even if you use resource files, you have a lack of control over your service. You need to create an application configuration file that will store the settings for your application. Not only will this solve the hard-coding issue, but it will also shorten your code because it allows you to perform almost all the actions in a single loop.

Updating the *<OnStop>* Method

The last thing we need to update is the *<OnStop>* method. Currently we are using the *Join* method of the global m_WorkerThread to validate that processing is complete. In this new case we have multiple threads running at the same time.

We must perform several steps to update this method:

1. Set the thread state to Stopped.

2. Ask the SCM for extra time so that we can perform the required cleanup.

3.   Attempt to join each thread to validate that it has shut down, requesting additional time from the SCM for each thread we join. This might cause the service to take as much as 45 seconds to shut down, because the time-out is 15 seconds and we have five threads. However, this additional time helps to ensure that we are shutting down properly and causes the SCM to believe we processed the shutdown request properly. If the SCM believes we have not responded to the shutdown request properly, it will display an error stating that the service did not respond to the request in a timely manner. At this point you may need to use Task Manager to end the service process, unless you were using all background threads, which would be cleaned up automatically once the service instance shut down.

> **Note**   Because the worker threads are background threads, if a *Join* times out, we exit the *<OnStop>* method and the service ends, these threads will be cleaned up, unlike non-background threads, which would keep the service running.

Listing 4-22 demonstrates how to properly join each thread and attempt to shut down the service gracefully.

Listing 4-22   Update *<OnStop>* method to shut down smoothly.

```
Protected Overrides Sub OnStop()
   Try
        WriteLogEvent(My.Resources.ServiceStopping, ONSTOP_INFO, _
                      EventLogEntryType.Information, My.Resources.Source)
        m_ThreadAction.StopThread = True
        For Each fw As FileWorker In m_WorkerThreads
            Me.RequestAdditionalTime(THIRTY_SECONDS)
            fw.WorkerThread.Join(TIME_OUT)
        Next
   Catch ex As Exception
        WriteLogEvent(My.Resources.ServiceStopping + ex.ToString(), _
                      ONSTOP_ERROR, EventLogEntryType.Error, _
                      My.Resources.Source)
   End Try
End Sub
```

Installation and Verification

Now you can compile and install the latest version of the service. Remember to create the five folder locations that we specified in the resource settings. Depending on the file locations you created and the file types you are monitoring for, you have to remember to create files for your service to monitor and process.

For each file that you add to your monitoring folders, you will see the file move to your output folder and an entry in the event log. Once you have verified the service, stop and remove it before moving to the next section.

> **Note**   Remember not to set two instances to the same file type—this will produce unexpected results, such as FileIOExceptions, because one thread has already moved a file that another thread just became aware of and tried to process.

Using Configuration Files

Using a resource file to store configuration information is not always the best solution. Therefore we will implement once last change to the service: We will add a configuration file.

Actually, we will create two configuration files. The first will be the application-specific configuration file that is supported by default in all .NET applications. This is where system and technology settings modify the behavior of the application. The other configuration file is an application-processing configuration file that will store information for preparing the options that the service will use to perform its tasks. Currently, we have three such options: Input, Output, and FileType.

We will use XML for both the application-processing file and the application-specific configuration file as required by .NET.

Application-Specific Configuration File

To create our application-specific configuration file, go to the Properties window of the project and select Settings. Create a key/value pair named **Configuration** with a value of **Configuration.Xml**. Then save and compile your code. \[note] If you are going to store the configuration file in the same folder as the service executable, you don't need to put in the %path%. Instead, just set the value to **Configuration.xml**; the service will look for the file locally by default.

When you look in your debug or release bin folder—depending on which type of build you are performing—you will see Tutorials.Exe.Config. All application-specific configuration files must be named in following the format: *servicename*.exe.config, where *servicename* is the name of the service executable, not the service name itself. In this situation the application-specific configuration will be named Tutorials.exe.config.

You may also notice that you now have a file called App.config in your project, stored with the rest of the source code. This is fine—you can ignore it. Do not edit the App.Config directly from the development environment; instead use the Settings Tab of the Project Properties to add or remove values. The App.config is used at design time by the Microsoft Visual Basic IDE, and the servicename.exe.config file is used at runtime. You can, , updated the runtime config file manually after you release your code.

For Listing 4-23, please refer to the App.Config file in your project folder for a full file listing. Here we will focus on the ApplicationSettings section only.

Listing 4-23   An example of an application-specific configuration file.

```xml
<?xml version="1.0" encoding="utf-8" ?>
<configuration>
    <applicationSettings>
        <Tutorials.My.MySettings>
            <setting name="Configuration" serializeAs="String">
                <value>Configuration.Xml</value>
            </setting>
        </Tutorials.My.MySettings>
    </applicationSettings>
</configuration>
```

In Listing 4-23, you can see a new configuration item called Configuration with a value of Tutorials.Xml in the Tutorials.My.MySettings scope. This item allows us to access this property through the My object, which is what we want to do in the *<Tutorials.ThreadFunc>* method.

We need to provide access to the configuration file at run time from the Tutorials service by adding the code in Listing 4-24 to the Tutorials.vb file.

Listing 4-24   Accessing My.Settings application settings.

```vb
Dim configstr As String = My.Settings.Configuration
```

This will return the value of the Configuration setting, which will point to the configuration file.

The Application-Processing Configuration File

The next step is to create the application-processing configuration file that will store Input, Output, and FileType information for each *FileWorker* class instance. This step allows us to avoid hard-coding or trying to use a resource file to store this information, which requires a recompile each time a change is needed. Listing 4-25 shows a copy of the Configuration.xml file that I created. You will need to also create this file because the system will not generate it automatically. You can use any standard editor, such as Notepad, to generate this file, or you can generate it in Visual Studio itself.

Listing 4-25   User-generated configuration file.

```xml
<?xml version="1.0" encoding="utf-8" ?>
<Configuration>
  <FileWorkerOptions>
    <FileWorkerOption>
      <IncomingPath>c:\temp\incoming</IncomingPath>
      <OutgoingPath>c:\temp\outgoing</OutgoingPath>
      <FileType>*.txt</FileType>
    </FileWorkerOption>
    <FileWorkerOption>
      <IncomingPath>c:\temp\incoming2</IncomingPath>
      <OutgoingPath>c:\temp\outgoing</OutgoingPath>
      <FileType>*.dat</FileType>
    </FileWorkerOption>
```

```
    <FileWorkerOption>
      <IncomingPath>c:\temp\incoming3</IncomingPath>
      <OutgoingPath>c:\temp\outgoing</OutgoingPath>
      <FileType>*.ico</FileType>
    </FileWorkerOption>
    <FileWorkerOption>
      <IncomingPath>c:\temp\incoming4/</IncomingPath>
      <OutgoingPath>c:\temp\outgoing</OutgoingPath>
      <FileType>*.bat</FileType>
    </FileWorkerOption>
    <FileWorkerOption>
      <IncomingPath>c:\temp\incoming5</IncomingPath>
      <OutgoingPath>c:\temp\outgoing</OutgoingPath>
      <FileType>*.inf</FileType>
    </FileWorkerOption>
  </FileWorkerOptions>
</Configuration>
```

We have created a simple XML file that allows us to avoid hard-coding configuration settings, to configure a single incoming folder to have multiple threads monitoring for different file types.

In the configuration file listed previously, I have created the same five entries that I hard-coded in the *<Tutorials.ThreadFunc>* method.

Next we have to update the *<Tutorials.ThreadFunc>* so that it uses a configuration file, instead of hard-coded values.

Updating *<Tutorials.ThreadFunc>*

The change to *<ThreadFunc>* will allow us to read the configuration file, create *FileWorkerOption* instances, create *FileWorker* instances, and then start the worker threads.

Before we read the configuration file, which is in XML, we want to add the import shown in Listing 4-26 to the top of the Tutorial.vb, allowing us to directly instantiate the classes in the namespace.

Listing 4-26   Adding the Xml namespace import.
```
Imports System.Xml
```

With the Xml namespace import in Listing 4-26 added we can make the code changes required to utilize the new configuration file and *updated <ThreadFunc>* method listed in Listing 4-27.

Listing 4-27   Using the new *<ThreadFunc>* method.
```
Private Sub ThreadFunc()
  Try
    'Load our Configuration File
    Dim Doc As XmlDocument = New XmlDocument()
    Doc.Load(My.Settings.Configuration)
    Dim Options As XmlNode
```

```
                'Get a pointer to the Outer Node
                Options = _
                    Doc.SelectSingleNode("//*[local-name()='FileWorkerOptions']")
                If (Not Options Is Nothing) Then
                    'Get a pointer to the first
                    'child node of FileWorkerOptions
                    Dim tmpOptions As System.Xml.XPath.XPathNavigator = _
                    Options.FirstChild.CreateNavigator()
                    If (Not tmpOptions Is Nothing) Then
                        Dim FWOptions As New FileWorkerOptions
                        Dim children As System.Xml.XPath.XPathNavigator
                        'Looop through each childe node (FileWorkerOption) and
                        'get the values. Create a new FileWorkerOptions
                        'instance and FileWorkerOption instance
                        Do
                          Try
                            children = tmpOptions.SelectSingleNode("IncomingPath")
                            FWOptions.Input = children.Value
                            children = tmpOptions.SelectSingleNode("OutgoingPath")
                            FWOptions.Output = children.Value
                            children = tmpOptions.SelectSingleNode("FileType")
                            FWOptions.FileType = children.Value
                            Dim tmpFW As New FileWorker(m_ThreadAction, FWOptions)
                            m_WorkerThreads.Add(tmpFW)
                            tmpFW.Start()
                          Catch ex As Exception
                            WriteLogEvent("Could not read key/value pair", _
                            ONSTART_ERROR, EventLogEntryType.Error, _
                            My.Resources.Source)
                          End Try
                        Loop While (tmpOptions.MoveToNext)
                    End If
                End If
            Catch ex As Exception
                WriteLogEvent(ex.ToString(), ONSTART_ERROR, _
                    EventLogEntryType.Error, My.Resources.Source)
                Me.Stop()
            End Try
    End Sub
```

The <ThreadFunc> version shown in Listing 4-27 allows us to create and run any number of *FileWorkerOptions* and *FileWorker* instances. It is configurable based on the number of entries that are included in the configuration.xml file. If you want to have multiple threads run against the same IncomingPath, you can easily configure more than one entry.

First we open the configuration file using the My object. Next we create a cursor into the XML file by loading it into memory and then pointing to the first parent node, <FileWorkerOptions>. Next we loop through the <FileWorkerOption> element children and read the values from the XML document. After each entry is read, we create an instance of the *FileWorker* class, pass in the values, and then start the internal class worker thread. We then repeat these actions until all instances are started. If at any point a failure occurs, we log an event, and if the document itself is invalid or unavailable, we log an event and also stop the service.

Using XML configuration and application-specific configuration files helps to extend the capabilities beyond hard-coding values, which are much harder to keep track of and impossible to update during run time.

Installation and Verification

Compile and install the new service. Make sure that the application-specific file configuration setting reflects where the configuration.xml file is stored. Make sure that the configuration.xml file is configured properly per Listing 4-5.

Add some files to your incoming folders matching the extension or file type with the location and settings in your configuration.xml file. Once you have created several files for each type, start the service. For each file found of the given type in the file input location, as configured in the configuration.xml, the file will be moved to the output folder and an event logged in the event log.

Summary

- Visual Basic 2008 provides easy access to file and system objects through several sets of classes such as *System.IO* and *System.Text*.

- Services or applications written to access these objects must be written with security in mind.

- Accessing file system objects and processing files on multiple threads requires a clear development strategy, otherwise locks and security access violations can occur. (Future chapters will focus on this issue.)

- Configuration files add extensibility to a service, as well as easy configuration.

- Avoid hard-coding values into your service or using resource files instead of configuration files.

- Application-specific configuration files can exist for any application that you code, including services, and can exist at the computer level itself. The effect a configuration file has on a computer, a service, or a stand-alone application depends on the type of configuration file and its implementation.

- Security is not based on an application alone, but also the thread level. Making sure that each thread is secure or that each thread runs in a required context requires thought and strategy.

Chapter 5

Processing and Notification

In most scenarios, whether for reporting, debugging, or administrative purposes, not only do you want your service to perform some type of processing function, but you also must be able to report on the processing status. This could mean reporting errors, current status, or even a summary of the service actions. Because you can easily program a service to run at different periods of time, or in intervals, the reporting or notification mechanism you choose can provide as little or as much detail as you want.

This chapter focuses on how you can implement socket-based services that support notifications using Simple Mail Transport Protocol (SMTP). SMTP is a standard used all over the world and is implemented in all major mail systems, such as Microsoft Exchange. Not only does Microsoft provide an SMTP Connector, allowing it to send and receive straight SMTP protocol messages, but almost every operating system that Microsoft has produced in the past five years has the built-in Microsoft SMTP Services. These services can be used in conjunction with Post Office Protocol 3 (POP3) services, also provided by Microsoft Operating Systems.

In this chapter you will need access to an SMTP-enabled server, or you can install and configure Microsoft SMTP service. For help with this, see Appendix C, "Microsoft SMTP Service."

SMTP Notifications

This section focuses on extending the capabilities from Chapter 4, "Services and Polling," to include notifications when files are received and processed by the service. To accomplish this, we need three things:

- We must add some text files with data in them to our incoming folder.
- We need to add code to read the data out of the text files.
- We need to add code to send the data to an SMTP server for relay to recipients.

I have added a class called *SMTP* that has a built-in SMTP e-mail sender.

Listing 5-1 is a simple SMTP implementation using standard Microsoft TCP/IP and .NET technologies. Because we will be extending the Chapter 4 code, you will want to add the code from Listing 5-1 as a new class file to the current tutorials project, calling it **SMTP**.

Listing 5-1 *SMTP* mail class code.

```
Imports System.Net.Mail
Imports System.Net

Public Class SMTP
    Private m_SmtpServer As String
    Private m_SmtpPort As Integer
    Private m_Sender As String
    Private m_Subject As String
    Private m_Message As String
    Private m_Recipient As String
    Private Const SMTP_ERROR As Integer = 15000
    Private m_SmtpClient As New SmtpClient

    Public Sub New()
    End Sub

    Public Property SmtpServer() As String
        Get
            Return m_SmtpServer
        End Get
        Set(ByVal value As String)
            m_SmtpServer = value
        End Set
    End Property

    Public Property SmtpPort() As Integer
        Get
            Return m_SmtpPort
        End Get
        Set(ByVal value As Integer)
            m_SmtpPort = value
        End Set
    End Property

    Public Property Sender() As String
        Get
            Return m_Sender
        End Get
        Set(ByVal value As String)
            m_Sender = value
        End Set
    End Property

    Public Property Subject() As String
        Get
            Return m_Subject
        End Get
        Set(ByVal value As String)
            m_Subject = value
        End Set
```

```vbnet
        End Property

    Public Property Message() As String
        Get
            Return m_Message
        End Get
        Set(ByVal value As String)
            m_Message = value
        End Set
    End Property

    Public Property Recipient() As String
        Get
            Return m_Recipient
        End Get
        Set(ByVal value As String)
            m_Recipient = value
        End Set
    End Property

    Public Function SendMail(ByVal sender As String, ByVal rcpt As String, _
ByVal server As String, ByVal port As Integer, ByVal subject As String, _
 ByVal message As String) As Boolean
        Return Send(sender, rcpt, server, port, subject, message)
    End Function
    Public Function SendMail() As Boolean
        Return Send(m_Sender, m_Recipient, m_SmtpServer, _
                  m_SmtpPort, m_Subject, m_Message)
    End Function

    Private Function Send(ByVal sender As String, ByVal rcpt As String, _
          ByVal server As String, ByVal port As Integer, _
          ByVal subject As String, ByVal message As String) As Boolean
        Try
            If ((String.IsNullOrEmpty(sender)) Or (String.IsNullOrEmpty(rcpt)) _
     Or (String.IsNullOrEmpty(server)) Or (port <= 0 Or port >= 65000) Or _
    (String.IsNullOrEmpty(subject)) Or (String.IsNullOrEmpty(message))) Then
                System.Diagnostics.EventLog.WriteEntry("Tutorials SMTP Class", _
                  "Error sending Email - Invalid Parameters", _
                  EventLogEntryType.Error, SMTP_ERROR)
                Return False
            End If
            m_SmtpClient.Host = server
            m_SmtpClient.DeliveryMethod = SmtpDeliveryMethod.Network
            m_SmtpClient.Port = port
            m_SmtpClient.Credentials = CredentialCache.DefaultNetworkCredentials
            m_SmtpClient.Send(sender, rcpt, subject, message)
        Catch ex As Exception
            System.Diagnostics.EventLog.WriteEntry("Tutorials SMTP Class", _
    "Error Sending Email - " + ex.ToString, EventLogEntryType.Error, SMTP_ERROR)
            Return False
        End Try
    End Function

End Class
```

File Processing

In this section we will move the files from Incoming to Outgoing folders, where they will be processed. We will then send an e-mail to the designated recipient. After the file is processed and the notification sent, we will move the file to the new Processed folder.

First we need to create a folder called Processed in the temp folder, in the same place as the Incoming and Outgoing folders. Since we are continuing on with the Chapter 4 code, we want to update Configuration.xml to add the new element, which we will call *ProcessedPath*. The *ProcessedPath* element will go under the current *<FileWorkerOption>* element because it will be configured on a per-file basis. In Listing 5-2 you can see the new element added to our configuration file.

Listing 5-2 Updated configuration file supporting the *ProcessedPath* element.

```xml
<?xml version="1.0" encoding="utf-8" ?>
<Configuration>
  <FileWorkerOptions>
    <FileWorkerOption>
      <IncomingPath>c:\temp\incoming</IncomingPath>
      <OutgoingPath>c:\temp\outgoing</OutgoingPath>
      <ProcessedPath>c:\temp\processed</ProcessedPath>
      <FileType>*.txt</FileType>
    </FileWorkerOption>
  </FileWorkerOptions>
</Configuration>
```

You'll see a demonstration of these changes later in the chapter.

Configuring Our New SMTP Class

In a real application (which we'll create shortly), the files that you process may contain the information required to send them, such as the Login ID, the Sender, Receiver, Server, the Message, and any other information required. However, we will configure the SMTP properties in the configuration XML file so that each file type gets its own SMTP recipient. You can, of course, configure them all to have the same information. I am modifying the configuration file *<FileWorkerOption>* to include the new SMTP information. The code shown in Listing 5-3 not only includes the SMTP properties, but also an enabled property. Having the SMTP options on a per-file configuration will allow you to enable or disable SMTP notifications on a per-file-type basis scaling both the notifications and allow you to manage notifications independently.

Listing 5-3 Updated user configuration file supporting the new SMTP values.

```xml
<?xml version="1.0" encoding="utf-8" ?>
<Configuration>
  <FileWorkerOptions>
    <FileWorkerOption>
      <IncomingPath>c:\temp\incoming</IncomingPath>
      <OutgoingPath>c:\temp\outgoing</OutgoingPath>
      <ProcessedPath>c:\temp\processed</ProcessedPath>
      <FileType>*.txt</FileType>
```

```
          <SmtpServer>test.com</SmtpServer>
          <Subject>Test Subject</Subject>
          <Message>Found Message</Message>
          <Sender>Michael@test.com</Sender>
          <Recipient>Michael@test.com</Recipient>
          <SmtpPort>25</SmtpPort>
          <MailEnabled>true</MailEnabled>
      </FileWorkerOption>
    </FileWorkerOptions>
</Configuration>
```

Remember that if you don't have an SMTP server available, but you are running Windows XP, Windows 2000, Windows Server 2003, or Windows Vista, you can install the SMTP service. Please see Appendix C for more information.

Updating the *FileWorkerOptions* Class

We need to update the *FileWorkerOptions* class to reflect the new ProcessedPath requirement. Listing 5-4 shows the code I have added to the class.

Listing 5-4   Adding the ProcessedPath property.
```
Public Property ProcessedPath() As String
  Get
     Return m_Processed
     End Get
  Set(ByVal value As String)
     m_Processed = value
  End Set
End Property
Private mProcessed As String
```

We use this property and private variable to access and set the ProcessedPath location, which is in our configuration XML file.

Updating the *FileWorker* Class

Now that we've added the SMTP class, we want to implement its use. For each file type or File-Worker class we'll have a separate *SMTP* class instance that will send e-mail for that thread.

To implement these changes I have added the code shown in Listing 5-5 to *FileWorker*.

Listing 5-5   SMTP mail support changes for the *FileWorker* class.
```
Private m_MailEnabled As Boolean
Private m_SmtpClient As New SMTP
Public Property MailEnabled() As Boolean
   Get
      Return m_MailEnabled
   End Get
   Set(ByVal value As Boolean)
      m_MailEnabled = value
   End Set
End Property
```

```
Public ReadOnly Property SmtpClient() As SMTP
    Get
        Return m_SmtpClient
    End Get
End Property
```

Updating the *FileWorker* Class Constructor

With the addition of the *ProcessedPath* element to our configuration file, and the Processed property to the *FileWorkerOptions* class, the *FileWorker* class constructor, which sets the instances local *FileWorkerOptions* properties, needs to reflect the additional property setting.

The code in Listing 5-6 demonstrates what the new *FileWorker* class constructor should look like.

Listing 5-6 *FileWorker* constructor change to support the ProcessedPath configuration elements.

```
Public Sub New(ByRef threadaction As ThreadActionState, _
               ByVal fileworkeroptions As FileWorkerOptions)
    m_ThreadAction = threadaction

    m_FileWorkerOptions.Input = fileworkeroptions.Input
    m_FileWorkerOptions.Output = fileworkeroptions.Output
    m_FileWorkerOptions.FileType = fileworkeroptions.FileType
    m_FileWorkerOptions.ProcessedPath = fileworkeroptions.ProcessedPath
End Sub
```

The code in Listing 5-6 sets the locally cached instance of the *FileWorkerOptions*, of the *FileWorker* class, property ProcessedPath to the passed in value created in the Tutorials.vb <*ThreadFunc*> method.

Updating the <*FileWorker.ThreadFunc*> Method

Now we need to modify the <*ThreadFunc*> code so that we can read, process, and move the files in the outgoing folder to the Process folder. It may seem redundant to move files from incoming to outgoing, process them, and then move them again. However, as is common, we may receive a file at a later time in the incoming folder with the same name as a file already received. If we don't move the existing files from the incoming to the outgoing folders, when new files come in, previous files could get overwritten and we could lose data.

In Listing 5-7 we will add in the code required for processing files and sending notifications.

Listing 5-7 Updated <*FileWorker.ThreadFunc*> method with ProcessedPath support.*ThreadFunc*.

```
Private Sub ThreadFunc()
    While Not m_ThreadAction.StopThread
        If Not m_ThreadAction.Pause Then
            Try
                For Each TextFile As String In My.Computer.FileSystem.GetFiles( _
                    m_FileWorkerOptions.Input, _
                    FileIO.SearchOption.SearchTopLevelOnly, _
                    m_FileWorkerOptions.FileType)

                    If m_ThreadAction.Pause Or m_ThreadAction.StopThread Then
```

```vb
                    Exit For
                End If
                Try
                    Dim tmpGuid As String = Guid.NewGuid().ToString()
                    Dim OutputFile As String = m_FileWorkerOptions.Output _
                        + "\" + tmpGuid + "_" +
                        My.Computer.FileSystem.GetName(TextFile)

                    Dim ProcessFile As String = _
                        m_FileWorkerOptions.ProcessedPath _
                        + "\" + tmpGuid + "_" +
                        My.Computer.FileSystem.GetName(TextFile)
                    My.Computer.FileSystem.MoveFile(TextFile, OutputFile)
                    'File is moved so lets read it out of the Output Folder
                    If (Me.MailEnabled) Then
                        Dim message As String
                        Try
                            message = "Processing File Data:[" + _
                            My.Computer.FileSystem.ReadAllText(OutputFile) + _
                            "] From File - "
                        Catch ex As Exception
                            message = "Unable to read from file - "
                        End Try
                        'Send the Email and then move it
                        again to the processed Folder
                        m_SmtpClient.Message = message + OutputFile
                            m_SmtpClient.SendMail()
                    End If
                    My.Computer.FileSystem.MoveFile(OutputFile, ProcessFile)
                    WriteLogEvent(My.Resources.ThreadMessage + TextFile,
                        THREAD_INFO, EventLogEntryType.Information,
                        My.Resources.Source)
                Catch ex As Exception
                    WriteLogEvent(My.Resources.ThreadErrorMessage +
                        Now.ToString, THREAD_ERROR, _
                        EventLogEntryType.Error, My.Resources.Source)
                End Try
            Next
        Catch fio As IOException
            WriteLogEvent(My.Resources.ThreadIOError + Now.ToString,
                THREAD_ABORT_ERROR, EventLogEntryType.Error,
                My.Resources.Source)
        Catch tab As ThreadAbortException
            WriteLogEvent(My.Resources.ThreadAbortMessage + Now.ToString,
                THREAD_ABORT_ERROR, EventLogEntryType.Error,
                My.Resources.Source)
        Catch ex As Exception
            WriteLogEvent(My.Resources.ThreadErrorMessage + Now.ToString,
                THREAD_ERROR, EventLogEntryType.Error, My.Resources.Source)
        End Try
    End If

    If Not m_ThreadAction.StopThread Then
        Thread.Sleep(THREAD_WAIT)
    End If
  End While
End Sub
```

We have extended the Chapter 4 code so that we are looping through the files, generating both the path for Outgoing folder and Processed folder move operations. After a file has been placed in the output folder, we check to see if mail is enabled for that *FileWorker* class instance. If mail is enabled, we read the text from the text file that was found, set the message, and then attempt to send the mail. Notice that I am resetting the message. This is not required, but because we're processing the files, it's good to show we really can process them.

After the e-mail notification is sent, we then move the file to the Processed folder.

One important thing to note about this method update is that the method appends a new globally unique identifier (GUID) to each file that the service attempts to process. Using a GUID ensures that if a file is not processed properly, or not moved to the processed folder, it will not block the processing of a new file in the incoming folder with the same name as a previous file in the outgoing folder.

Updating the *Tutorials* Class

The *Tutorials* class must be updated to read, validate, and configure the new e-mail capabilities of the service. We need to update the <*ThreadFunc*> method to read the updated configuration file and set the e-mail properties for each <*FileWorker*> class we create.

Updating the <*Tutorials.ThreadFunc*> Method

Before we can actually send the mail notifications and use the new Processed folder function-ality, we need to update the processing of the configuration.xml. In addition to the ability to process the new configuration format and properties, we need to add the ability to process the new mail settings and enable the mail functionality in our code based on those settings. Before we review the Listing 5-7 code changes we need to add another constant to our modService.vb file. This constant, CONFIG_READ_ERROR, will be used for errors when processing the new configuration.xml file format. In the modService.vb file, with the rest of the constants, add the code shown in Listing 5-8.

Listing 5-8 Event ID declaration for xml configuration file processing errors.

```
Public Const CONFIG_READ_ERROR As Integer = 11000
```

Listing 5-9 shows the changes for <*ThreadFunc*>. It supports the new configuration format and e-mail configuration properties.

Listing 5-9 <*Tutorials.ThreadFunc*> code required to read the new configuration.xml file.

```
Private Sub ThreadFunc()
  Try
    'Load our Configuration File
    Dim Doc As XmlDocument = New dXmlDocument()
    Doc.Load(My.Settings.Configuration)
    Dim Options As XmlNode
    'Get a pointer to the Outer Node
    Options = Doc.SelectSingleNode("//*[local-
            name()='FileWorkerProperties']")
```

```vbnet
        If (Not Options Is Nothing) Then
          'Get a pointer to the first child node of FileWorkerOptions
          Dim tmpOptions As System.Xml.XPath.XPathNavigator _
             = Options.FirstChild.CreateNavigator()
          If (Not tmpOptions Is Nothing) Then
            Dim FWOptions As New FileWorkerOptions
            Dim children As System.Xml.XPath.XPathNavigator
            'Loop through each childe node (FileWorkerOption) and
            'get the values. Create a new FileWorkerOptions instance and
            'FileWorkerOption instance
            Do
              Try
                children = tmpOptions.SelectSingleNode("IncomingPath")
                FWOptions.Input = children.Value
                children = tmpOptions.SelectSingleNode("OutgoingPath")
                FWOptions.Output = children.Value
                children =
                    tmpOptions.SelectSingleNode("ProcessedPath")
                FWOptions.ProcessedPath = children.Value
                children = tmpOptions.SelectSingleNode("FileType")
                FWOptions.FileType = children.Value
                Dim tmpFW As New FileWorker(m_ThreadAction, FWOptions)
                children = tmpOptions.SelectSingleNode("Message")
                tmpFW.SmtpClient.Message = children.Value
                children = tmpOptions.SelectSingleNode("Subject")
                tmpFW.SmtpClient.Subject = children.Value
                children = tmpOptions.SelectSingleNode("Sender")
                tmpFW.SmtpClient.Sender = children.Value
                children = tmpOptions.SelectSingleNode("Recipient")
                tmpFW.SmtpClient.Recipient = children.Value
                children = tmpOptions.SelectSingleNode("SmtpPort")
                tmpFW.SmtpClient.SmtpPort = children.Value
                children = tmpOptions.SelectSingleNode("SmtpServer")
                tmpFW.SmtpClient.SmtpServer = children.Value
                children = tmpOptions.SelectSingleNode("MailEnabled ")
                tmpFW.MailEnabled = Convert.ToBoolean(children.Value)
                m_WorkerThreads.Add(tmpFW)
                tmpFW.Start()
              Catch ex As Exception
                WriteLogEvent(ex.ToString(), CONFIG_READ_ERROR,
                    EventLogEntryType.Error, My.Resources.Source)
              End Try
            Loop While (tmpOptions.MoveToNext)
          End If
        End If
    Catch ex As Exception
      WriteLogEvent(ex.ToString(), ONSTART_ERROR, _
          EventLogEntryType.Error, My.Resources.Source)
      Me.Stop()
    End Try
  End Sub
```

The code shown in Listing 5-9 selects the new *FileWorkerProperties* node in the configuration file and loops through, assigning the values to the appropriate properties. You will notice that I'm using the the read-only SMTP property of the *FileWorker* class to access the correct SMTP object, then I set the properties on that SMTP object. If an error occurs, we log an error and continue to the next file type.

In this way, an e-mail notification will be sent to the specified address for every incoming file processed by this service.

Installation and Verification

Compile, copy, and install the new service, but don't start it yet. First we want to add a few things to the incoming directories. Open Windows Explorer, browse to your temp folder, find the Incoming folder, and create a few text (*.txt) files in that folder. The content of the files in this case should be some random plain text for validation purposes. In the future you could write the service to support different encodings and formats.

Now start the service. When the service is running, all text files placed in the Incoming folder will be moved to the Outgoing folder, processed, and then moved to the Processed folder. An e-mail should appear for each file processed. The message should contain the text you typed into the file.

Stop the service and you'll also see the events logged in the Application Log. If you don't, try clearing the EventViewer Application log. To do this, right-click the Application Log, select Clear All Events, and click No when prompted to save the entries first. Restart the service and verify that you've achieved the desired results.

Advanced Processing

We have added threads, processing, and other features to the service. However, although a synchronous process may suffice, what if we had multiple directories with incoming files, or what if we want to speed up the processing? If we had a larger number of files in the incoming folder, with possibly a larger amount of data in those files, we may want to make the service more efficient.

Before you go any Further, understand that the more threads and actions you add to your service, the more care you have to take. For example, if you have multiple actions happening that all use the same data, it's very easy to corrupt the data on a separate thread from the one actively using that data.

You get around this issue by synchronizing your access to that data. This means that even though you may use multiple threads—all of which can perform actions almost simultaneously—all the threads you have created might need to be synchronized, to control accessing the same data from multiple threads simultaneously. Synchronization can be costly. Imagine blocking 30 or more worker threads from doing anything while you waited for access to the data. If the data were to be blocked for a very long period of time, adding multiple threads could add overhead of administration and development, possibly slowing down the service. Using a single thread requires less overhead, administration, and development effort. Be sure to decide what actions have to take place and how those actions have to get accomplished.

What actions are we accomplishing currently?

- Moving a file from an Incoming folder to an Outgoing folder
- Reading a file in an Outgoing folder and sending e-mail notification
- Moving a file from an Outgoing folder to a Processed folder

Which of these actions are separate actions and don't need to be synchronized or asynchronous?

Imagine that you have 500 files in the Incoming folder. You are not required to move a single file, process it, and move it again before moving another file from the Incoming folder to the Outgoing folder. However, a file must exist in the Outgoing folder before it is processed. When a file is found in the Outgoing folder, that file is processed and then moved again. The processing, e-mailing, and moving must all happen in the same order—but not necessarily on the same thread—on a per-file basis.

We then have to decide how to maximize the use of the threads without causing too much overhead and administrative effort. So how can we do that? Let's explore a couple of ways.

Exploring Processing Options

First let's understand threads a little better. Threads are like mini-processes within a process—not unlike your arms and legs. Each limb can do its own thing, but they all belong to your body. Threads are essentially a way to create smaller processes within the same application so that information, data, and results can be shared. Each thread can have its own security context. You can create a thread and have it run in an alternative context, so that the thread—and only that thread or thread pool—can execute with special privileges while the other threads and the main application run as another context.

Optimizing Processing

First, we must move files to the outgoing folder before the service processes them. However, is it a requirement that all files must be moved before processing begins? In our case, moving the file from the Incoming folder to the Outgoing folder doesn't require us to move all files before the application processes them. Therefore, we can create one thread that moves the files from the Incoming folder to the Outgoing folder, and does only this. This thread will remain totally unaware of what the rest of the service is doing.

The other option is to create a group of threads that pick up files from the same folder. Your current code will already do this, but only on a per-file-type basis, meaning that you can set up any number of threads based on how many file types you have. What you can't do is set up more than one thread to work against the same file type on the same folder.

Scenario 1: Synchronization with Threads and Queues

The choice you make to optimize processing depends on information about your files, such as size and the maximum time you expect the file move operation will take to complete. One choice is to have a single thread that reads all the filenames and then pushes them to a queue. Once in the queue the files would be read out one by one by several threads and then moved. This choice would also demonstrate the use of synchronized lists because you end up with at least one producer and at least one consumer. All of this happens outside of the thread functionality that processes these files, sends an e-mail, and then moves them to the Processed folder, making this a more robust multithreaded application. This would give you at minimum two threads per folder per file type, which might well be all you need.

Scenario 2: Optimizing Peformance with Delegates and Events

Another way to optimize processing is to implement events and delegates. You can use events so that when a file is found in the Incoming folder, it would be moved and then the service could raise an event, which would then execute whatever code you required to process, e-mail, and once again move the file.

The ability of delegates to be used by multiple threads and/or creating a multicast delegate that allows you to call multiple methods that can act against the same file can be a power solution. In our case multicasting wouldn't make a lot of sense as we wouldn't want the file being moved at the same time we are trying to read its contents to send an e-mail, but multi-casting can be a very powerful feature of your service when used appropriately.

Scenario 3: Combing Synchronized Queues and Eventing

Yet another option for optimizing processing is to combine a queue for the incoming files with the use of events and another queue for the outgoing file processing.

One problem is that when you use a queue to move files from one place to another—and you have a single thread monitoring a folder—you run the risk of writing the same file to the queue more than once.

Let's say you read the filenames from a folder and created a queue that had 20 files in it. Now imagine that for some reason the worker threads don't process the files. When your polling interval occurs again, you'll merely write the same files again and now have 40 files, of which 20 are duplicates. One solution is to code around the fact that this may occur and ignore FileIO errors for FilesNotFound.

Why not just remove duplicates from the list? This would seem to make sense because duplicates should never exist. You just have to ask yourself if you coded properly to avoid adding duplicates to your list. If the answer is absolutely yes, you are okay. However it's always possible that the same filename can reappear later—but it should never reappear in the same active list, which would happen if the system reuses names or processing puts the files into the Incoming folder.

A more optimized approach might be to just allow duplicates because removing them would require the list to be locked while it's being de-duped. In a sense you would be coding to the error, meaning that you expect some errors might occur but they won't be fatal, and you would know up front to ignore them. I don't recommend purposely ignoring errors, but this solution is used in many applications.

Deciding on the Best Solution

I haven't mentioned all the ways to handle this situation. Each technique has its pros and cons. Each one has fewer or greater synchronization requirements, processing requirements, coding, and support requirements.

In most cases your goal should be to determine what things are grouped as actions and cannot be decoupled without requiring so much complexity that the potential gains don't outweigh the efforts to create a viable solution.

Implementing a Solution

For our solution we will offer a staggered approach. First we will separate the incoming processing of files—which entails moving them to the outgoing path—from the processing of the files, the e-mail being sent, and the actual movement into the Processed folder.

Creating a New *<FileWorker.ProcessingIncoming>* Method

Creating a new *<FileWorker.ProcessingIncome>* method is fairly straightforward. In this case we take the *FileWorker* class and implement the code shown in Listing 5-10 by replacing the *FileWorker* class *<ThreadFunc>* method.

Listing 5-10   The new *<ProcessIncoming>* thread method.

```
Private Sub ProcessIncoming()
  While Not m_ThreadAction.StopThread
    If Not m_ThreadAction.Pause Then
      Try
        For Each TextFile As String In My.Computer.FileSystem.GetFiles( _
          m_FileWorkerOptions.Input, _
          FileIO.SearchOption.SearchTopLevelOnly, _
          m_FileWorkerOptions.FileType)
          If m_ThreadAction.Pause Or m_ThreadAction.StopThread Then
            Exit For
          End If
          Try
            Dim tmpGuid As String = Guid.NewGuid().ToString()
            Dim OutputFile As String = m_FileWorkerOptions.Output _
              + "\" + tmpGuid + "_" + _
              My.Computer.FileSystem.GetName(TextFile)

            My.Computer.FileSystem.MoveFile(TextFile, OutputFile)
            WriteLogEvent(My.Resources.ThreadMessage + TextFile, _
```

```
                        THREAD_INFO, _
                    EventLogEntryType.Information, My.Resources.Source)

                    System.Threading.Thread.Sleep(0)
                Catch ex As Exception
                    WriteLogEvent(My.Resources.ThreadErrorMessage + " " + _
                        ex.ToString + " " + Now.ToString, THREAD_ERROR, _
                        EventLogEntryType.Error, My.Resources.Source)
                End Try
            Next
        Catch fio As IOException
         WriteLogEvent(My.Resources.ThreadIOError + " " + fio.ToString + " " _
            + Now.ToString, THREAD_ABORT_ERROR, EventLogEntryType.Error, _
            My.Resources.Source)
        Catch tab As ThreadAbortException
            'this must be listed first as Exception is the master catch
            'Clean up thread here
         WriteLogEvent(My.Resources.ThreadAbortMessage + " " + _
            tab.ToString + _" " + Now.ToString, THREAD_ABORT_ERROR, _
            EventLogEntryType.Error, My.Resources.Source)
        Catch ex As Exception
            WriteLogEvent(My.Resources.ThreadErrorMessage + " " + _
                ex.ToString + _" " + Now.ToString, THREAD_ERROR, _
                EventLogEntryType.Error, My.Resources.Source)
        End Try
        End If
        If Not m_ThreadAction.StopThread Then
         Thread.Sleep(THREAD_WAIT)
        End If
    End While
End Sub
```

The code in Listing 5-10 is almost identical to the original *<ThreadFunc>* code, except that in the original code we only wrote an event to the event log. Here we are moving the file to the Outgoing folder and then writing an event.

Creating a New *<FileWorker.ProcessFiles>* Method

After we have separated the code that handles incoming files, we need to also create the method that will process the files, send the e-mail notification, and move the file to our Processed folder. Listing 5-11 shows the code for the new method.

Listing 5-11   The new *<ProcessFiles>* method.

```
Private Sub ProcessFiles()
  While Not m_ThreadAction.StopThread
    If Not m_ThreadAction.Pause Then
      Try
        For Each TextFile As String In My.Computer.FileSystem.GetFiles( _
            m_FileWorkerOptions.Output, _
            FileIO.SearchOption.SearchTopLevelOnly, _
            m_FileWorkerOptions.FileType)
            If m_ThreadAction.Pause Or m_ThreadAction.StopThread Then
```

```vb
                Exit For
            End If
            Try
                Dim tmpGuid As String = Guid.NewGuid().ToString()

                Dim ProcessFile As String = m_FileWorkerOptions.ProcessedPath _
                    + "\" + tmpGuid + "_" + _
                    My.Computer.FileSystem.GetName(TextFile)

                'File is moved so lets read it out of the Output Folder
                If (Me.MailEnabled) Then
                    Dim message As String
                    Try
                        message = "Processing File Data:[" + _
                        My.Computer.FileSystem.ReadAllText(ProcessFile) + _
                        "]] From File - "
                    Catch ex As Exception
                        message = "Unable to read from file - "
                    End Try
            'Send the Email and then move it again to the processed Folder
                    m_FileWorkerOptions.EmailProperties.Message = message
                    m_SmtpClient.QueueMail(m_FileWorkerOptions.EmailProperties)
                End If
                My.Computer.FileSystem.MoveFile(TextFile, ProcessFile)
                System.Threading.Thread.Sleep(0)
                WriteLogEvent(My.Resources.ThreadMessage + TextFile, THREAD_INFO,    _
        EventLogEntryType.Information, My.Resources.Source)
            Catch ex As Exception
                WriteLogEvent(My.Resources.ThreadErrorMessage + Now.ToString, _
                THREAD_ERROR, EventLogEntryType.Error, My.Resources.Source)
            End Try
        Next
        Catch fio As IOException
            WriteLogEvent(My.Resources.ThreadIOError + " " + fio.ToString _
                + " " + Now.ToString, THREAD_ABORT_ERROR, _
                EventLogEntryType.Error, My.Resources.Source)
        Catch tab As ThreadAbortException
            'this must be listed first as Exception is the master catch
            'Clean up thread here
            WriteLogEvent(My.Resources.ThreadAbortMessage + " " + _
            tab.ToString + " " + Now.ToString, THREAD_ABORT_ERROR, _
            EventLogEntryType.Error, My.Resources.Source)
        Catch ex As Exception
            WriteLogEvent(My.Resources.ThreadErrorMessage + " " + _
                ex.ToString + " " + Now.ToString, THREAD_ERROR, _
                EventLogEntryType.Error, My.Resources.Source)
        End Try
        End If
        If Not m_ThreadAction.StopThread Then
            Thread.Sleep(THREAD_WAIT)
        End If
    End While
End Sub
```

The logic in the *<ProcessFiles>* method is almost identical to the logic in the *<ProcessIncoming>* method. We again are looping through the available files, but this time in our Outgoing folder. When a file is found, we send an e-mail to the configured recipient and then move the file to our Processed folder as normal.

Separating the functionality of moving a file when it hits the incoming folder from actually processing the files has now allotted us one thread working to move files into the outgoing path and one thread for processing these files. With the layout of the current service we now have two threads per file type, per folder. If you had four file types, you would have a total of eight threads processing those files. Let's complete the changes required to make this work properly.

Updating *FileWorker* Class Thread Property Support

With the changes to our *FileWorker* class methods we'll need to modify the property and class members to support these changes. We'll need to have another thread available to run the *<ProcessFiles>* method. We are also going to rename the current m_WorkerThread member to reflect the change in thread functions. Finally we need to add in a new property that exposes the secondary worker thread so that Tutorials.vb can do a join to it when shutting down the service and cleaning up the threads. Lastly, we need to update the *<OnStart>* method to reflect the usage of the two new threads used by the *<ProcessFiles>* and *<ProcessIncoming>* methods.

Listing 5-12 shows the changes to the *FileWorker* class.

Listing 5-12   FileWorker property and thread declaration support.

```
Private m_Incoming As Thread = Nothing
Private m_Outgoing As Thread = Nothing
Public ReadOnly Property Incoming() As Thread
    Get
        Return m_Incoming
    End Get
End Property
Public ReadOnly Property Outgoing() As Thread
    Get
        Return m_Outgoing
    End Get
End Property
Public Sub Start()
    m_Incoming = New Thread(AddressOf ProcessIncoming)
    m_Incoming.Priority = ThreadPriority.Normal
    m_Incoming.IsBackground = True
    m_Incoming.Start()

    m_Outgoing = New Thread(AddressOf ProcessFiles)
    m_Outgoing.Priority = ThreadPriority.Normal
    m_Outgoing.IsBackground = True
    m_Outgoing.Start()
End Sub
```

With a new property and exposed threads, we can make the last required change, which is to the *<Tutorials. OnStop>* method.

Updating the *<Tutorials.OnStop>* Method

The service should be written in such a way that when it is told to shut down it attempts to clean up any active threads. In our *FileWorker* class the threads that have been created are exposed as a read-only property that the service can access. Updating the service to clean up—or at least attempt to clean up—those threads is relatively simple. Change the code to reflect that shown in Listing 5-13, which shows the list of changes to the *<OnStop>* method.

Listing 5-13   Changes to the *<OnStop>* method.

```
Protected Overrides Sub OnStop()
' Add code here to perform any tear-down necessary to stop your service.
  Try
    If (Not m_WorkerThread Is Nothing) Then
      Try
        WriteLogEvent(My.Resources.ServiceStopping, ONSTOP_INFO, _
          EventLogEntryType.Information, My.Resources.Source)

        m_ThreadAction.StopThread = True

        For Each fw As FileWorker In m_WorkerThreads
          Me.RequestAdditionalTime(THIRTY_SECONDS)
          fw.Incoming.Join(TIME_OUT)
          Me.RequestAdditionalTime(THIRTY_SECONDS)
          fw.Outgoing.Join(TIME_OUT)
        Next
      Catch ex As Exception
        m_WorkerThread = Nothing
      End Try
    End If

  Catch ex As Exception
    'We Catch the Exception
    'to avoid any unhandled errors
    'since we are stopping and
    'logging an event is what failed
    'we will merely write the output
    'to the debug window
    m_WorkerThread = Nothing
    Debug.WriteLine("Error stopping service: " + ex.ToString())
  End Try
End Sub
```

These last changes allow us to do a join on each worker thread in the *FileWorker* class instance and to request additional time just in case the thread join times out. (Because the state changes should cause all threads to exit within a few seconds of each other, this shouldn't happen.)

Queueing E-mail Notifications

We have advanced the service greatly from the generic version we created at the beginning of Chapter 1, "Writing Your First Service in Visual Basic 2008." The problem now is that the processing, e-mail notification, and final move are all on the same thread. This is okay, but not optimal—even from a single-threaded standpoint.

To resolve this, we need to be able to break down the processing further to determine which parts are required to be serialized and which parts aren't. This raises a question: Does the success of the e-mail notification determine whether the file should be moved? The next section explores this issue.

Decoupling Notifications Implementation Questions

If the answer to the question at the end of the preceding section is yes, you cannot decouple the e-mail notification from the file move because you would never know for sure if you succeeded. Or could you?

Do Notifications have to be successful before a file is moved?

The answer to this question has many parts. Again, remember that you have a mechanism that is polling the file system. Currently it is serializing the reading, processing, e-mail and the final move, so duplicate messages aren't really an issue. However, if you require that a message be e-mailed successfully before its final move, and you want to decouple the processing from the work of sending the notification, you must have a clean mechanism in the middle that will allow you to guarantee that not only was the message delivered, but also that the same file doesn't end up in the processing queue again. If it did, it would cause a duplication of work and create a problem.

Can notifications be asynchronous to the file being moved?

You can also look at this question from the eventing model. When a file is processed, an event can be triggered that would pick up where the processing left off, sending the e-mail notification, and then either moving the file itself or fire off another event that would then move the file. Because you can raise events or use delegates, you can easily create parameterized events or delegates and pass the filename to the next processing step.

This is all possible, but again, is the synchronization processing and overhead worth it? Let's review a possible solution to the decoupling scenario.

Decoupling: An Example

For the sake of this demonstration, let's assume that the e-mail notification itself is not a requirement for the move—all that is required is a successful queueing of the message to be sent. This would mean that you should implement some sort of auditing procedure that can identify that you are queueing a message to be sent, or that the queuing is done in a transaction or a transaction-like methodology. This is so that if the e-mail doesn't go out, you can retrieve the information and resend it later, or at least report on it.

Although I have decoupled the requirement to wait for an e-mail acknowledgement, I still have to acknowledge that the e-mail was queued to be delivered. I still need to tightly couple the processing of the file with the final move. Again, this is not because it is an absolute requirement but because the complexity to guarantee delivery with no duplicates is more than we need to worry about now.

SMTP Queueing Solution

Now we need to separate the ability to send mail from the ability to queue mail. Currently we're exposing two versions of <*SMTP.Send*> with two different signatures. We're going to have to add another method that will queue the e-mail instead of sending it immediately.

For this to work, the internal *SMTP* class not only has to implement a queue, but must also implement a method that can synchronize the list of e-mails to send while a worker thread constantly looks for e-mails to send. This means we have one producer—our service—and one consumer: the *SMTP* class itself.

One final design note. We need to be able to avoid long blocking calls made into the queueing method that would cause the service to stop processing. This is not a requirement, but it is something you should consider. For now we won't worry about it—for the purposes of this example it's not an issue. We will only be synchronizing on dequeueing of the queue itself, not on the processing of the result of dequeueing, which will be fast.

The Queue

First we have to decide what we want to use for a queueing mechanism. .NET and Visual Basic 2008 provide a synchronized version of the *Queue* class which acts as a first in, first out (FIFO) list. The great thing about this is that we can have any number of threads that read and write to this queue—we simply have to make sure we use the synchronized version.

The only downside to the synchronized *Queue* is that if you decide that you want to iterate through *Queue* itself you must protect the list. Even though *Queue* is synchronized, the enumeration capability of the *Queue* is not synchronized. The *Queue* will throw an error if items are added or deleted while iterating through the list. This means you need to lock the list, iterate through it, and then unlock it. Of course during this time you are blocking the producers and the consumers from populating and reading off the list. To create the *Queue* class, add the code shown in Listing 5-14 to the top of the *SMTP* Class.

Listing 5-14   Required SMTP class variables for *Queue* support.

```
Private m_Queue As New System.Collections.Queue
Private m_SyncQueue As Queue = Queue.Synchronized(m_Queue)
```

This will be added to the top of the class before the constructor.

This code may seem redundant, but the first definition creates our *Queue* and the second creates a thread-safe synchronous pointer into the *Queue*. We will use the synchronous pointer.

The Data

Using *Queue* to store the e-mail notification information is great, not only from a processing perspective but also because the list is FIFO-oriented, it allows any number of consumers and producers, and it allows us to store reference types (i.e. pointers to class instances).

Although a class is not a requirement, I have created the public class shown in Listing 5-15 because I want to avoid unnecessary boxing. This class is part of the SMTP.vb file and will be used to store information about an incoming message so that it can later be retrieved and processed. Understanding boxing is important, but from a deep level understanding all the specific performance related issues is beyond the scope of this book. However, it is important to understand the purpose of changing this structure from a structure to a class.

In .NET, structures are considered Value Types, where classes are considered Reference Types. At the most simplistic, this means that a Reference Type is like a pointer in C++. You can pass a pointer to an object around quickly and efficiently without doing any special marshalling. However, when you have a Value Type, it must be casted or boxed into a Reference Type, or pointer , and then it has to be unboxed or casted back into the original type on the other side of the call. With a small number of objects this will not have a huge affect, however, over time and with a larger quantity of items, it can have a tremendous performance impact to your service.

> **Note**   It is possible .to place any of the classes that are created in this book into their own class files. Just remember to make them public and available to the rest of the service.

Listing 5-15 *EmailDetail* class for storing e-mail configuration data.

```
Public Class EmailDetail
  Private m_SmtpServer As String
  Private m_SmtpPort As Integer
  Private m_Sender As String
  Private m_Subject As String
  Private m_Message As String
  Private m_Recipient As String
  Public Sub New()
  End Sub
  Public Property SmtpServer() As String
    Get
        Return m_SmtpServer
    End Get
    Set(ByVal value As String)
        m_SmtpServer = value
    End Set
  End Property
  Public Property SmtpPort() As Integer
    Get
        Return m_SmtpPort
    End Get
    Set(ByVal value As Integer)
        m_SmtpPort = value
    End Set
  End Property
  Public Property Sender() As String
    Get
```

```
            Return m_Sender
        End Get
        Set(ByVal value As String)
            m_Sender = value
        End Set
    End Property
    Public Property Subject() As String
        Get
            Return m_Subject
        End Get
        Set(ByVal value As String)
            m_Subject = value
        End Set
    End Property
    Public Property Message() As String
        Get
            Return m_Message
        End Get
        Set(ByVal value As String)
            m_Message = value
        End Set
    End Property
    Public Property Recipient() As String
        Get
            Return m_Recipient
        End Get
        Set(ByVal value As String)
            m_Recipient = value
        End Set
    End Property
    Public Shared Function Copy(ByVal incdetail As EmailDetail) As EmailDetail
        Dim tmpDetail As New EmailDetail
        tmpDetail.Message = incdetail.Message
        tmpDetail.Recipient = incdetail.Recipient
        tmpDetail.Sender = incdetail.Sender
        tmpDetail.SmtpPort = incdetail.SmtpPort
        tmpDetail.SmtpServer = incdetail.SmtpServer
        tmpDetail.Subject = incdetail.Subject
        Return tmpDetail
    End Function
End Class
```

You may notice that this class has the same properties as the original *SMTP* class. This allows me to create a *Queue* class that can store all the information on a per e-mail basis and also allows me to remove the code from the *SMTP* class itself, requiring it to only store a *Queue* of these instances. This means the queue can have 0, 1, or many pending e-mails at any given time, processing them in order.

Listing 5-16 shows the entire SMTP class instance with the correct class definition, method definitions, and the removal of the properties that have been moved to the *EmailDetail* class. Initially the compiler will generate an error because the current method implementations require those properties. This will be covered in the next section and Listing 5-16.

Updating the *SMTP* Class

We need to make some significant changes to the *SMTP* class to make it effective. We have removed the previously exposed properties from *SMTP* because we want to be able to send more than one e-mail at a time. We now want to queue the e-mail requests and send them as we see fit: in real time, in intervals, or even on a schedule that we create.

Because we are going to use a queue, we need to modify the <*SendMail*> methods. Currently, we are exposing one version, allowing us to pass in the required parameters—such as recipient— along with another version that assumed we had set the properties in advance. Now we must keep in mind that we have not only removed our exposed properties, but also replaced them with a separate class that we will use to populate a queue.

Instead of exposing two methods, we will expose one that will allow users to pass in an *Email-Detail* class and send an e-mail in real time, and a secondary private method that will be used internally by our queueing code to send e-mails. Listing 5-16 shows these modifications.

Listing 5-16   Updated SMTP class> to support the *EmailDetail* class.

```
Imports System.Net.Mail
Imports System.Net

Public Class SMTP
   Private Const SMTP_ERROR As Integer = 15000
   Private m_SmtpClient As New SmtpClient
   Private m_Queue As New System.Collections.Queue
   Private m_SyncQueue As Queue = Queue.Synchronized(m_Queue)

   Public Sub New()
   End Sub

   Public Function SendMail(ByVal sender As String, ByVal rcpt As String, _
   ByVal server As String, ByVal port As Integer, ByVal subject As String, _
   ByVal message As String) As Boolean
      Return Send(sender, rcpt, server, port, subject, message)
   End Function

   Public Function SendMail(ByVal emaildetail As EmailDetail) As Boolean
      Try
         Return Send(emaildetail.Sender, emaildetail.Recipient, _
            emaildetail.SmtpServer, emaildetail.SmtpPort, _
            emaildetail.Subject, emaildetail.Message)
      Catch ex As Exception
         System.Diagnostics.EventLog.WriteEntry("SMTP Tutorials Class", _
         ex.ToString(), EventLogEntryType.Error, SMTP_ERROR)
         Return False
      End Try
   End Function

   Private Function SendMail() As Boolean
      Try
         Dim tmpDetail As EmailDetail
         tmpDetail = m_SyncQueue.Dequeue
         Return SendMail(tmpDetail)
```

```
      Catch ex As Exception
          System.Diagnostics.EventLog.WriteEntry("SMTP Tutorials Class", _
              ex.ToString(), EventLogEntryType.Error, SMTP_ERROR)
          Return False
      End Try
  End Function


    Private Function Send(ByVal sender As String, ByVal rcpt As String, _
        ByVal server As String, ByVal port As Integer, _
        ByVal subject As String, ByVal message As String) As Boolean
      Try
        If ((String.IsNullOrEmpty(sender)) Or (String.IsNullOrEmpty(rcpt)) _
        Or (String.IsNullOrEmpty(server)) Or (port <= 0 Or port >= 65000) Or _
        (String.IsNullOrEmpty(subject)) Or (String.IsNullOrEmpty(message))) Then
            System.Diagnostics.EventLog.WriteEntry("Tutorials SMTP Class", _
            "Error sending Email - Invalid Parameters", _
            EventLogEntryType.Error, SMTP_ERROR)
            Return False
        End If
        m_SmtpClient.Host = server
        m_SmtpClient.DeliveryMethod = SmtpDeliveryMethod.Network
        m_SmtpClient.Port = port
        m_SmtpClient.Credentials = CredentialCache.DefaultNetworkCredentials
        m_SmtpClient.Send(sender, rcpt, subject, message)
      Catch ex As Exception
          System.Diagnostics.EventLog.WriteEntry("Tutorials SMTP Class", _
          "Error Sending Email - " + ex.ToString, EventLogEntryType.Error, _
          SMTP_ERROR)
          Return False
      End Try
  End Function
End Class
```

The first method is a wrapper to our private method, <Send>, from our first implementation. The second method wraps the publicly exposed <SendMail> version. It will remove a single instance of the *EmailDetail* class off the queue and pass it to the public <SendMail> method, which in turn sends the mail.

Now that we have created new <SendMail> implementations, we have to create the method that users will call to place outgoing e-mail requests onto the queue, shown in Listing 5-17. This code method should be added to the SMTP class.

Listing 5-17   <QueueMail> code implementation listing.

```
Public Function QueueMail(ByVal emaildetail As EmailDetail) As Boolean
  Try
    m_SyncQueue.Enqueue(emaildetail)
    System.Threading.ThreadPool.QueueUserWorkItem(AddressOf MailThread)
    Return True
  Catch ex As Exception
    System.Diagnostics.EventLog.WriteEntry("SMTP Tutorials Class", _
              ex.ToString(), EventLogEntryType.Error, SMTP_ERROR)
    Return False
  End Try
End Function
```

This method takes in an *EmailDetail* instance and places it on the queue. Again, we need to make sure that we use the synchronous queue to protect ourselves from data corruption or internal exceptions. After we add the entry into the queue, we create a queued worker thread item to perform the mail send.

Now we have to create both the delegate and the thread function, which will process the e-mails off the queue. First we create our thread method in the SMTP class, as shown in Listing 5-18.

Listing 5-18   *<MailThread>* implementation code.

```
Private Sub MailThread(ByVal state As Object)
  Try
    If (m_SyncQueue.Count > 0) Then
      Dim sqm As SendQueuedMail = New SendQueuedMail(AddressOf SendMail)
      Dim ed As EmailDetail = m_SyncQueue.Dequeue()
      sqm.Invoke(ed)
    End If
  Catch ex As Exception
    System.Diagnostics.EventLog.WriteEntry("SMTP Tutorials Class", _
           ex.ToString(), EventLogEntryType.Error, SMTP_ERROR)
  End Try
End Sub
```

This method validates that there are records on the queue and then creates an instance of the delegate shown in Listing 5-19, which must be added to the SMTP class.

Listing 5-19   Creating the *<SendQueuedMail>* delegate.

```
Private Delegate Function SendQueuedMail(ByVal emaildetail As EmailDetail) _
  As Boolean
```

This delegate will be used to point to the *SendMail* method, which takes in an *EmailDetail* class.

You may notice that we have the parameter **ByVal state As Object** parameter definition. This is because we're going to use the *ThreadPool* class to create worker item threads to call this method. This parameter allows information to be passed by the system as well, but we are only declaring it, not using it.

Finally, as shown in Listing 5-20, we need to update the *Send* method, which sends the e-mail.

Listing 5-20   New *<Send>* mail implementation supporting the Queue.

```
Private Function Send(ByVal sender As String, ByVal rcpt As String, _
  ByVal server As String, ByVal port As Integer, _
ByVal subject As String, ByVal message As String) As Boolean
  Try
    If ((String.IsNullOrEmpty(sender)) Or (String.IsNullOrEmpty(rcpt)) _
Or (String.IsNullOrEmpty(server)) Or (port <= 0 Or port >= 65000) Or _
(String.IsNullOrEmpty(subject)) Or (String.IsNullOrEmpty(message))) Then
      System.Diagnostics.EventLog.WriteEntry("Tutorials SMTP Class", _
"Error sending Email - Invalid Parameters", EventLogEntryType.Error, _
SMTP_ERROR)
      Return False
    End If
    Dim bSent As Boolean
    SyncLock (m_SmtpClient)
```

```
      Try
        m_SmtpClient.Host = server
        m_SmtpClient.DeliveryMethod = SmtpDeliveryMethod.NETwork
        m_SmtpClient.Port = port
        m_SmtpClient.Credentials = CredentialCache.DefaultNetworkCredentials
        m_SmtpClient.Send(sender, rcpt, subject, message)
        bSent = True
      Catch ex As Exception
        bSent = False
        System.Diagnostics.EventLog.WriteEntry("Tutorials SMTP Class", _
    "Error Sending Email - " + ex.ToString, EventLogEntryType.Error, SMTP_ERROR)
      End Try
    End SyncLock
    Return bSent
  Catch ex As Exception
    System.Diagnostics.EventLog.WriteEntry("Tutorials SMTP Class", _
"Error Sending Email - " + ex.ToString, EventLogEntryType.Error, SMTP_ERROR)
    Return False
  End Try
End Function
```

The change that you see in Listing 5-19 is that we now have to synchronize the use of *SMTP-Client*. Because we only have one *SMTPClient* for the class, we can only send one e-mail at a time. If we try to throw more than one thread at this method at a time, we will cause a failure because the instance will be busy. This does, of course, slow down our processing overall because the threads are serialized. However, this technique still speeds up other sections of the code. You could have also created a local instance of *SMTPClient* instead of a member variable in which you could send multiple e-mails at once. This would be an easy change (but not one I will do here). Remember, though, that this is not a shared class, so each *FileWorker* actually gets its own mail queue.

With this model, we don't have to worry about creating a pool of threads and controlling them ourselves, or avoiding any blocking calls required to send the mail directly. Therefore, we can send multiple e-mails at one time without requiring much effort decoupling the processing, e-mailing, and finally moving to our Processed folder.

Updating the *FileWorkerOptions* Class

The *FileWorkerOptions* class will store the information used by that *FileWorker* class instance to send e-mail. Although we can change the message and subject based on the details in the file itself, we are going to fill these in with the data from configuration.xml, as shown in Listing 5-21.

Listing 5-21   Code to support the new EmailProperties property.

```
Public Property EmailProperties() As EmailDetail
    Get
        Return m_MailDetail
    End Get
    Set(ByVal value As EmailDetail)
        m_MailDetail = EmailDetail.Copy(value)
    End Set
End Property
```

The EmailProperties property allows us to pass in an *EmailDetail* and assign it to the local variable declared as m_MailDetail. I have defined this at the top of the *FileWorkerOptions* class, as shown in Listing 5-22.

Listing 5-22   Updated *FileWorkerOptions* with *EmailDetail* class definition.
```
Private m_MailDetail As EmailDetail
```

You will notice that I am calling the *<Copy>* method of the *EmailDetail* class. I added this method in this chapter.

The copy method takes in an instance of an already existing *EmailDetail*, creates a new one, copies the values from the input parameter, and returns the new instance.

Updating the *<Tutorials.ThreadFunc>* Method

As shown in Listing 5-23, we have to update our *<Tutorials.ThreadFunc>* class to read in our e-mail properties, create an instance of our new *EmailDetail*, and associate the values so that we can pass it into our *FileWorker* class instance.

Listing 5-23   Updated service code to use the *EmailProperties* class.
```
Private Sub ThreadFunc()
  Try
    'Load our Configuration File
    Dim Doc As XmlDocument = New XmlDocument()
    Doc.Load(My.Settings.Configuration)
    Dim Options As XmlNode
    'Get a pointer to the Outer Node
    Options = Doc.SelectSingleNode("//*[local-
        name()='FileWorkerOptions']")
    If (Not Options Is Nothing) Then
      'Get a pointer to the first child node of FileWorkerOptions
      Dim tmpOptions As System.Xml.XPath.XPathNavigator _
          = Options.FirstChild.CreateNavigator()
    If (Not tmpOptions Is Nothing) Then
        Dim FWOptions As New FileWorkerOptions
        Dim children As System.Xml.XPath.XPathNavigator
        'Loop through each childe node (FileWorkerOption) and
        'get the values. Create a new FileWorkerOptions instance and
        'FileWorkerOption instance
        Do
          Try
            children = tmpOptions.SelectSingleNode("IncomingPath")
            FWOptions.Input = children.Value

            children = tmpOptions.SelectSingleNode("OutgoingPath")
            FWOptions.Output = children.Value

            children = tmpOptions.SelectSingleNode("FileType")
            FWOptions.FileType = children.Value

            children = tmpOptions.SelectSingleNode("ProcessedPath")
            FWOptions.ProcessedPath = children.Value
```

```
                    Dim tmpDetail As New EmailDetail
                    children = tmpOptions.SelectSingleNode("Message")
                    tmpDetail.Message = children.Value

                    children = tmpOptions.SelectSingleNode("Subject")
                    tmpDetail.Subject = children.Value

                    children = tmpOptions.SelectSingleNode("Sender")
                    tmpDetail.Sender = children.Value

                    children = tmpOptions.SelectSingleNode("Recipient")
                    tmpDetail.Recipient = children.Value

                    children = tmpOptions.SelectSingleNode("SmtpPort")
                    tmpDetail.SmtpPort = children.Value

                    children = tmpOptions.SelectSingleNode("SmtpServer")
                    tmpDetail.SmtpServer = children.Value

                    FWOptions.EmailProperties = tmpDetail

                    Dim tmpFW As New FileWorker(m_ThreadAction, FWOptions)

                    children = tmpOptions.SelectSingleNode("MailEnabled")
                    tmpFW.MailEnabled = Convert.ToBoolean(children.Value)

                    m_WorkerThreads.Add(tmpFW)
                    tmpFW.Start()
                Catch ex As Exception
                    WriteLogEvent(ex.ToString(), CONFIG_READ_ERROR, _
                      EventLogEntryType.Error, _
                      My.Resources.Source)
                End Try
            Loop While (tmpOptions.MoveToNext)
        End If
    End If
  Catch ex As Exception
    WriteLogEvent(ex.ToString(), ONSTART_ERROR, _
      EventLogEntryType.Error, My.Resources.Source)
    Me.Stop()
  End Try
End Sub
```

Updating the *<FileWorker>* Constructor

With the inclusion of the *EmailDetail* class into the solution we need to update the constructor
to utilize these new properties that are associated with the EmailDetail class. In Listing 5-24
the constructor has been modified to assign the passed in *<FileWorkerOptions>* *EmailDetail*
class to the *<FileWorker>* class instance of *<FileWorkerOptions>*.

Listing 5-24   Updated *<FileWorker>* constructor with *EmailDetail* support modifications.
```
Public Sub New( _
  ByRef threadaction As ThreadActionState, _
  ByVal fileworkeroptions As FileWorkerOptions)
  m_ThreadAction = threadaction
```

```
    m_FileWorkerOptions.Input = fileworkeroptions.Input
    m_FileWorkerOptions.Output = fileworkeroptions.Output
    m_FileWorkerOptions.FileType = fileworkeroptions.FileType
    m_FileWorkerOptions.ProcessedPath = fileworkeroptions.ProcessedPath
    m_FileWorkerOptions.EmailProperties = fileworkeroptions.EmailProperties
End Sub
```

In the current constructor I am passing in an instance of specific class types, that are required for the *<FileWorker>* class. In the service's Tutorials.vb *<ThreadFunc>* method we are creating instances of the *FileWorkerOptions* class and the *EmailDetail* class.

In this final change, we have now successfully tied together the reading of our e-mail properties with the queueing code required to queue, and also sent e-mail notifications based on the files that are placed into the Outgoing folder.

Balance and Performance

More doesn't always mean better when it comes to threading and resources. Sometimes you need to balance not only the work items you need to perform, but also the processing power of your system, your memory, and the volume and velocity of the required work.

If your volume is really low and the processing time requirement on that work is relatively long, instant processing with massive amounts of queues and worker threads is not always the best solution. A service's manageability is a key factor in how you decide to implement your service—not just in terms of design, but in the code itself.

Installation and Verification

Compile and install the new service. Make sure that you have moved the .txt files from the processed folder back to the incoming folder before you start the service again.

When you start the service you should notice simultaneous movement and processing of the files and the e-mail notifications instead of a serialization of that process. If you add more files, or a lot of files, you will notice the simultaneous processing even more.

However, because of the size and number of our files, you may not see a huge increase in our service from when everything was single-threaded. But even if you added larger size or volume of files with only two threads, you would definitely see a difference. If you add more or larger files, you can now process one file while copying one file, meaning that you are doing two things at once. With more threads and synchronization you could shave off even more time, but only if you add a lot more complexity to your service.

If you know you are going to be receiving and processing more or larger files, having a complex service may be worthwhile. Remember that each thread takes up memory and stack space. Remember also that whatever the processing thread is attaching to—whether SQL Server or SMTP—these services will have a limited number of connections they will accept at one time.

You have to code knowing that you cannot assume external services can accept 500 or any number connections at a time. More threads do not mean performance increases. Actually, the more threads you have, the more your CPUs have to switch between those threads to allow them to do their work. This can cause a bottleneck of thread-context switches.

How to balance between multiple threads versus a single thread is fairly straightforward. However, deciding how many threads and how to best resource and administer those threads is a much bigger question and requires much thought and proper coding techniques.

Summary

- Visual Basic 2008 has native support for client-written and server-written socket-based applications.

- Visual Basic 2008 supports a practically unlimited protocol set for sockets, including UDP, TCP/IP (including the new Internet Protocol Version 6 standard), secured sockets and more.

- Data transferred over a client/server architecture is based on an application-defined protocol standard. Custom-written applications that communicate with a custom server must internally supply this definition so that the client/server can communicate properly and effectively.

- SMTP is a powerful communication protocol for sending information to single or multiple recipients.

- Use the *ThreadPool* class when possible to avoid difficult synchronization and management code.

Chapter 6

User Input, Desktop Interaction, and Feedback

Services are designed to run in the background while you perform actions in the foreground. In the real world, many services run on servers where almost no foreground processing—word processing, games, or any other action—is taking place. Services are never intended to interact with the users or the desktop, nor are they meant to receive input from these sources. This is very important to understand. In this chapter, I will explain the circumstances in which you might decide to write services that interact with the desktop and are looking for interaction with the users on the desktop. Keep in mind that although some situations may draw you into designing services that do this, I would avoid it at all costs. For reasons that I will explain in this chapter, it is a dangerous practice.

Understanding Service Feedback

When we looked at the account used to start the service, we had an option when using the Local System Account to Allow Service To Interact With Desktop. This option is very important. By default, services run in the background. They don't run on the same workstation as the user that is logged on. What this means is that by default these services can't display messages, pop-ups, error dialogs, or notifications like a regular application would. This is both for security and for practical purposes. Services are neither designed nor intended to wait for user input or feedback.

Imagine you have written a service such as an installation wizard. What if at some point it presents a dialog box and asks for user input or for the user to select a predefined option? What if no one is logged on? Who would see the input or selection options? Worse, what if someone is logged on, and walks away and forgets that she is logged on? The prompt would sit there blocking the service as it waited for input. Now imagine that someone tries to stop the service on another workstation, or in another administrative terminal service client.

For these reasons you should avoid creating services that are intended to interact with the desktop. However, it is possible to do this, and in very specific cases it could be useful. Again, this must be done with such care that I would only very rarely recommend it. I am explaining this for demonstration purposes only.

Configuring a Service to Interact with the Desktop

By selecting Allow Service To Interact With Desktop, you will be able to send user input, such as keyboard input, dialog boxes, and so on, to the currently logged-on user. So you should only use this configuration to send information to a user who you know is logged on to the computer.

Before we begin I must again reiterate that this should only be done under required circumstances. The following code should *never* be placed onto a production system.

Getting Started with Creating the Interactive Service

Clear the application event log. To do this, Click Start, click Run, and type **eventvwr** at the command prompt. Right-click Application Log and choose Clear All Entries. Click No when prompted to save events before clearing.

Many changes must be made to the current service. We are going to create a form that will be displayed, presenting the user with information about the files that are processed. It's important to understand that this form must reside on its own thread to function properly. I say "properly" because the form can, of course, be created from anywhere, such as one of our worker threads or even the main thread. However, because our main thread is actually released back to the SCM and does nothing until another action is issued (such as Pause, Stop, or Continue), there is no way a paint event can be raised on that thread. Therefore there is no way for the form to be updated visually—it would just sit there with a non-responsive, busy cursor.

In our case, because our projects are already object-oriented and multithread-supported, we are going to create as many form instances as *FileWorker* class instances we create.

We are going to use the code from Chapter 4, "Services and Polling," so please shut down your Chapter 5, "Processing and Notification," code and reload your Chapter 4 project.

Creating a Feedback Form

We are going to create a form that will be presented to the user, providing feedback about the files that we are processing. First, we add a form to our project and change its name to frmFeedBack, as shown in the following steps:

1.   Select Project from the Visual Studio menu bar.

2.   Select Add Windows Form.

3.   Name the form **frmFeedBack** and click Add.

4.   Select the ToolBox, Components, Common Controls, and then Textbox. Drag a text box onto the new form. Right-click the text box and choose Properties. Under Name, enter **txtFeedback**. Right-click the form and select Properties.

❑   Set the form property FormBorderStyle to FixedToolWindow.

❑   Set the ControlBox property to False.

You can make the form and the text box any size you want, but I suggest a size of about 324, 262 for the form, Then fit the text box to scale inside the form. Set the Multiline property of the text box to True.

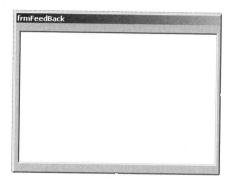

Adding Text Selection Code

Once you have renamed the text box, double-click it. The code designer will appear and add a changedtext event. Inside this event, modify the code as shown in Listing 6-1.

Listing 6-1   *<TextChanged>* event code to properly display output.

```
Private Sub txtFeedBack_TextChanged(ByVal sender As System.Object, _
ByVal e As System.EventArgs) Handles txtFeedBack.TextChanged
  Try
    txtFeedBack.SelectionStart = txtFeedBack.TextLength
    txtFeedBack.ScrollToCaret()
  Catch ex As Exception
    txtFeedBack.Text = ""
  End Try
End Sub
```

This code will clear the text box when and if the text buffer overflows, and it will also make sure that we are always looking at the last entry in the list instead of the first. We could have reversed the order in which the text displayed, so that entries were placed on top of the text box list instead of the bottom.

Adding a Delegate Method

To properly update the Windows form, we need to add a deletegate method to the form that our *FileWorker* class can invoke on the form so that it will update the text of the text box on the creation thread itself. Listing 6-2 shows how to do this.

Listing 6-2   Service feedback window Event Delegate update method.

```
Public Sub UpdateTextBox(ByVal text As String)
    Try
        txtFeedBack.Text += text
    Catch ex As Exception
    End Try
End Sub
```

You may notice that there is no code in the error handler. The delegate code is simple and for demonstration purposes, and requires no further processing if there is an error processing the delegate update.

Adding Required References

Within our project we need to make sure that we are able to access properties, objects, and classes related to creating Windows forms. By default these references would not be part of a service project, so we need to add the following references:

- System.Windows.Forms
- System.Drawing

Making the Form Visible to the Service

In this example we want to display output on a per-*FileWorker* class instance. Therefore we need to create an instance of our feedback form in our *FileWorker* class, so we will add a variable instance to our *FileWorker* class as shown in Listing 6-3.

Listing 6-3   Creating a variable to store our form instance.

```
Private m_Feedback As frmFeedBack
```

The form variable is required because services don't contain user interface components. To allow the service to display such a component we first have to create the form, and then we create a variable that the service will use to instantiate and make visible an instance of the form. Like other .NET classes, our form is an object and therefore is created the same way as other class instances.

Updating the *FileWorker* Class

We need to update the *FileWorker* class to take advantage of the new form and to create the code required to make it functional for the service.

Creating a Delegate

We have created an instance of the form, but now we need to create a delegate that will be able to invoke the <*frmFeedback.UpdateText*> method. At the top of the *FileWorker* class add the code shown in Listing 6-4.

Listing 6-4   Creating a delegate for the service to update the form.

```
Private Delegate Sub UpdateText(ByVal text As String)
```

In the next section we will use this delegate to update our FileWorker.m_Feedback instance on a per-*FileWorker* class instance.

Creating the *<FrmThread>* Method

We have to create the form on a different thread than the class or service runs on. If we don't, we won't be able to update the form and it will hang. To avoid this we will add the method shown in Listing 6-5 to our *FileWorker* class.

Listing 6-5   Creating a separate thread to update the form.

```
Private Sub frmThread()
  Do
    Dim FORM_WAIT As Integer = 10
    Try
      If m_Feedback Is Nothing Then
        Try
            m_Feedback = New frmFeedBack
            m_Feedback.Show()
        Catch ex As Exception
            WriteLogEvent(ex.ToString, THREAD_ERROR,_
            EventLogEntryType.Error, My.Resources.Source)
        End Try
      Else
        m_Feedback.Update()
        System.Windows.Forms.Application.DoEvents()
      End If
      Catch tab As ThreadAbortException
        Try
          m_Feedback.Dispose()
          m_Feedback = Nothing
        Catch ex As Exception
          m_Feedback = Nothing
        End Try
      Catch ex As Exception
        WriteLogEvent(ex.ToString, THREAD_ERROR, _
          EventLogEntryType.Error, My.Resources.Source)
      End Try
    Thread.Sleep(FORM_WAIT)
  Loop
End Sub
```

This method will validate that the form is available and, if it isn't, create it. The method will then update the screen and temporarily switch back to any other system threads waiting to perform processing with DoEvents. Finally, the method sleeps for 10 milliseconds. This way you won't overload the CPU while it processes the updates to the screen.

Creating a Thread Instance in *FileWorker* Class

We are going to create an instance of the thread that will run the *<frmThread>* method at the top of the class definition, as shown in Listing 6-6.

Listing 6-6 Adding a feedback thread to update the form.
```
Private m_FeedbackThread As Thread
```

Updating *<FileWorker.Start>*

Now that we have a thread definition we need to start the thread by updating the *<Start>* method, which is called by *<Tutorials.ThreadFunc>*, as shown in Listing 6-7.

Listing 6-7 Updating the *<Start>* method to start a new feedback thread.
```
Public Sub Start()
    m_WorkerThread = New Thread(AddressOf ThreadFunc)
    m_WorkerThread.Priority = ThreadPriority.Normal
    m_WorkerThread.IsBackground = True
    m_WorkerThread.Start()
    m_FeedbackThread = New Thread(AddressOf frmThread)
    m_FeedbackThread.Priority = ThreadPriority.Normal
    m_FeedbackThread.IsBackground = True
    m_FeedbackThread.Start()
End Sub
```

Adding the *UpdateForm* Method to the *FileWorker* Class

The *FileWorker* class needs a method that the new thread instance we created can execute. In Listing 6-8 the new method, called *UpdateForm*, will be created to call the new Windows form delegate to update the form's text box.

Listing 6-8 The *FileWorker UpdateForm* method.
```
Private Sub UpdateForm(ByVal file As Object)
    Try
        Dim update As New UpdateText(AddressOf m_Feedback.UpdateTextBox)

        Dim FileOutput As String = Convert.ToString(file)

        SyncLock (m_Feedback)
            Try
                m_Feedback.Invoke(update, "Thread Function Processed File - " _
                + FileOutput + " at " + Now.ToString + vbCrLf)
            Catch ex As Exception
                WriteLogEvent(My.Resources.ThreadErrorMessage + Now.ToString, _
                THREAD_ERROR, EventLogEntryType.Error, My.Resources.Source)
            End Try
        End SyncLock
    Catch ex As Exception
        'We do not need to process the error here
        'However you can add functionality here to write an event log
        'to extend this code.
    End Try
End Sub
```

The code in Listing 6-8 creates an instance of the UpdateText delegate used to update the text box on the Windows feedback form. Next, the code creates a string instance of the data passed to the *UpdateForm* method, places a sync lock on the global shared feedback form variable, and invokes the delegate method to update the text box on the feedback form. Now we have to update the <*ThreadFunc*> method to instantiate the thread instance to run this method.

Updating <*FileWorker.ThreadFunc*>

Currently <*ThreadFunc*> only moves the file to the process folder. However, we want to update the specific FileWorker.m_Feedback form instance with the file that we processed. To do this we have to update the function as shown in Listing 6-9.

Listing 6-9   Updated thread function with *UpdateForm* method support.

```
Private Sub TThreadFunc()
  While Not m_ThreadAction.StopThread
    If Not m_ThreadAction.Pause Then
      Try
        For Each TextFile As String In My.Computer.FileSystem.GetFiles( _
            m_FileWorkerOptions.Input, _
            FileIO.SearchOption.SearchTopLevelOnly, _
            m_FileWorkerOptions.FileType)
          If m_ThreadAction.Pause Or m_ThreadAction.StopThread Then
              Exit For
          End If
          Try
              Dim FileOutput As String = My.Resources.OutgoingPath + _
                "\" + My.Computer.FileSystem.GetName(TextFile)
              My.Computer.FileSystem.MoveFile(TextFile, FileOutput)
              Dim tmpThread As Thread = New Thread(AddressOf UpdateForm)
              tmpThread.IsBackground = True
              tmpThread.Start(FileOutput)
              WriteLogEvent(My.Resources.ThreadMessage + TextFile,_
                    THREAD_INFO, EventLogEntryType.Information, _
                    My.Resources.Source)
          Catch ex As Exception
              WriteLogEvent(My.Resources.ThreadErrorMessage + _
              Now.ToString, THREAD_ERROR, EventLogEntryType.Error,_
              My.Resources.Source)
          End Try
        Next
      Catch fio As IOException
        WriteLogEvent(My.Resources.ThreadIOError + _
          Now.ToString, THREAD_ABORT_ERROR, EventLogEntryType.Error,_
          My.Resources.Source)
      Catch tab As ThreadAbortException
          'this must be listed first as Exception is the master catch
          'Clean up thread here
        WriteLogEvent(My.Resources.ThreadAbortMessage + _
          Now.ToString, THREAD_ABORT_ERROR, EventLogEntryType.Error,_
          My.Resources.Source)
      Catch ex As Exception
```

```
        WriteLogEvent(My.Resources.ThreadErrorMessage + _
            Now.ToString, THREAD_ERROR, EventLogEntryType.Error,_
            My.Resources.Source)
      End Try
    End If
    If Not m_ThreadAction.StopThread Then
        Thread.Sleep(THREAD_WAIT)
    End If
  End While
End Sub
```

In the bolded code in Listing 6-9, we are taking the form instance variable and creating a lock on it. We then invoke the delegate, passing it the updated status information about the current file we have processed.

I wrapped this delegate in a Try/Catch block to avoid losing the sync lock and causing a hang in the service.

Install, Configure, and Verify

Creating services that interact with the desktop—even a remote desktop—is dangerous and should be avoided. Proper error handling and threading are required to give the most supportable solution, avoiding dangerous system hangs or, even worse, crashes.

Build the service and install it, making sure that you have removed the old version. Remember to go to Administrative Tools, Control Panel, and then Services Panel. Right-click the service, select Properties, click the Log On tab, make sure that Local System is selected, and then select Allow Service To Interact With Desktop.

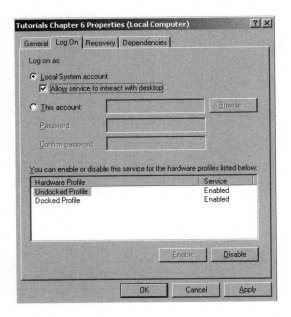

If you don't set the Interact With Desktop option, you will see nothing but a large number of errors in your Application Log. With the new service installed, make sure that you have your .txt files back in your incoming folder and then start the service. You will see the form immediately display even before the service has fully started. A few seconds later you should see entries for the files you are moving. After that, you should see entries stating that there are no files. Stop and uninstall the service and move to the next chapter.

Make sure that you have configured your Configuration.xml file with the locations of any folders and file types that you want to monitor and report on.

> **Note**   While you're running this service, some files might not appear to be updating the form when you first start. This is because the service starts quickly and the form isn't displayed while files are actually processed. While you run the service, add more files and it will update correctly.

Summary

- Direct input from and to a service from any user has to be designed carefully.

- System output from a service to the desktop or workstation should be limited to situations with interactive users or imperative system events that must be visible to administrators.

- When a service has privileges to interact with the desktop, any messages, boxes, or windows that require user interaction can be extremely dangerous if no user is currently logged on, or a user is logged on but away from his desk.

- Never use forms in your services—they are never a supported strategy. User feedback should be provided through other notification channels such as the NT Event Log, Simple Network Management Protocol, SQL Server, SMTP, or any other logging mechanism.

Chapter 7

Data Logging: Processing and Storing Data in SQL Server 2005

In our previous examples, we were able to monitor for incoming data and then process and e-mail it to someone. Services can also be a great way to log data found on the local computer, a remote computer, or even a remote set of computers. You can use services to monitor for a large subset of data that you need to transfer from flat files into a storage location such as Microsoft SQL Server or placed into an MSMQ Queue.

In this chapter we will use our service to gather data from several different locations and then store it in SQL Server. Microsoft Visual Studio comes with a version of SQL Server for development, or you can download a trial copy from Microsoft. You will need SQL Server to run some of the sections in this chapter. If you don't have SQL Server 2000 or SQL Server 2005, you can study the code here and modify it to work with your database, such as a Microsoft Access database.

Note Because of all the changes that we made in our code in Chapter 6, "User Input, Desktop Interaction, and Feedback," I will revert to the code in Chapter 5, "Processing and Notification."

Configuring Microsoft SQL Server

The first thing we need to do is configure SQL Server. As you will see in the screen shots, I am using SQL Server 2005.

Creating a Tutorials Database

First we need to create our database. From SQL Server Management Studio, connect to your Database Engine instance. Right-click Database, choose New Database, and name the database **Tutorials**.

Creating a Users Table

In this example we'll log user data received in our incoming folders into SQL Server. To do this we need to create a table to store the data.

Click the plus sign (+) before the Databases header. Select the plus sign near the Tutorials database listing. Right-click the Tables header, and choose New Table. Enter the column values and sizes shown in Listing 7-1, making sure to clear the Allow Nulls option.

Listing 7-1 User table implementation details.

```
Column Name Data type        Allow nulls
UserID      uniqueidentifier Unchecked
FirstName   nvarchar(50)     Unchecked
LastName    nvarchar(50)     Unchecked
Address1    nvarchar(100)    Unchecked
Address2    nvarchar(100)    Unchecked
City        nvarchar(50)     Unchecked
State       nvarchar(50)     Unchecked
Zipcode     nvarchar(10)     Unchecked
Phone       nvarchar(15)     Unchecked
```

Save the table, naming it **Users**.

Creating a User Stored Procedure

We are going to create a stored procedure that we can call from our code. Although we could insert records using dynamic SQL, using T-SQL and stored procedures provide better scalability, performance, and manageability.

Right-click the Programmability option, right-click Stored Procedures, and choose New Stored Procedure. Listing 7-2 shows the create procedure statement.

Listing 7-2 Microsoft SQL Server SaveUser stored procedure T-SQL code implementation.

```
SET ANSI_NULLS ON
GO
SET QUOTED_IDENTIFIER ON
GO
```

```
CREATE PROCEDURE [dbo].[SaveUser]
@FirstName    nvarchar(50),
@LastName     nvarchar(50),
@Address1     nvarchar(100),
@Address2     nvarchar(100),
@City         nvarchar(50),
@State        nvarchar(50),
@Zipcode      nvarchar(10),
@Phone        nvarchar(15),
@UserID       uniqueidentifier

AS
BEGIN
    SET NOCOUNT ON;

    INSERT INTO Users (UserID, FirstName, LastName, Address1, Address2, City,
[State]
,     ZipCode, Phone)
    Values
      (@UserID, @FirstName,@LastName,@Address1,@Address2,@City,@State,@Zipcode,@Phone)

    RETURN @@IDENTITY
END
```

In this chapter, we need to write code that will populate the Users table. To make this easier we are going to develop a class called *LINQTOSQL* that will handle all of our database interaction.

Understanding a *LINQSQL* Class

In Listing 7-2, I am creating a stored procedure in the Tutorials database called SaveUser that takes in the list of required parameters, inserts the record into our users table, and then returns back the identity value of the newly inserted record.

The caller can use the newly created GUID to reference the newly inserted record.

Using LINQ To SQL

There are multiple forms of LINQ when using Microsoft Visual Basic, such as LINQ for DataSets and LINQ To SQL. We will use LINQ To SQL, which is one technology that extends the abilities of Visual Basic 2008.

LINQ To SQL is a way for Visual Basic to create classes that represent data entities. You can use these entitites to describe a table in which you then use LINQ to query or manipulate the underlying data or structure. You define a class that represents the implementation of the SQL structure and attributes.

I will describe one way to create the Data Entity class implementation for LINQ To SQL.

Creating the Users Table Data Entity Class with LINQ To SQL File

The easiest method of creating the class is to use the LINQ To SQL tool built into Visual Studio 2008. To do this, select your project header, right-click, and choose New Item. Select LINQ To SQL File, and in the File Name box type **Users.dbml,** and click Add.

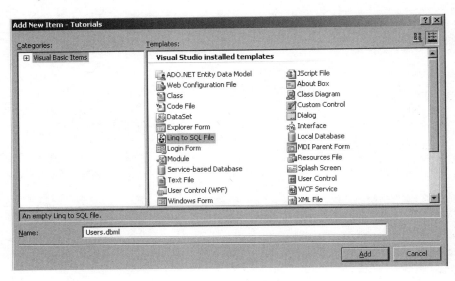

Now that you have a new blank file, you need to be able to drag entities onto the canvas. Therefore you must create a connection to SQL Server that has the objects that you want to represent in LINQ syntax. By default you won't have a connection to any Microsoft SQL Server database servers so we need to create one.

Click the Server Explorer tab. Right-click Data Connections and select Add Connection. Fill in the appropriate Connection Type, which in my case is a local Microsoft SQL Server database server using Windows Authentication.

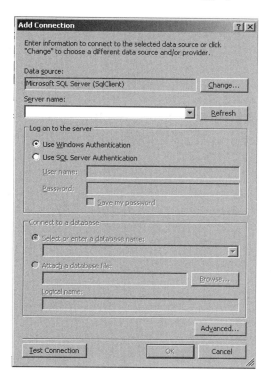

Enter your SQL Server name and authentication type. In the Database drop-down box, select your Tutorials database and click OK.

A connection to the database is now added, and the available tables, stored procedures, and other database objects are available to drag onto the Users.dbml designer window.

Drag the Users table and the SaveUser stored procedure onto the canvas. You will see the table added to the canvas directly, but when you drag the stored procedure it will appear in a list, in a split window to the right of the table listings. At the top left of the dbml file you will see a Method Pane button, which will turn off viewing the stored procedure list pane.

When you add tables, stored procedures, or other objects to the dbml file and then save the file, the tool automatically generates the code information that links LINQ to the SQL entities it describes. Visual Studio 2008 will then generate an Application.Settings entry which will be used by the newly generated LINQ class as the connection string. If you go to your project's properties and click the Settings tab, you will see the newly created entry.

If you want to view the code of the dbml file, you can choose File, Open File, browse to your solution file folder, and then open the Users.designer.vb file. This file is not listed in your project list and is not accessible by clicking the dbml file.

You will see a *UsersDataContext* class and a *Users* class, which have been generated to support the LINQ To SQL code. The *UsersDataContext* class represents our connection to the underlying data entity as well as our usage of defined stored procedures. The *Users* class represents the data entity and describes the table and its columns, indexes, and keys.

Because the file is extremely large, I won't copy the entire file here, but Listing 7-3 shows a snippet of what it looks like.

Listing 7-3   UsersDataContext LINQ To SQL implementation.

```
Partial Public Class UsersDataContext
    Inherits Global.System.Data.Linq.DataContext

    <Global.System.Diagnostics.DebuggerNonUserCodeAttribute()> _
    Public Sub New(ByVal connection As String)
        MyBase.New(connection)
    End Sub

    <Global.System.Diagnostics.DebuggerNonUserCodeAttribute()> _
    Public Sub New(ByVal connection As Global.System.Data.IDbConnection)
        MyBase.New(connection)
    End Sub

    <Global.System.Diagnostics.DebuggerNonUserCodeAttribute()> _
    Public Sub New()
        MyBase.New(Global.Tutorials.My.MySettings.Default.TutorialsConnectionString)
    End Sub

    Public ReadOnly Property Users() As Global.System.Data.Linq.Table(Of User)
        Get
            Return Me.GetTable(Of User)
        End Get
    End Property
```

The snippet represents the *UsersDataContext* class, which creates our connection to the database and also implements the ability for us to retrieve an instance of the *Users* class represented in Listing 7-4.

Listing 7-4   LINQ To SQL *Users* class DataEntity implementation.

```
<Global.System.Data.Linq.Table(Name:="dbo.Users")> _
Partial Public Class User
    Inherits Object
    Implements Global.System.Data.Linq.INotifyPropertyChanging,
      Global.System.ComponentModel.INotifyPropertyChanged
```

The *Users* class is the real meat of the LINQ project. Without it, we could not interact with or use our underlying entity.

Creating a SQL Class

Now that we have LINQ code generated—connecting us to our data source and entities—we need to generate the Visual Basic code that will allow us to query, retrieve, and insert new records into our Users table.

Add a new class file to your project and call it SQL.vb. This class will be the layer between our LINQ To SQL class code and the Microsoft SQL Server database data source.

For the first example we will use a fairly straightforward class that will allow us to call an overloaded *<InsertRecord>* method, as shown in Listing 7-5.

Listing 7-5   LINQSQL wrapper class for integration with Users.dbml.

```
Public Class LINQSQL
    Public Sub New()
    End Sub
    Public Function InsertRecord( _
                                ByVal First As String, _
                                ByVal Last As String, _
                                ByVal Address1 As String, _
                                ByVal Address2 As String, _
                                ByVal City As String, _
                                ByVal State As String, _
                                ByVal Zip As String, _
                                ByVal phone As String, _
                                ByVal UserID As String _
                                ) As Boolean
        Try
            Dim newuser As User = New User()

            newuser.UserID = New Guid(UserID)
            newuser.FirstName = First
            newuser.LastName = Last
            newuser.Address1 = Address1
            newuser.Address2 = Address2
            newuser.City = City
            newuser.State = State
            newuser.Zipcode = Zip
            newuser.Phone = phone

            m_UDC.Users.Add(newuser)
            m_UDC.SubmitChanges()

            Return True
        Catch ex As Exception
            Throw New Exception(ex.ToString)
        End Try
    End Function

    Public Function InsertRecord(ByVal pszRecord As String) As Boolean
        Try
            Dim pszQuery As String = Nothing
            Dim pszVars() As String = Split(pszRecord, ",")
            Dim newuser As User = New User()

            newuser.FirstName = pszVars(0)
            newuser.LastName = pszVars(1)
            newuser.Address1 = pszVars(2)
            newuser.Address2 = pszVars(3)
            newuser.City = pszVars(4)
```

```
            newuser.State = pszVars(5)
            newuser.Zipcode = pszVars(6)
            newuser.Phone = pszVars(7)
            newuser.UserID = New Guid(pszVars(8))

            m_UDC.Users.Add(newuser)
            m_UDC.SubmitChanges()

            Return True
        Catch ex As Exception
            Throw New Exception(ex.ToString)
        End Try
    End Function
End Class
```

The code in Listing 7-5 is very simple. The overloaded method takes in either a string or a breakdown of the values of a new *Users* class instance and then inserts that record into the database. This is done by creating a new underlying connection to the database through the *UsersDataContext* object and the default connection string, which is listed in our My.Settings project properties.

Unlike in normal database interactions using LINQ, we create an object instead of our *User* class and set the approriate values for a new record. When we finish setting those values we have to call the *Add* method on the db.Users object instance, where *db* represents our *UsersDataContext* and *Users* represents a static instance of the *Users* class.

Finally, we call SubmitChanges on our UsersDataContext instance to save the record and changes to our Tutorials database. If you don't call SubmitChanges, the data will not be written to the database.

Updating the *FileWorker* Class

To make the additions useful, we have to update the *FileWorker* class to read and insert the records into our Tutorials database.

Updating *<FileWorker.ProcessFiles>*

We need to create an instance of our *LINQSQL* class and then use the file that we found while polling our process folder to populate a new user record for each line in the process file. To do this we will update the *<ProcessFiles>* method, which is where we query the outgoing folder, send an e-mail, and then move the file to our processed folder. Listing 7-6 shows the changes required for *<ProcessFiles>*.

Listing 7-6   FileWorker updated ProcessFiles method to support the *LINQSQL* class implementation.

```
Private Sub ProcessFiles()
  Dim LinqSql As LINQSQL = New LINQSQL()
  While Not m_ThreadAction.StopThread
    If Not m_ThreadAction.Pause Then
      Try
```

```vb
For Each TextFile As String In My.Computer.FileSystem.GetFiles( _
    m_FileWorkerOptions.Output, _
    FileIO.SearchOption.SearchTopLevelOnly, _
    m_FileWorkerOptions.FileType)
    If m_ThreadAction.Pause Or m_ThreadAction.StopThread Then
        Exit For
    End If
    Try
        Dim ProcessFile As String = _
        m_FileWorkerOptions.ProcessedPath("\" + _
        My.Computer.FileSystem.GetName(TextFile))
        'File is moved so lets read it out of the Output Folder
        If (Me.MailEnabled) Then
            Dim message As String
            Try
                message = "Processing File Data:[" + _
                    My.Computer.FileSystem.ReadAllText(TextFile) + _
                    "]] From File - "
            Catch ex As Exception
                message = "Unable to read from file - "
            End Try
    'Send the Email and then move it again to the processed Folder
            m_FileWorkerOptions.EmailProperties.Message = message
            m_SmtpClient.QueueMail(m_FileWorkerOptions.EmailProperties)
        End If
        Dim records As StreamReader = _
        My.Computer.FileSystem.OpenTextFileReader(TextFile)
        Dim record As String
        record = records.ReadLine()
        While (Not record Is Nothing)
            Try
                LinqSql.InsertRecord(record)
            Catch ex As Exception
                WriteLogEvent(My.Resources.ThreadIOError + _
        "_" + ex.ToString + "_" + Now.ToString, THREAD_ERROR, _
                EventLogEntryType.Error, My.Resources.Source)
            End Try
            record = records.ReadLine
        End While
        records.Close()
                records.Dispose()
        My.Computer.FileSystem.MoveFile(TextFile, ProcessFile, True)
        System.Threading.Thread.Sleep(0)
        WriteLogEvent(My.Resources.ThreadMessage + _
    TextFile, THREAD_INFO, EventLogEntryType.Information, _
My.Resources.Source)
    Catch ex As Exception
        WriteLogEvent(My.Resources.ThreadErrorMessage + _
    "_" + ex.ToString + "_" + Now.ToString, THREAD_ERROR, _
    EventLogEntryType.Error, My.Resources.Source)
    End Try
Next
Catch fio As IOException
WriteLogEvent(My.Resources.ThreadIOError + "_" + fio.ToString _
    + "_" + Now.ToString, THREAD_ABORT_ERROR, _
```

```
                    EventLogEntryType.Error, My.Resources.Source)
          Catch tab As ThreadAbortException
            'this must be listed first as Exception is the master catch
            'Clean up thread here
            WriteLogEvent(My.Resources.ThreadAbortMessage + "_" _
            + tab.ToString + "_" + Now.ToString, THREAD_ABORT_ERROR, _
            EventLogEntryType.Error, My.Resources.Source)
          Catch ex As Exception
            WriteLogEvent(My.Resources.ThreadErrorMessage + "_" + _
                ex.ToString + "_" + Now.ToString, THREAD_ERROR, _
                EventLogEntryType.Error, My.Resources.Source)
          End Try
      End If
      If Not m_ThreadAction.StopThread Then
          Thread.Sleep(THREAD_WAIT)
      End If
  End While
End Sub
```

The bolded code in Listing 7-6 creates an instance of our *LINQSQL* class before we enter our thread loop because we only need one instance of this class.

When a file is found, we open the file and iterate through it, passing each line to our *<InsertRecord>* method on the LINQSQL instance. This will populate the database with a new User instance. If the insertion fails, we log an event and move the file.

Install and Verify

To validate that the service can read files and create records for the system to insert, I have modified my configuration.xml file so that it only points to the incoming folder and looks for *.txt files.

I have created three files with five records each. Listing 7-7 is a sample from one of the text files.

Listing 7-7   Demonstration data used for service verification.
```
FirstName,LastName,111 South Street,NA,TestCity,TT,00000,555-1212
FirstName2,LastName,111 South Street,NA,TestCity,TT,00000,555-1212
FirstName3,LastName,111 South Street,NA,TestCity,TT,00000,555-1212
FirstName4,LastName,111 South Street,NA,TestCity,TT,00000,555-1212
FirstName5,LastName,111 South Street,NA,TestCity,TT,00000,555-1212
```

For each file I added five records. Because there are no unique index constraints on any columns but the UniqueIdentifier field, or GUID, the data shown in Listing 7-7 is appropriate.

You can run these files through as many times as you like by merely cutting and pasting them back into your incoming folder each time they are processed successfully.

Data Tracking Validation

The preceding section demonstrated how to monitor for data and then insert it into the database. However, if a record failed to be inserted, nothing stops that record from being lost to us forever. Yes, you could look in the Application log, but this is tedious and not a very good solution. Therefore we are going to add some extra validation, logging, and notification.

Creating Process Error Folder

First we need to create a directory to store our records that fail to get inserted. In the same directory as our incoming directory, add a directory called ProcessError. This is where we will store our records that fail.

You can store the failed records two ways:

- Create a file per failed record.
- Create one file and add all failed records to it.

Error Processing Solution

Each solution has its pros and cons. I'm going to use a single file per record because I want to avoid any locking that could occur if I were to have a secondary automated process collecting this data or trying to reprocess it.

For each file we will use a format of fail_record_Guid.fri for failed record information. The GUID portion of our file assures us that no record will be overwritten. We could use DateTime.Now.Ticks as an identifier, but with multiple threads and faster processors running in parallel, it is possible to overwrite files that you are creating because each thread uses the same Ticks value.

Updating the *FileWorkerOptions* Class

We need to add our process file location to our *FileWorkerOptions* class so that for each record we create in the database we will know the location of where to save it. Make the changes shown in Listing 7-8 to your *FileWorkerOptions* class to add a property that we can set or retrieve as needed.

Listing 7-8   ProcessError property implementation.

```
Private m_ProcessError As String

Public Property ProcessError() As String
    Get
        Return m_ProcessError
    End Get
    Set(ByVal value As String)
        m_ProcessError = value
    End Set
End Property
```

Updating Our configuration.xml File

For each incoming folder we need to configure the ProcessError folder that we will use for it. Listing 7-9 shows an example of what your file should now look like.

Listing 7-9   ProcessError modification in configuration.xml file.

```xml
<?xml version="1.0" encoding="utf-8" ?>
<Configuration>
  <FileWorkerOptions>
    <FileWorkerProperties>
      <IncomingPath>c:\tutorials\incoming</IncomingPath>
      <OutgoingPath>c:\tutorials\outgoing</OutgoingPath>
      <ProcessedFolder>c:\tutorials\processed</ProcessedFolder>
      <FileType>*.txt</FileType>
      <SmtpServer>testserver</SmtpServer>
      <Subject>Test Subject</Subject>
      <Message>Found Message</Message>
      <Sender>Michael@testing.com</Sender>
      <Recipient>Michael@testing.com</Recipient>
      <SmtpPort>25</SmtpPort>
      <MailEnabled>true</MailEnabled>
      <ProcessedError>c:\tutorials\processerror</ProcessedError>
    </FileWorkerProperties>
  </FileWorkerOptions>
</Configuration>
```

You can see that I have added the *<ProcessError>* element and set it equal to my newly created folder path. Each record that fails in my incoming folder or outgoing folder will be written to the ProcessError folder as a separate file.

Updating the *FileWorker* Class

We will modify several things from the current *FileWorker* implementation to support additional threading, processing, and notifications. The following sections are required to update the *FileWorker* class.

Updating the *FileWorker* Class Constructor

To reflect the support for the new ProcessError property in the *FileWorker* class, the constructor needs to be updated. In Listing 7-10, the constructor has been updated to update the local ProcessError property based on the passed in *FileWorkerOptions* instance.

Listing 7-10   Updated *FileWorker* class constructor.

```
    Public Sub New(ByRef threadaction As ThreadActionState, ByVal
 fileworkeroptions As FileWorkerOptions)
        m_ThreadAction = threadaction

        m_FileWorkerOptions.Input = fileworkeroptions.Input
        m_FileWorkerOptions.Output = fileworkeroptions.Output
        m_FileWorkerOptions.FileType = fileworkeroptions.FileType
        m_FileWorkerOptions.ProcessedPath = fileworkeroptions.ProcessedPath
        m_FileWorkerOptions.EmailProperties = fileworkeroptions.EmailProperties
```

```
            m_FileWorkerOptions.ProcessError = fileworkeroptions.ProcessError
    End Sub
```

Updating the *<Tutorials.threadFunc>* Method

Now that we have created our property to store the location internally and added the value to our configuration file, we have to link the two together using the *<threadFunc>* method.

In your current *threadFunc* method, add the bolded code shown in Listing 7-11; the other non-bolded lines should already exist.

Listing 7-11   *<ThreadFunc>* XML configuration read changes.

```
Private Sub ThreadFunc()
    Try
        'Load our Configuration File
        Dim Doc As XmlDocument = New XmlDocument()
        Doc.Load(My.Settings.Configuration)
        Dim Options As XmlNode
        'Get a pointer to the Outer Node
        Options = Doc.SelectSingleNode("//*[local-name()='FileWorkerOptions']")
        If (Not Options Is Nothing) Then
            'Get a pointer to the first child node of FileWorkerOptions
            Dim tmpOptions As System.Xml.XPath.XPathNavigator _
            = Options.FirstChild.CreateNavigator()
            If (Not tmpOptions Is Nothing) Then
                Dim FWOptions As New FileWorkerOptions
                Dim children As System.Xml.XPath.XPathNavigator
                'Loop through each childe node (FileWorkerOption) and
                'get the values. Create a new FileWorkerOptions instance and
                'FileWorkerOption instance
                Do
                    Try
                        children = tmpOptions.SelectSingleNode("IncomingPath")
                        FWOptions.Input = children.Value

                        children = tmpOptions.SelectSingleNode("OutgoingPath")
                        FWOptions.Output = children.Value

                        children = tmpOptions.SelectSingleNode("FileType")
                        FWOptions.FileType = children.Value

                        children = tmpOptions.SelectSingleNode("ProcessedPath")
                        FWOptions.ProcessedPath = children.Value

                        children = tmpOptions.SelectSingleNode("ProcessedError")
                        FWOptions.ProcessError = children.Value

                        Dim tmpDetail As New EmailDetail
                        children = tmpOptions.SelectSingleNode("Message")
                        tmpDetail.Message = children.Value

                        children = tmpOptions.SelectSingleNode("Subject")
                        tmpDetail.Subject = children.Value
```

```
                            children = tmpOptions.SelectSingleNode("Sender")
                            tmpDetail.Sender = children.Value

                            children = tmpOptions.SelectSingleNode("Recipient")
                            tmpDetail.Recipient = children.Value

                            children = tmpOptions.SelectSingleNode("SmtpPort")
                            tmpDetail.SmtpPort = children.Value

                            children = tmpOptions.SelectSingleNode("SmtpServer")
                            tmpDetail.SmtpServer = children.Value

                            FWOptions.EmailProperties = tmpDetail

                            Dim tmpFW As New FileWorker(m_ThreadAction, FWOptions)

                            children = tmpOptions.SelectSingleNode("MailEnabled")
                            tmpFW.MailEnabled = Convert.ToBoolean(children.Value)

                            m_WorkerThreads.Add(tmpFW)
                            tmpFW.Start()
                        Catch ex As Exception
                            WriteLogEvent(ex.ToString(), CONFIG_READ_ERROR, _
        EventLogEntryType.Error, _
                                    My.Resources.Source)
                        End Try
                    Loop While (tmpOptions.MoveToNext)
                End If
            End If
        Catch ex As Exception
            WriteLogEvent(ex.ToString(), ONSTART_ERROR, _
                        EventLogEntryType.Error, My.Resources.Source)
            Me.Stop()
        End Try
    End Sub
```

Now that we have successfully retrieved and set our property value we need to make the code functional.

Implementing the Record Failure Code

We need to make some significant changes to the current implementation to add functionality to the code. I will outline each change in the following sections. Remember that for each failure you will need to find a way to reprocess that record. In our case we are providing storage and notification but not reprocessing. Because of the unlimited number of reasons why something could fail, we have no surefire way to assure a single reprocessing solution.

Adding a Process *Failure* Method

For this solution to work we have to look at different ways to implement the processing of the failed data. The power of Visual Studio 2008 and Visual Basic provides unlimited possibilities;

however, together they provide an implementation model that gives us everything we need with little work.

How we decide to use that implementation model, however, can enhance or decrease its value. Internally, .NET supports the notion of the *ThreadPool* class. This class provides us with the ability to create managed threads without having to create the infrastructure code around managing the threads. This can be both good and bad. If you have a situation where something needs to run once and only once, this is great. If you have a situation where you need a large number of threads and you are not concerned with monitoring those threads or having to deal with synchronizing or optimizing their wait states by using Sleep, this is also good. However, if you need to be able to directly monitor a thread so that if it fails you can restart that thread, using a run once logic for a given thread would be an issue.

However, even this issue is easy to overcome and should not be seen as a hindrance to the importance and power using the *ThreadPool* class gives us. We will use the *ThreadPool* class once again, as we did in our SMTP class.

To implement using the *ThreadPool* class solution we need two things:

- An implementation of a method that can be used by *ThreadPool*.
- The code necessary to generate the thread itself.

Listing 7-12 shows the method I have implemented and added to the *FileWorker* class instance.

Listing 7-12   ProcessFailures method implementation.

```
Private Sub ProcessFailures(ByVal args As Object)
    Try
        If m_ThreadAction.StopThread Then Return
        Dim failurefile As StreamWriter = _
        My.Computer.FileSystem.OpenTextFileWriter(m_FileWorkerOptions.ProcessError +
"\Failure_File_" _
        + Guid.NewGuid().ToString + ".fri", False)

        failurefile.WriteLine(args.ToString())
        failurefile.Flush()
        failurefile.Close()
        failurefile.Dispose()
        If (Me.MailEnabled) Then
            Dim message As String
            Try
                message = "Error Processing File Data:[" + args.ToString + "] - "
            Catch ex As Exception
                message = "Unable to specify data - " + ex.ToString + vbCrLf
            End Try
            'Send the Email and then move it again to the processed Folder
            m_FileWorkerOptions.EmailProperties.Message = message
            m_SmtpClient.QueueMail(m_FileWorkerOptions.EmailProperties)
        End If
    Catch ex As IOException
```

```
            WriteLogEvent(My.Resources.ThreadErrorMessage + "_" + ex.ToString _
            + "_" + Now.ToString, THREAD_ERROR, EventLogEntryType.Error, _
        My.Resources.Source)
    Catch ex As Exception
        WriteLogEvent(My.Resources.ThreadErrorMessage + "_" + ex.ToString _
            + "_" + Now.ToString, THREAD_ERROR, EventLogEntryType.Error, _
            My.Resources.Source)
    End Try
End Sub
```

We then use the Visual Basic 2008 *My* class to create a text-based streamwriter that we use to write our record data to before closing the file. Last, we ensure that e-mail notifications are enabled and, if so, we send an e-mail notification about the specified data that has failed.

Note that I am creating a new GUID for each file that we produce so that everything is written uniquely.

The Worker Thread

Now we need to update our *<ProcessFiles>* method to create the worker thread necessary to process the failure request. Listing 7-13 shows the code.

Listing 7-13   ProcessFiles code update for new queue thread.

```
Private Sub ProcessFiles()
    Dim LinqSql As LINQSQL = New LINQSQL()

    While Not m_ThreadAction.StopThread
        If Not m_ThreadAction.Pause Then
            Try
                For Each TextFile As String In My.Computer.FileSystem.GetFiles( _
                    m_FileWorkerOptions.Output, _
                    FileIO.SearchOption.SearchTopLevelOnly, _
                    m_FileWorkerOptions.FileType)
                    If m_ThreadAction.Pause Or m_ThreadAction.StopThread Then
                        Exit For
                    End If
                    Try
                        Dim tmpGuid As String = Guid.NewGuid().ToString()

                        Dim ProcessFile As String =
                          m_FileWorkerOptions.ProcessedPath _
                            + "\" + tmpGuid + "_" +
                        My.Computer.FileSystem.GetName(TextFile)

                        'File is moved so lets read it out of the Output Folder
                        If (Me.MailEnabled) Then
                            Dim message As String
                            Try
                                message = "Processing File Data:[" + _
                                    My.Computer.FileSystem.ReadAllText(TextFile) + _
                                    "]] From File - "
                            Catch ex As Exception
                                message = "Unable to read from file - "
```

```vbnet
                    End Try
                    'Send the Email and then move it again to the
                processed Folder
                    m_FileWorkerOptions.EmailProperties.Message = message
m_SmtpClient.QueueMail(m_FileWorkerOptions.EmailProperties)
                End If
                Dim records As StreamReader = _
                My.Computer.FileSystem.OpenTextFileReader(TextFile)
                Dim record As String
                record = records.ReadLine()
                While (Not record Is Nothing)
                    Try
                        Dim insert As Boolean = LinqSql.InsertRecord(record)
                        If Not insert Then
                            'Save it
                            System.Threading.ThreadPool.QueueUserWorkItem( _
                New WaitCallback(AddressOf ProcessFailures), record)
                        End If
                    Catch ex As Exception
                        'Save it
                        System.Threading.ThreadPool.QueueUserWorkItem(
                                        New WaitCallback( _
                            My.Resources.Source)
                    End Try
                    record = records.ReadLine
                End While

                records.Close()
                records.Dispose()
                My.Computer.FileSystem.MoveFile(TextFile, ProcessFile, True)
                System.Threading.Thread.Sleep(0)
                WriteLogEvent(My.Resources.ThreadMessage + _
            TextFile, THREAD_INFO, EventLogEntryType.Information, _
            My.Resources.Source)
                Catch ex As Exception
                    WriteLogEvent(My.Resources.ThreadErrorMessage + _
            "_" + ex.ToString + "_" + Now.ToString, THREAD_ERROR, _
            EventLogEntryType.Error, My.Resources.Source)
                End Try
            Next
        Catch fio As IOException
            WriteLogEvent(My.Resources.ThreadIOError + "_" + fio.ToString _
                + "_" + Now.ToString, THREAD_ABORT_ERROR, _
                EventLogEntryType.Error, My.Resources.Source)
        Catch tab As ThreadAbortException
            'this must be listed first as Exception is the master catch
            'Clean up thread here
            WriteLogEvent(My.Resources.ThreadAbortMessage + "_" _
        + tab.ToString + "_" + Now.ToString, THREAD_ABORT_ERROR, _
            EventLogEntryType.Error, My.Resources.Source)
        Catch ex As Exception
            WriteLogEvent(My.Resources.ThreadErrorMessage + "_" + _
                ex.ToString + "_" + Now.ToString, THREAD_ERROR, _
                EventLogEntryType.Error, My.Resources.Source)
        End Try
```

```
            End If
            If Not m_ThreadAction.StopThread Then
                Thread.Sleep(THREAD_WAIT)
            End If
        End While
End Sub
```

Our *<LINQSQL.InsertRecord>* method returns a Boolean; however, it also will throw certain errors. To take the return value and the possible exception thrown into account, I have added a Boolean validation of the result that then creates a worker thread in our *ThreadPool*, passing it our record data.

In our exception handler, where we will either capture a thrown error or some internal failure, we again create a worker thread and pass it not only the record information but also the error message that we received.

Install and Verify

Install and run the new service. Using the sample files and by saving our data we are at least assured that we can review that data later on, and if necessary, copy the data back into our incoming directory and reprocess it when the server is up again, the network is up again, or whatever issue that caused the failure has been resolved.

Data Migration from One Data Store to Another Data Store

At times you might need to monitor for data that has been stored in SQL Server. Sometimes data needs to be migrated from one place to another. If you need to transfer data from a database server to a back-end database server, you have several options. One way is to have your service monitor for the data and then query the records, create a file with the data, and wait for another application to pick that file up and process it. Another way is to have your service not only pick up the data, but also process the data. I have already covered submitting data to SQL Server, but now let's create an example of monitoring SQL Server for data to send to a simulated back-end server.

As in previous chapters, the goal should always be to try and optimize your service's interactions with the system and your data. In this case, because you are monitoring a database table for data, it doesn't make sense to have more than one thread for this—you have to synchronize your data reads as well as remember what data you have already queried.

Suppose you have a database table full of customer data from a Web site. You want to move this data to your mainframe. You have many options, including using Host Integration Server or other transport layers. A service is a fairly robust and simplistic solution. However, if you are copying records from the table into a flat file or XML format for your mainframe or other back-end server, you have to be able to keep track of records you have already copied. You could have a shadow table in the database where you copy records and they will be deleted when the transaction is complete. Another solution is to have a bit field in the database table that specifies whether the data has been copied out. For our example we will use a simple query method to grab the data and write it to our flat file. We will not be concerned in this section with grabbing duplicate data.

Creating the Back-End Data Store

In this section we'll create a duplicate of the original Users table. However, we will do so by creating a secondary database called BackEnd.

In Microsoft SQL Server, create a secondary database and name it **BackEnd**. If you are unsure of the steps for creating a database, please review "Creating a Tutorials Database" earlier in this chapter.

Next you want to create a table called **Users,** using the exact structure with which you created the original Users table in our Tutorials database, as well as the SaveUser stored procedure. Once again, if you are unsure how to do this, please review "Creating a Users Table" earlier in the chapter. The only difference between the original and new configurations should be the name of the database.

Creating a New Connection String

Now that we have our data store, we need to create a new connection string to use with our current Users.dbml. Because these are identical objects we can reuse the current implementation. We do, however, need to distinguish the underlying UserDataContext object to connect to the appropriate data store.

On the Properties tab of the service, select Settings. You will see our current TutorialsConnectionString. Add a new settings entry called **BackEndConnectionString**. Set the type to Connection String, set the level to Application, and then copy the **TutorialsConnectionString** value into our new entry. Change the database name in the copied value from Tutorials to **BackEnd** and close the Properties window. Save the service.

Updating the LINQSQL Class Connectionstring

Now that we have a new connection string we need to update our *LINQSQL* class, which is currently set to only use the default connection string. To do this, we add a data member of type UsersDataContext and then modify our constructor to accept the connection string. Listing 7-14 shows the modified *LINQSQL* class.

Listing 7-14   Updating the *LINQSQL* class and constructor.

```
Public Class LINQSQL
  Private m_UDC As UsersDataContext

  Public Sub New(ByVal ConnectionString As String)
     m_UDC = New UsersDataContext(ConnectionString)
  End Sub
```

Now that we have our new data member, we have to update our methods to use that new data member instead of the local variable instance we've been using.

Updating InsertRecord Implementations

For both *<InsertRecord>* implementations we want to update the code to use the class data member instance. This step enhances our code because now it will not need to initialize a new instance on each call. Listing 7-15 shows the new implementation of the code.

Listing 7-15   The new *<InsertRecord>* implementations.

```
Public Function InsertRecord( _
                        ByVal First As String, _
                        ByVal Last As String, _
                        ByVal Address1 As String, _
                        ByVal Address2 As String, _
                        ByVal City As String, _
                        ByVal State As String, _
                        ByVal Zip As String, _
                        ByVal phone As String, _
                        ByVal UserID As Guid _
                        ) As Boolean
Try
    Dim newuser As User = New User()

    newuser.UserID = UserID
    newuser.FirstName = First
    newuser.LastName = Last
    newuser.Address1 = Address1
    newuser.Address2 = Address2
    newuser.City = City
    newuser.State = State
    newuser.Zipcode = Zip
    newuser.Phone = phone

    m_UDC.Users.Add(newuser)
    m_UDC.SubmitChanges()

    Return True
Catch sqlex As SqlClient.SqlException
    If sqlex.Number = 2627 Then
        'It was a duplicate.
        Return True
    End If
Catch ex As Exception
    Throw New Exception(ex.ToString)
End Try
End Function

Public Function InsertRecord(ByVal pszRecord As String) As Boolean
Try
    Dim pszQuery As String = Nothing
    Dim pszVars() As String = Split(pszRecord, ",")
```

```
        Dim newuser As User = New User()

        newuser.FirstName = pszVars(0)
        newuser.LastName = pszVars(1)
        newuser.Address1 = pszVars(2)
        newuser.Address2 = pszVars(3)
        newuser.City = pszVars(4)
        newuser.State = pszVars(5)
        newuser.Zipcode = pszVars(6)
        newuser.Phone = pszVars(7)
        newuser.UserID = Guid.NewGuid()

        m_UDC.Users.Add(newuser)
        m_UDC.SubmitChanges()

        Return True
    Catch sqlex As SqlClient.SqlException
        If sqlex.Number = 2627 Then
            'It was a duplicate.
            Return True
        End If
    Catch ex As Exception
        Throw New Exception(ex.ToString)
    End Try
End Function
```

These changes are important because we will now connect to a secondary database implementation that uses the same format as our source database.

Implementing a *Dispose* Method for the *LINQSQL* Class

Now that we are using a class member, we want to make sure we can also clean it up, so we add the method shown in Listing 7-16.

Listing 7-16 Implementing the *<Dispose>* method.

```
Public Sub Dispose()
  Try
    m_UDC.Dispose()
  Catch ex As Exception
    m_UDC = Nothing
  End Try
End Sub
```

We will need to also update any instance of this object created in any external code to call this method. In our case, we will want to call this in our *FileWorker* class.

Updating the *<FileWorker.ProcessFiles>* Method

Now that we are required to pass in the connection string, we need to update the *<ProcessFiles>* method to reflect this change, as shown in Listing 7-17.

Listing 7-17   Updating the call to *<InsertRecord>* from *<ProcessFiles>*.

```vb
Private Sub ProcessFiles()
    Dim LinqSql As LINQSQL = New LINQSQL(My.Settings.TutorialsConnectionString)

    While Not m_ThreadAction.StopThread
        If Not m_ThreadAction.Pause Then
            Try
                For Each TextFile As String In My.Computer.FileSystem.GetFiles( _
                    m_FileWorkerOptions.Output, _
                    FileIO.SearchOption.SearchTopLevelOnly, _
                    m_FileWorkerOptions.FileType)
                If m_ThreadAction.Pause Or m_ThreadAction.StopThread Then
                    Exit For
                End If
                Try
                    Dim tmpGuid As String = Guid.NewGuid().ToString()

                    Dim ProcessFile As String =
m_FileWorkerOptions.ProcessedPath _
                        + "\" + tmpGuid + "_" +
My.Computer.FileSystem.GetName(TextFile)

                            'File is moved so lets read it out of the Output Folder
                            If (Me.MailEnabled) Then
                                Dim message As String
                                Try
                                    message = "Processing File Data:[" + _
                                        My.Computer.FileSystem.ReadAllText(TextFile)
                                        + _"]] From File - "
                                Catch ex As Exception
                                    message = "Unable to read from file - "
                                End Try
                                'Send the Email and then move it again to the processed Folder
                                m_FileWorkerOptions.EmailProperties.Message = message
m_SmtpClient.QueueMail(m_FileWorkerOptions.EmailProperties)
                            End If
                            Dim records As StreamReader = _
                            My.Computer.FileSystem.OpenTextFileReader(TextFile)
                            Dim record As String
                            record = records.ReadLine()
                            While (Not record Is Nothing)
                                Try
                                    Dim insert As Boolean =
                                LinqSql.InsertRecord(record)

                                    If Not insert Then
                                        'Save it
                                        System.Threading.ThreadPool.QueueUserWorkItem( _
            New WaitCallback(AddressOf ProcessFailures), record)
                                    End If
                                Catch ex As Exception
                                    'Save it
                                    System.Threading.ThreadPool.QueueUserWorkItem( _
                                        New WaitCallback(AddressOf ProcessFailures),
                                        _
```

```
                                      record + "-" + ex.ToString)
                            WriteLogEvent(My.Resources.ThreadIOError + "_" +
ex.ToString _
                                + "_" + Now.ToString, THREAD_ERROR, EventLogEntryType.
Error, _
                                    My.Resources.Source)
                        End Try

                        record = records.ReadLine
                    End While


                    records.Close()
                    records.Dispose()
                    My.Computer.FileSystem.MoveFile(TextFile, ProcessFile,
True)
                    System.Threading.Thread.Sleep(0)
                    WriteLogEvent(My.Resources.ThreadMessage + _
                TextFile, THREAD_INFO, EventLogEntryType.Information, _
                My.Resources.Source)
                    Catch ex As Exception
                        WriteLogEvent(My.Resources.ThreadErrorMessage + _
                "_" + ex.ToString + "_" + Now.ToString, THREAD_ERROR, _
                EventLogEntryType.Error, My.Resources.Source)
                    End Try
                Next
            Catch fio As IOException
                WriteLogEvent(My.Resources.ThreadIOError + "_" + fio.ToString _
                    + "_" + Now.ToString, THREAD_ABORT_ERROR, _
                    EventLogEntryType.Error, My.Resources.Source)
            Catch tab As ThreadAbortException
                'this must be listed first as Exception is the master catch
                'Clean up thread here
                WriteLogEvent(My.Resources.ThreadAbortMessage + "_" _
                + tab.ToString + "_" + Now.ToString, THREAD_ABORT_ERROR, _
                    EventLogEntryType.Error, My.Resources.Source)
            Catch ex As Exception
                WriteLogEvent(My.Resources.ThreadErrorMessage + "_" + _
                    ex.ToString + "_" + Now.ToString, THREAD_ERROR, _
                    EventLogEntryType.Error, My.Resources.Source)
            End Try
        End If
        If Not m_ThreadAction.StopThread Then
            Thread.Sleep(THREAD_WAIT)
        End If
    End While
End Sub
```

I'm updating this method because in this demonstration we want to emulate a situation in which newly created records are being inserted into a source database and then migrated to our back-end data store.

Creating a New *<ProcessRecords>* Method

At this point we can insert records into our source database; now we need to add a method that can then process these records by moving them to our back-end store. Of course in this example we could simply add the same record to our primary and back-end stores. If the situation called for it—if we were to get in a single record with a multi-destination requirement—that solution makes sense. But in our case, we want to show a migration of the data. We are emulating a circumstance in which the record may already exist, or going directly from the source to the destination is not possible. Listing 7-18 shows the new *<ProcessRecords>* method.

Listing 7-18 Updated *<ProcessRecords>* with support for data migration.

```
Private Sub ProcessRecords()
    While Not (m_ThreadAction.StopThread)
        If Not (m_ThreadAction.Pause) Then
            Try
                Dim source As LINQSQL = New _
                LINQSQL(My.Settings.TutorialsConnectionString)

                Dim destination As LINQSQL = New _
                LINQSQL(My.Settings.BackEndConnectionString)

                Dim AllUsers() As User = source.GetUsers

                For Each user In AllUsers
                    Try
                        destination.InsertRecord(user.FirstName, user.LastName, _
                            user.Address1, user.Address2, user.City, user.State, _
                            user.Zipcode, user.Phone, user.UserID)
                    Catch ex As Exception
                        WriteLogEvent(My.Resources.ThreadErrorMessage + ex.ToString, _
                            THREAD_ERROR, EventLogEntryType.Error, My.Resources.Source)
                    End Try
                Next

                source.Dispose()
                destination.Dispose()
            Catch ex As Exception
                WriteLogEvent(My.Resources.ThreadErrorMessage + ex.ToString, _
            THREAD_ERROR, EventLogEntryType.Error, My.Resources.Source)
            End Try
        End If
        If Not m_ThreadAction.StopThread Then
            Thread.Sleep(THREAD_WAIT)
        End If
    End While
End Sub
```

As with other methods, we are going to loop, looking for new records to migrate, while also validating whether we are supposed to return or pause.

We are also creating two instances of our *LINQSQL* class, one for each data store we are connecting to. Our source instance is where we will query our records from, and our destination is where we will migrate to.

Note two things about this new method:

■ We are using our source instance to query the records and then looping through the current users. This is a new method, which I will demonstrate shortly.

■ I am looping through all the instances of the source and then calling the *<InsertRecord>* method on the destination.

Now that we have our *ProcessRecords* method, I need to show the changes to the *LINQSQL* class so that we can return the records we need to query from our source.

Updating the *FileWorker* Class

We need to add thread support for the new method in Listing 7-18. We need to add a new thread definition to our *FileWorker* class, a new property that we will use to expose this new thread to the service, and an update to the *<Start>* method, as in the code in Listing 7-19.

Listing 7-19   Updated *FileWorker* class with *<CopyRecords>* method thread support.

```
Private m_CopyRecords As Thread = Nothing

Public Sub Start()
    m_Incoming = New Thread(AddressOf ProcessIncoming)
    m_Incoming.Priority = ThreadPriority.Normal
    m_Incoming.IsBackground = True
    m_Incoming.Start()

    m_Outgoing = New Thread(AddressOf ProcessFiles)
    m_Outgoing.Priority = ThreadPriority.Normal
    m_Outgoing.IsBackground = True
    m_Outgoing.Start()

    m_CopyRecords = New Thread(AddressOf ProcessRecords)
    m_CopyRecords.Priority = ThreadPriority.Normal
    m_CopyRecords.IsBackground = True
    m_CopyRecords.Start()
End Sub

Public ReadOnly Property CopyRecords() As Thread
    Get
        Return m_CopyRecords
    End Get
End Property
```

Each piece of code in Listing 7-19 reflects a change to the current *FileWorker* implementation. The *<Start>* method has been updated to utilize the newly created m_CopyThreads thread variable to run an instance of the *<CopyRecords>* method.

With the changes in Listing 7-19, we need to make an update to the Tutorials.vb class to clean up the newly created FileWorker thread.

Listing 7-20 shows the updates to the *Tutorials.OnStop* method.

Listing 7-20 Updated Tutorials.vb *<OnStop>* with FileWorker CopyRecords thread cleanup support.

```
Protected Overrides Sub OnStop()
    ' Add code here to perform any tear-down necessary to stop your service.
    Try
        If (Not m_WorkerThread Is Nothing) Then
            Try
                WriteLogEvent(My.Resources.ServiceStopping, ONSTOP_INFO, _
                    EventLogEntryType.Information, My.Resources.Source)

                m_ThreadAction.StopThread = True

                For Each fw As FileWorker In m_WorkerThreads
                    Me.RequestAdditionalTime(THIRTY_SECONDS)
                    fw.Incoming.Join(TIME_OUT)

                    Me.RequestAdditionalTime(THIRTY_SECONDS)
                    fw.Outgoing.Join(TIME_OUT)

                    Me.RequestAdditionalTime(THIRTY_SECONDS)
                    fw.CopyRecords.Join(TIME_OUT)
                Next
            Catch ex As Exception
                m_WorkerThread = Nothing
            End Try
        End If
    Catch ex As Exception
        'We Catch the Exception
        'to avoid any unhandled errors
        'since we are stopping and
        'logging an event is what failed
        'we will merely write the output
        'to the debug window
        m_WorkerThread = Nothing
        Debug.WriteLine("Error stopping service: " + ex.ToString())
    End Try
End Sub
```

The updated code shuts down the CopyRecords thread gracefully when a request to shut down the service is generated by the system or a user.

Creating the New *<LINQSQL.GetUsers>* Method

We need to be able to easily query our source records in a reusable manner. For this reason I have implemented the code shown in Listing 7-21.

Listing 7-21 *<GetUsers>* data-retrieval implementation.

```
Public Function GetUsers() As User()
    Try
        Dim AllUsers = (From ausers In m_UDC.Users Select ausers).ToArray

        Return AllUsers
```

```
  Catch ex As Exception
    Throw New Exception(ex.ToString)
  End Try
End Function
```

Understanding LINQ syntax will help clarify the point of this query. LINQ, which is designed for generic source data retrieval, supports a syntax similar to T-SQL. However, note that the order of the query and the keywords are reversed.

Another important thing to note is that by default you don't define the object type you are querying in your declaration. Nor do you define an array collection. Instead, you query the records into a variable instance and then use a For Each loop to iterate through the enumeration that is created for you automatically. However, in this case I want the iteration to occur in the calling method and not from the source method. To make this work, I tell the LINQ generator that I want to create an Array by wrapping the query, which occurs when the line is encountered, in a ToArray cast. This allows me to pass an array of User types back to the caller, where I am iterating through the collection as defined in the *<ProcessRecords>* method.

Install and Verify

Compile and install the service. Remember to place some records in your incoming folder if you don't have any records in your source database.

> **Note**   You will actually be inserting the same records over and over into your destination data store.

One way to resolve duplicating records is to place a unique primary key constraint on your destination table preventing insertion of duplicate records based on that key. The uniqueness should be based on a combination of columns you choose, such as First, Last, and Address.

The flaw in this solution is that even though we won't get any duplicates, our query will always pull back every record in our source table. The more records that we return, the more processing time it will take and the more resources over time are needed to pull back all the unprocessed and already processed records.

Reporting Processing Failures

As with the *ProcessFiles* method, a record might fail to be migrated into our destination table. Depending on the mechanism you use to track which records have or have not been successfully inserted into the destination table, you may not have to create any cleanup code.

For instance, if you have a flag on the source table to specify whether a record has been processed, and you fail to migrate the record, you most likely didn't mark it as complete. If you did, it is probably a bug in your service or database implementation because record duplication should not occur. Therefore the only thing to do is log an error, because the next time you query unprocessed records, any that had failed previously will be attempted again.

The flaw here is that if a record really is broken, you will just keep querying that same record. Therefore you may want to mark records as complete with a specific status and then have an offline process monitor for any records that have been completed but completed with a failure.

Optimizing the *LINQSQL* Class

The *LINQSQL* class provides a wrapper around the Users table implementation in both the source and destination databases. Using the *<InsertRecord>* methods, we can migrate records into our destination database or create records in our source table.

However, look at our current implementations: We're creating a new instance of the *User* class and then mapping the values from the source to the destination through the instance itself.

Recall that when we created Users.dbml you implemented the SaveUser stored procedure. The reason for that will now be clear. I want to use the stored procedure call on our LINQ To SQL implementation instead of creating a new instance of the user record, mapping the values, and then calling Commitchanges.

What's nice is that although the code shown in Listing 7-22 uses the stored procedure call instead of the user mappings, the procedure implementation is exactly the same—there is no change to the calling methods.

Listing 7-22   New *<InsertRecord>* implementations.

```
Public Function InsertRecord(ByVal pszRecord As String) As Boolean
    Try
        Dim pszQuery As String = Nothing
        Dim pszVars() As String = Split(pszRecord, ",")

        m_UDC.SaveUser(pszVars(0), pszVars(1), _
                       pszVars(2), pszVars(3), _
                       pszVars(4), pszVars(5), _
                       pszVars(6), pszVars(7), _
                       Guid.NewGuid())
        m_UDC.SubmitChanges()

        Return True
    Catch sqlex As SqlClient.SqlException
        If sqlex.Number = 2627 Then
            Return True
        End If
    Catch ex As Exception
        Throw New Exception(ex.ToString)
    End Try
End Function

Public Function InsertRecord( _
                    ByVal First As String, _
                    ByVal Last As String, _
                    ByVal Address1 As String, _
                    ByVal Address2 As String, _
```

```
                         ByVal City As String, _
                         ByVal State As String, _
                         ByVal Zip As String, _
                         ByVal phone As String, _
                         ByVal UserID As Guid _
                         ) As Boolean
        Try
            m_UDC.SaveUser(First, Last, Address1, _
                         Address2, City, State, Zip, phone, UserID)

            m_UDC.SubmitChanges()

            Return True
        Catch sqlex As SqlClient.SqlException
            If sqlex.Number = 2627 Then
                Return True
            End If
        Catch ex As Exception
            Throw New Exception(ex.ToString)
        End Try
    End Function
```

To the calling methods there is no difference. However, within the method there is one important difference: I no longer specify the UserID because it will be created automatically when the stored procedure inserts a record into the database. This is different than creating an instance of the user class, which expects you to populate the data.

This gives less to debug, and more control over what happens to the data inserted by the stored procedure, without having to do any modifications to the method that inserts the data.

Install and Verify

Although it may seem simple in this case to migrate from one data store to another, you might find dozens of practical uses when the source is not a database. It could very well be an XML file, a flat file, a totally different data store, or any combination of these.

The ability to easily monitor for and successfully and automatically migrate this data is key to the use of a service.

Install and run the new service. Create files with some sample records, which— after you insert them into the primary database and table—will be replicated into the secondary data store.

Summary

- Data stores, with the proper drivers installed on the server and client, can be accessed using Visual Basic 2008, which has built-in support for many data storage technologies, such as ODBC, OLEDB, SQL Server, and many more.

- Support classes, such as *System.Data, System.Data.OLEDB, System.Data.ODBC*, and *System.Data.SQL*, allow for connectivity to a nearly limitless set of database storage services, such as Microsoft SQL Server, Oracle, IBM DB2, and any other OLEDB or ODBC–compliant server systems.

■ Microsoft Visual Basic 2008 has built-in objects that you can use to access an array of data stores with a wide variety of data manipulation, memory storage, and collaboration capabilities through the use of Microsoft ADO and ADO.NET objects and classes.

■ Services can be securely written to access both local and remote data stores for migrating and processing data.

■ Data stores such as SQL Server 2005 are extensive, user-friendly, and scaleable enterprise solutions for storing data and writing reporting and archival services.

Part III
Services That Support IT and the Business

Chapter 8
Monitoring and Reporting with WMI

Windows Management Instrumentation (WMI) is a powerful set of methods, properties, classes, and data that you can use to gather information about local computers, applications, processes, memory, and remote computers. You can use WMI to perform powerful data gathering and maintenance procedures on any system with WMI enabled, along with the proper security rights.

Using WMI with Services

In this chapter, we will use WMI to gather information about the local system and then use that information to create an entry in the Application log. Your service can also use the data collected to perform actions, such as terminating processes and rebooting the system, or even on remote systems to start processes or log events.

You can use WMI and Microsoft Visual Basic 2008 to create self-monitoring services that report information to administrators, or log events that are being monitored for by other enterprise applications. You can create these services, or *agents*, that run on the local computer, perform tasks, report results, and act as a very powerful tool. In some cases you can handle these situations with an out-of-the-box solution. However, sometimes these solutions are costly and require maintenance, licensing, and external training. Self-produced solutions can help you create a rich set of operational tools.

Suppose you want to monitor a system's available memory and report an error if that memory drops below a certain point. You could easily do this with other existing applications, but the steps taken in reaction by those applications may not fit with your needs. Some solutions have both client and server pieces: You can use the server piece to monitor for SNMP trap messages or NT Events logged by your service and then have it react to those messages. In some of these instances, purchasing client or agent licenses may cost extra. If you could produce this agent yourself, knowing that it is a required component of your monitoring, you could save your company time and money. Because the code is yours, you could more easily distribute it or share and reuse it elsewhere. Documentation and support is also more readily available with internal resource knowledge of the application.

The great thing about WMI is that it comes with Windows XP, the Microsoft Windows 2000 server series, the Microsoft Windows 2003 server series, and other Microsoft operating systems. In some cases, you must install specific service packs to obtain this, but it is a default for Windows XP, Windows 2000, and Windows Server 2003. For this chapter we will revert to the code in Chapter 4, "Services and Polling" and build from there.

> **Note** Although we will be starting with the code from Chapter 4, you will need the also SMTP.vb class file from Chapter 5, "Processing and Notification."

WMI Architecture

The WMI implementation architecture is fairly simple in terms of how it is exposed. WMI creates computer- and application-level classes that provide access to built-in system and application-defined objects.

To access WMI you have to know the fully qualified domain name (FDQN) of the object you are attempting to access in WMI terms. Everything starts at the root node or namespace for a given object. You first connect to that root node and then use that interface to connect, add, retrieve, update, and execute methods and properties that are exposed by classes that exist in the given node or namespace.

Whether you are using the Management namespace from .NET or the COM interfaces exposed by Windows and WMI, the usage and syntax are very similar. The technology used to connect to WMI doesn't necessarily create any WMI syntax differences, but it does create code-specific differences because the objects you are using to talk to WMI are implemented differently.

Adding the WMI Class Reference

When you use the WMI object model in non-.NET languages, it is used through COM interfaces and classes. When you use WMI with .NET, you can use the System.Management namespace. If the Management namespace is not part of your project you will need to add its reference in your project. Select Project, select Add Reference, and then select the System.Management .NET DLL. Now we can create the WMI class.

Once you have added the System.Management reference to the project you will need to add an Imports System.Management declaration to the top of the Tutorials.vb class.

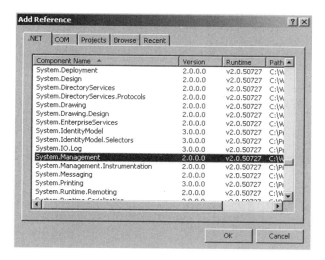

Creating the Generic WMI Class

We are going to use a generic WMI class to query information about the current processes running on our system and then record that information into the Application log. In later sections we will monitor for certain applications and then take actions based on those applications. Listing 8-1 shows the code required for our WMI generic class.

Listing 8-1   Generic class with Microsoft WMI support.

```
Imports System.Management
Imports System.Threading
Public Class WMI
  Private m_Error As String = Nothing
  Private m_Scope As ManagementScope = Nothing
  Private m_Path As ManagementPath = Nothing
  Private m_MOC As ManagementObjectCollection = Nothing

  Public Sub New()
  End Sub

  Private Const Processes As String = "Select * from Win32_Process"
  Private Const BootInfo As String = "select * from Win32_BootConfiguration"
  Private Const LogicalDisk As String = "select * from Win32_LogicalDisk"
  Private Const SystemInfo As String = "select * from Win32_ComputerSystem"

  Public Enum Management_Query_Type
    Processes = 1
    LogicalDisks = 2
    BootInfo = 3
    SystemINfo = 4
  End Enum

  Public Function Connect(ByVal pszServer As String) As Boolean
      Try
```

```
            If Not m_Path Is Nothing Then
                Try
                    m_Path = Nothing
                Catch ex As Exception
                    m_Error = ex.ToString
                End Try
            End If
            If Not m_Scope Is Nothing Then
                Try
                    m_Scope = Nothing
                Catch ex As Exception
                    m_Error = ex.ToString
                End Try
            End If
            m_Path = New ManagementPath("\\" + pszServer + "\root\cimv2")
            m_Scope = New ManagementScope(m_Path)
            m_Scope.Connect()
            Return True
        Catch ex As Exception
            m_Error = ex.ToString
            Return False
        End Try
    End Function

    Public Function Query( _
        ByVal pszQuery As String, _
        Optional ByVal iType As Management_Query_Type = _
         Management_Query_Type.Processes) _
        As ManagementObjectCollection
        Try
          Dim tmpQuery As New ObjectQuery
            If Not pszQuery Is Nothing Then
                tmpQuery.QueryString = pszQuery
            Else
                Select Case iType
                    Case Management_Query_Type.BootInfo
                        tmpQuery.QueryString = BootINfo
                    Case Management_Query_Type.LogicalDisks
                        tmpQuery.QueryString = LogicalDisk
                    Case Management_Query_Type.Processes
                        tmpQuery.QueryString = Processes
                    Case Management_Query_Type.SystemINfo
                        tmpQuery.QueryString = SystemInfo
                    Case Else
                        m_Error = "Invalid Query Type"
                        Return Nothing
                End Select
            End If
            Dim MOS As ManagementObjectSearcher = New
    ManagementObjectSearcher(m_Scope, tmpQuery)
            m_MOC = MOS.Get()
            tmpQuery = Nothing
            Return m_MOC
        Catch ex As Exception
            m_Error = ex.ToString
```

```
            Return Nothing
        End Try
    End Function

    Public Function GetError() As String
        Try
            Return m_Error
        Catch ex As Exception
            Return ex.ToString
        End Try
    End Function
End Class
```

The code in Listing 8-1 will connect to the local or remote server and then run the predefined query of your choice, returning the result set to the caller. The class exposes a simple *<Connect>* method that will connect to the local or remote WMI RPC services at the root specified and return an error if it fails. Then the class provides a simple method called *<Query>*, which can retrieve information about a query, either passed into the method or from the predefined WMI queries.

You can use WMI for monitoring and reporting in many ways. We are going to use WMI to look at specific system information. In our WMI class we don't have specific methods to process the data that we retrieve. This is because although we could create a generic wrapper around all the WMI object and property data collections, we are only focusing on a small subset of specific information. First let's review how WMI works so that you can better understand what you can do with it.

Understanding WMI Classes and Their Uses

WMI is a set of classes that represent system information in the form of objects, such as a logical disk, a CD-ROM, or even your physical memory. This data that WMI retrieves comes from another interface that WMI inherits from. However, although WMI lists nearly all of the properties of an object from its base or parent class, in some cases the data or property is not supported. This means that you can query for that data, but when you try to access the property data you get what WMI calls a DbNull. This is similar to what you would get in a SQL database query when a field is set to NULL.

Specific WMI and Custom Classes

The WMI classes are not just those that come with the base operating system. Developers can create a WMI interface for an application and expose those methods and properties. This means that our generic WMI class can pull data from any WMI-compatible object. We will use the following WMI classes in this chapter: *Win32_Process*, *Win32_BootConfiguration*, *Win32_LogicalDisk*, and *Win32_ComputerSystem*. These represent only a small portion of the available classes in WMI.

> **Note** For more information about WMI classes, methods, and object implementations, see *http://www.microsoft.com/whdc/system/pnppwr/wmi/default.mspx* .

Listing 8-2 shows the *Win32_ComputerSystem* class definition.

Listing 8-2 WMI *Win32_ComputerSystem* root node implementation.

```
class Win32_ComputerSystem : CIM_UnitaryComputerSystem
{
  uint16   AdminPasswordStatus;
  boolean  AutomaticResetBootOption;
  boolean  AutomaticResetCapability;
  uint16   BootOptionOnLimit;
  uint16   BootOptionOnWatchDog;
  boolean  BootROMSupported;
  string   BootupState;
  string   Caption;
  uint16   ChassisBootupState;
  string   CreationClassName;
  sint16   CurrentTimeZone;
  boolean  DaylightInEffect;
  string   Description;
  string   DNSHostName;
  string   Domain;
  uint16   DomainRole;
  boolean  EnableDaylightSavingsTime;
  uint16   FrontPanelResetStatus;
  boolean  InfraredSupported;
  string   InitialLoadInfo;
  datetime InstallDate;
  uint16   KeyboardPasswordStatus;
  string   LastLoadInfo;
  string   Manufacturer;
  string   Model;
  string   Name;
  string   NameFormat;
  boolean  NetworkServerModeEnabled;
  uint32   NumberOfProcessors;
  uint8    OEMLogoBitmap[];
  string   OEMStringArray[];
  boolean  PartOfDomain;
  sint64   PauseAfterReset;
  uint16   PowerManagementCapabilities[];
  boolean  PowerManagementSupported;
  uint16   PowerOnPasswordStatus;
  uint16   PowerState;
  uint16   PowerSupplyState;
  string   PrimaryOwnerContact;
  string   PrimaryOwnerName;
  uint16   ResetCapability;
  sint16   ResetCount;
  sint16   ResetLimit;
  string   Roles[];
  string   Status;
```

```
string   SupportContactDescription[];
uint16  SystemStartupDelay;
string   SystemStartupOptions[];
uint8   SystemStartupSetting;
string   SystemType;
uint16  ThermalState;
uint64  TotalPhysicalMemory;
string   UserName;
uint16  WakeUpType;
string   Workgroup;
};
```

The great thing about this class is that we can use it to query every computer on our network and gather information directly from the system, then use that information to compare it to information that administrators or the purchasing department has compiled. You could use this information, such as TotalPhysicalMemory, to verify that the equipment has what it is supposed to. It will also help to show what memory the operating system sees compared to how much memory is installed in the system

> **Note**   It is possible to modify the boot.ini to tell the Windows operating system to only use a certain amount of the total memory installed on the server motherboard.

We will use WMI to query Name, Domain, Status, NumberOfProcessors, and TotalPhysical-Memory and then report this information to the Application log.

Using the WMI Class

In this chapter we will use our WMI class to extend the code in Chapter 3, "Services and Security." We will use the code to collect information about the local system and log an event.

Adding New EventLog Constants

We will add the constants shown in Listing 8-3 to the top of the modService.vb file so that we can write the correct EventID to the Application log.

Listing 8-3   Application log EventID constants.
```
Public Const WMI_ERROR As Integer = 1010
Public Const WMI_INFO As Integer = 2007
Public Const CONFIG_READ_ERROR As Integer = 4000
```

Updating *<Tutorials.ThreadFunc>*

In this section we will add the WMI class to the Chapter 4 code and then write the code to use this class. Because we will build onto existing code, we do not need to create a new project. Listing 8-4 shows the updated *<ThreadFunc>* method.

Listing 8-4   Updated *<ThreadFunc>* method.

```
Private Sub ThreadFunc()
    While Not m_ThreadAction.StopThread
        If Not m_ThreadAction.Pause Then
            Try
                Dim tmpWMI As New WMI
                If Not tmpWMI.Connect(".") Then
                    WriteLogEvent("Thread WMI Connection Error - " +
            tmpWMI.GetError, WMI_ERROR, EventLogEntryType.Error, "Tutorials")
                Else
                    'Now process the file
                    Dim pMOC As ManagementObjectCollection
                    'Run our Query for SystemInfo
                    pMOC = tmpWMI.Query(Nothing, WMI.Management_Query_Type.SystemINfo)
                    If Not pMOC Is Nothing Then
                        Dim Name As String = Nothing
                        Dim Domain As String = Nothing
                        Dim Status As String = Nothing
                        Dim NumberOfProcessors As String = Nothing
                        Dim TotalPhysicalMemory As String = Nothing
                        Dim pMO As ManagementObject
                        For Each pMO In pMOC
                            Try
                                ReadProperty(pMO, "Name", Name)
                                ReadProperty(pMO, "Domain", Domain)
                                ReadProperty(pMO, "Status", Status)
                                ReadProperty(pMO, "NumberOfProcessors",
                                NumberOfProcessors)
                                ReadProperty(pMO, "TotalPhysicalMemory",
                                TotalPhysicalMemory)
                            Catch ex As Exception
                                Exit For
                            End Try
                            'Lets Log This Information
                            Dim pszOut As String
                            pszOut = "Name: " + Name.Trim
                            pszOut += ",Domain: " + Domain.Trim
                            pszOut += ",Status: " + Status.Trim
                            pszOut += ",NumberOfProcessors: " +
                            NumberOfProcessors.Trim
                            pszOut += ",TotalPhysicalMemory: " +
                            TotalPhysicalMemory.Trim + vbCrLf
                            WriteLogEvent(pszOut, WMI_INFO,
                            EventLogEntryType.Information, "Tutorials")
                        Next
                    Else
                        WriteLogEvent("Thread WMI query Error - " +
                        tmpWMI.GetError, WMI_ERROR, EventLogEntryType.Error,
                        "Tutorials")
                    End If
                End If
                WriteLogEvent("Thread Function Information - " +
                Now.ToString, 1005, EventLogEntryType.Information,
                "Tutorials")
            Catch tab As ThreadAbortException
```

```
    'this must be listed first as Exception is the master catch
    'Clean up the thread here
        WriteLogEvent("Thread Function Abort Error - " +
        Now.ToString, 1006, EventLogEntryType.Error, "Tutorials")
    Catch ex As Exception
        WriteLogEvent("Thread Function Error - " + Now.ToString,
        1005, EventLogEntryType.Error, "Tutorials")
    End Try
    End If
    If Not m_ThreadAction.StopThread Then
        Thread.Sleep(THREAD_WAIT)
    End If
    End While
End Sub
```

The example shown in Listing 8-4 allows us to read and then log information about the system that we have queried. One thing you'll notice about the WMI class is that we used the built-in query for *Win32_ComputerSystem*; however, because we knew exactly what information we were querying, we could have written the query ourselves to limit the amount of data that was returned. This is a very good idea when you are querying a large number of servers over a network interface. Not only will the amount of data traffic and memory requirements be reduced, but it will also speed up your application.

Adding the WMI Property Reader Method

When we use the WMI class implementation to run our predefined queries, we will be returned an object with a specific set of properties exposed. To manage the reading of these properties, I've implemented the code in Listing 8-5 to facilitate reading the property and returning the value to the calling method. This method will be added to our existing Tutorials.vb class implementation.

Listing 8-5   WMI property reading method implementation for Tutorials.vb.

```
Private Sub ReadProperty(ByRef pObject As ManagementObject,
        ByRef pProp As String, ByRef pszStr As String)
    Try
        pszStr = pObject.Properties(pProp).Value.ToString
    Catch ex As Exception
        pszStr = ""
    End Try
End Sub
```

This method attempts to read the value of the property defined in the parameter list called pProp, and setting the outgoing pointer, pszStr, to the string value of the property. If the property is not valid or an exception occurs, the return parameter is assigned a null value.

The previous code was fairly simple. We used a WMI class to connect to the server, and then we queried the WMI class that we wanted information about, assigning the result of that query to our local ManagementObjectCollection. When you call a WMI class using System.Management, nearly every object returns two types of collections: the objectname collection and the Enumerator collection. You can use either collection to access the objects that were returned. When you perform the query, you are returned a ManagementObject-Collection, which contains all the objects from your query, such as each Logicaldisk or Adapter. Each object within the collection has a Properties collection. The difference between the collection interface and the Enumerator collection interface is that the *Enumerator* class allows you to access objects within the collection as if it were a database result set, in that it holds a pointer to the previous and next objects available. When you use the standard collection, you would normally loop through with a For Each loop, but you have no direct bookmark into the collection, so accessing it initially and then accessing it later will not hold your place. Using the Enumerator rectifies this.

Extending the WMI Implementation

The current WMI implementation isn't a very scalable solution, so we'll implement the same strategies that we used for file monitoring.

Extending the WMI Class

We need to create a more robust and scalable WMI class that allows for multiple instances of monitored servers. In addition, we want to be able to predefine a query that we can use to retrieve specific information.

Because of the extensive nature of changes to the WMI class, I will reprint the code in Listing 8-6 and then review the changes.

Listing 8-6   Extended WMI class.

```
Public Class WMI
  Private m_Error As String = Nothing
  Private m_Scope As ManagementScope = Nothing
  Private m_Path As ManagementPath = Nothing
  Private m_Outgoing As Thread = Nothing
  Private m_ThreadAction As ThreadActionState
  Private m_WMIWorkerOptions As New WMIWorkerOptions

  Public Sub New(ByRef threadaction As ThreadActionState,
                      ByVal wwo As WMIWorkerOptions)
    m_ThreadAction = threadaction
    WMIWorkerOptions.Copy(m_WMIWorkerOptions, wwo)
    m_Path = New ManagementPath
    m_Scope = New ManagementScope
  End Sub

  Public Function Connect(ByVal pszServer As String,
              ByVal pszRoot As String) As Boolean
    Try
        If Not m_Scope Is Nothing Then
            Try
                If m_Scope.IsConnected Then
                    Return True
```

```vb
                        End If
                Catch ex As Exception
                    m_Error = ex.ToString
                End Try
            End If
            m_Path.Path = "\\" + pszServer + pszRoot
            m_Scope.Path = Me.Path
            m_Scope.Connect()
            Return True
        Catch ex As Exception
            m_Error = ex.ToString
            Return False
        End Try
    End Function

    Public Function Query( _
                        ByVal pszQuery As String) _
                        As ManagementObjectCollection
        Try
            If (String.IsNullOrEmpty(pszQuery)) Then
                Throw New ArgumentException("pszQuery")
            End If
            Dim tmpQuery As New ObjectQuery
            tmpQuery.QueryString = pszQuery
            Dim MOS As ManagementObjectSearcher = New
        ManagementObjectSearcher(Me.Scope, tmpQuery)
            Dim MOC As ManagementObjectCollection = MOS.Get()
            tmpQuery = Nothing
            MOS.Dispose()
            Return MOC
        Catch ex As Exception
            m_Error = ex.ToString
            Return Nothing
        End Try
    End Function

    Public Function GetError() As String
        Try
            Return m_Error
        Catch ex As Exception
            Return ex.ToString
        End Try
    End Function

    Private Sub ProcessWMIRequest()
        While Not m_ThreadAction.StopThread
            If Not m_ThreadAction.Pause Then
                Try
                    'Now process the file
                    Connect(m_WMIWorkerOptions.Server,
                    m_WMIWorkerOptions.WMIRoot)
                    Dim pMOC As ManagementObjectCollection
                    pMOC = Query(m_WMIWorkerOptions.Query)
                    If Not pMOC Is Nothing Then
                        Dim Name As String = Nothing
```

```vb
                              Dim Domain As String = Nothing
                              Dim Status As String = Nothing
                              Dim NumberOfProcessors As String = Nothing
                              Dim TotalPhysicalMemory As String = Nothing
                              Dim pMO As ManagementObject
                              For Each pMO In pMOC
                                  Try
                                      ReadProperty(pMO, "Name", Name)
                                      ReadProperty(pMO, "Domain", Domain)
                                      ReadProperty(pMO, "Status", Status)
                                      ReadProperty(pMO, "NumberOfProcessors",
                                          NumberOfProcessors)
                                          ReadProperty(pMO, "TotalPhysicalMemory",
                                          TotalPhysicalMemory)
                                  Catch ex As Exception
                                      Exit For
                                  End Try
                                  'Lets Log This Information
                                  Dim pszOut As String
                                  pszOut = "Name: " + Name.Trim
                                  pszOut += ",Domain: " + Domain.Trim
                                  pszOut += ",Status: " + Status.Trim
                                  pszOut += ",NumberOfProcessors: " +
                                  NumberOfProcessors.Trim
                                  pszOut += ",TotalPhysicalMemory: " +
                                      TotalPhysicalMemory.Trim + vbCrLf
                                  WriteLogEvent(pszOut, WMI_INFO,
                          EventLogEntryType.Information, "Tutorials")
                                      pMO.Dispose()
                                  Next
                              Else
                                  WriteLogEvent("Thread WMI query Error - " + GetError(),
                          WMI_ERROR, EventLogEntryType.Error, "Tutorials")
                              End If
                              pMOC.Dispose()
                          Catch tab As ThreadAbortException
                              'Clean up the thread here
                              WriteLogEvent("Thread Function Abort Error - " +
                      Now.ToString, WMI_ERROR, EventLogEntryType.Error, "Tutorials")
                          Catch ex As Exception
                              WriteLogEvent("Thread Function Error - " + Now.ToString,
                                  WMI_ERROR, EventLogEntryType.Error, "Tutorials")
                          End Try
                      End If
                      If Not m_ThreadAction.StopThread Then
                          Thread.Sleep(THREAD_WAIT)
                      End If
                  End While
              End Sub

          Private Sub ReadProperty(ByRef pObject As ManagementObject, ByRef pProp As
      String, ByRef pszStr As String)
              Try
                  pszStr = pObject.Properties(pProp).Value.ToString
              Catch ex As Exception
```

```
                pszStr = ""
        End Try
    End Sub


    Public ReadOnly Property Outgoing() As Thread
        Get
            Return m_Outgoing
        End Get
    End Property


    Public Sub Start()
        m_Outgoing = New Thread(AddressOf ProcessWMIRequest)
        m_Outgoing.Priority = ThreadPriority.Normal
        m_Outgoing.IsBackground = True
        m_Outgoing.Name = m_WMIWorkerOptions.Server + "-" +
                      m_WMIWorkerOptions.Query
        m_Outgoing.Start()
    End Sub


    Private Shared Sub WriteLogEvent(ByVal pszMessage As String, ByVal dwID As
        Long, ByVal iType As EventLogEntryType, ByVal pszSource As String)
        Try
            Dim eLog As EventLog = New EventLog("Application")
            eLog.Source = pszSource
            Dim eInstance As EventInstance = New EventInstance(dwID, 0, iType)
            Dim strArray() As String
            ReDim strArray(1)
            strArray(0) = pszMessage
            eLog.WriteEvent(eInstance, strArray)
            eLog.Dispose()
        Catch ex As Exception
            'Do not Catch here as it doesn't do any good for now
        End Try
    End Sub


    Public ReadOnly Property Scope() As ManagementScope
        Get
            Return m_Scope
        End Get
    End Property


    Public ReadOnly Property Path() As ManagementPath
        Get
            Return m_Path
        End Get
    End Property
End Class
```

New WMI Member Variables

As shown in Listing 8-7, we are going to add several new WMI member variables, which will hold the pointers to our internal WMI implementation, and our new thread-state management class instance.

Listing 8-7   WMI class member variables.

```
Private m_Error As String = Nothing
Private m_Scope As ManagementScope = Nothing
Private m_Path As ManagementPath = Nothing
Private m_Outgoing As Thread = Nothing
Private m_ThreadAction As ThreadActionState
Private m_WMIWorkerOptions As New WMIWorkerOptions
```

As you can see, we have only one thread per WMI instance because no e-mail or incoming file processing is required.

New and Updated WMI Class Member Methods

The new WMI class implementation has several properties that are used to relate to the WMI Management namespace in Microsoft Visual Studio. The following list includes these changes to the WMI class and a brief description of how they correlate to their WMI representations.

The *<New>* Constructor   Because we are now using thread state management, I have updated the *<New>* constructor so that, as with the *FileWorker* chapters, we can pass in a shared instance of the thread state management object, as well as the newly created *WMIWorkerOptions* class.

The *WMIWorkerOptions* Class   Note that the *WMIWorkerOptions* class is very close in design and detail to the *FileWorkerOptions* class. It is used for the same purpose—to store WMI specific configuration information on a per-class instance basis.

The WMI Properties   As with the *FileWorker* class, we need to store certain pieces of information outside the scope of our *WMIWorkerOptions* class, so we will implement it directly in our WMI class.

- **The WMI Path**   The WMI path represents the physical and logical connection to the local or remote computer where the WMI classes that you want to work with are implemented. ManagementPath is given a string to represent the FQDN of the root node and object you want to query. In our class, we defined this as the property Path.

- **The WMI Scope**   The WMI scope represents the connection to the root node as defined in the ManagementPath variable associated with the scope. This is where you will implement the underlying details of the connection to the computer and therefore to the WMI objects you want to interface with. In our class, we define this as the property Scope.

- **The *<ProcessWMIRequest>* Method**   The *<ProcessWMIRequest>* is like the *<ProcessFiles>* method in our *FileWorker* class. It defines the entry point for the thread created on a per-WMI instance basis. This is where we connect to the local or remote WMI services, query the data we are looking for, and then process the data.

Creating the *WMIWorkerOptions* Class

We need to be able to pass into our new WMI class the properties that we will define in our configuration file, which we will discuss in the next section. For this I have created the class shown in Listing 8-8.

Listing 8-8   *WMIWorkerOptions* class.

```
Public Class WMIWorkerOptions
  Private m_WMIRoot As String
  Private m_Query As String
  Private m_Server As String

  Public Property Server() As String
      Get
          Return m_Server
      End Get
      Set(ByVal value As String)
          m_Server = value
      End Set
  End Property

  Public Property Query() As String
      Get
          Return m_Query
      End Get
      Set(ByVal value As String)
          m_Query = value
      End Set
  End Property

  Public Property WMIRoot() As String
      Get
          Return m_WMIRoot
      End Get
      Set(ByVal value As String)
          m_WMIRoot = value
      End Set
  End Property

  Public Shared Sub Copy(ByVal wwo1 As WMIWorkerOptions,
                         ByVal wwo2 As WMIWorkerOptions)
      wwo1.Query = wwo2.Query
      wwo1.Server = wwo2.Server
      wwo1.WMIRoot = wwo2.WMIRoot
  End Sub
End Class
```

The Query Property

The Query property represents the WMI query that will be passed to this instance from our configuration file. The query may differ slightly based on the operating system.

The WMIRoot Property

The WMIRoot property represents the root node of the local or remote WMI class instance that you want to query. From here you can query or use other subordinate classes or methods.

The Server Property

The Server property represents the server that we want to connect to. It can also represent the local computer by either using the local computer name or by using a period, which also represents the local computer.

Creating the Configuration File

We will create a configuration file that we can use to identify the preceding properties to our WMI class instances. Listing 8-9 shows the XML file that we are using. Note that it contains the same format as the configuration file used in our *FileWorker* chapters.

Listing 8-9   WMI configuration XML file.

```
<?xml version="1.0" encoding="utf-8" ?>
<Configuration>
<WMIWorkerOptions>
  <WMIWorkerProperties>
    <Query>select * from Win32_ComputerSystem</Query>
    <WMIRoot>\root\cimv2</WMIRoot>
    <Server>mgern-D820</Server>
  </WMIWorkerProperties>
  <WMIWorkerProperties>
    <Query>select * from Win32_ComputerSystem</Query>
    <WMIRoot>\root\cimv2</WMIRoot>
    <Server>TestServer</Server>
    </WMIWorkerProperties>
  </WMIWorkerOptions>
</Configuration>
```

The configuration file shown previously in Listing 8-8 contains the matching properties from our *WMIWorkerOptions* class. You will notice that I have included the *WMIWorkerOptions* section twice. This is to test that we can get multiple threads to perform the work. Future implementations of the service can either point to different servers or use different queries to customize the service usage.

WMI Service Account

WMI communicates over RPC to the local and remote servers. You need to ensure that on the computer you want to communicate with, the service or the threads using WMI are running in the context of a user with the proper privileges.

After installing the service and implementing your own configuration file, you will see at least one Application log entry for each entry in the configuration file. The intent here is to show that you can use WMI to query both local and remote information.

WMI System Monitoring

Although WMI is great for gathering information, it can also be a very powerful monitoring and debugging tool. In this section we will use WMI to monitor the processes on our system and then use WMI to shut down an application that we define as behaving poorly. Because we don't want to negatively affect our system at the moment, we will simulate this sitation by using NotePad.exe.

Updating the Configuration File

We need to be able to store the process or processes that we want to monitor for. Listing 8-10 shows the updated configuration file with the process element added.

Listing 8-10   Process monitoring elements.

```
<Process>Notepad.exe</Process>
```

We can implement the process element in several ways, depending on the complexity that we want to create. You can choose from the following options:

- Create a master *<Processes>* element with subelements called *<Process>*. You'll need to modify the *<ThreadFunc>* method of your *Tutorials* class so that it can parse all the processes that have been entered. Then you'll have to update the *WMIWorkerOptions* class to store an array of process names.

- Create a single element (as I've done in the previous example). I called my element process, and then placed the specific process name that I want to monitor.

- Create a single element but place a delimited list of processes to monitor.

Any of these options will work, though some require more work than others. For demonstration purposes, I have taken what I consider the simplest approach and created a single element with a single process name, Notepad.

WMI *Win32_Process* Usage

In this section we will use the *Win32_Process* class (shown in Listing 8-11) from WMI to monitor for any application named Notepad.exe. When we find an instance of Notepad, we will use WMI to shut it down.

Listing 8-11   *Win32_Process* WMI class implemented in the .NET Framework in C#.

```
class Win32_Process : CIM_Process
{
  string  Caption;
  string  CommandLine;
  string  CreationClassName;
  datetime  CreationDate;
  string  CSCreationClassName;
  string  CSName;
  string  Description;
```

```
string   ExecutablePath;
uint16   ExecutionState;
string   Handle;
uint32   HandleCount;
datetime  InstallDate;
uint64   KernelModeTime;
uint32   MaximumWorkingSetSize;
uint32   MinimumWorkingSetSize;
string   Name;
string   OSCreationClassName;
string   OSName;
uint64   OtherOperationCount;
uint64   OtherTransferCount;
uint32   PageFaults;
uint32   PageFileUsage;
uint32   ParentProcessId;
uint32   PeakPageFileUsage;
uint64   PeakVirtualSize;
uint32   PeakWorkingSetSize;
uint32   Priority;
uint64   PrivatePageCount;
uint32   ProcessId;
uint32   QuotaNonPagedPoolUsage;
uint32   QuotaPagedPoolUsage;
uint32   QuotaPeakNonPagedPoolUsage;
uint32   QuotaPeakPagedPoolUsage;
uint64   ReadOperationCount;
uint64   ReadTransferCount;
uint32   SessionId;
string   Status;
datetime  TerminationDate;
uint32   ThreadCount;
uint64   UserModeTime;
uint64   VirtualSize;
string   WindowsVersion;
uint64   WorkingSetSize;
uint64   WriteOperationCount;
uint64   WriteTransferCount;
}
```

We will not use all of the class properties available to us. System administrators can use many things to monitor servers based on process performance: threads, handles, memory, virtual memory, CPU usage, and more. A well-written service can monitor a nearly unlimited number of processes per computer while tracking usage over time so that you can determine whether an application is causing a problem.

Although we will gather several pieces of information, we will only use the Name property to determine whether we should shut down the application. This demonstration is not intended to teach you how to design a monitor, but instead to give you an idea of what you can do within a service. When we find an application that matches our <Processes> element, we will shut down the application. We need to make several changes to support this functionality.

Updating the *WMIWorkerOptions* Class

We need to update the *WMIWorkerOptions* to store the new process element value that we created. Listing 8-12 shows the code required to store this information.

Listing 8-12   *WMIWorkerOptions* class process update.

```
Private m_Process As String

Public Property Process() As String
  Get
    Return m_Process
  End Get
  Set(ByVal value As String)
    m_Process = value
  End Set
End Property
```

I added a Process property that we will use to determine the process that we want to monitor for.

Updating the *<Tutorials.ThreadFunc>* Method

We need to read in the new value from our configuration.xml file and use our *WMIWorkerOptions* class to store it. We will update the *<ThreadFunc>* method, as shown in Listing 8-13.

Listing 8-13   *<ThreadFunc>* method update to read the process element.

```
Do
  Try
    children = tmpOptions.SelectSingleNode("Query")
    WWOptions.Query = children.Value

    children = tmpOptions.SelectSingleNode("Server")
    WWOptions.Server = children.Value

    children = tmpOptions.SelectSingleNode("WMIRoot")
    WWOptions.WMIRoot = children.Value

    children = tmpOptions.SelectSingleNode("Process")
    WWOptions.Process = children.Value

    Dim tmpWW As New WMI(m_ThreadAction, WWOptions)
    m_WorkerThreads.Add(tmpWW)
    tmpWW.Start()
  Catch ex As Exception
    WriteLogEvent(ex.ToString(), CONFIG_READ_ERROR, EventLogEntryType.Error, _
      My.Resources.Source)
  End Try
Loop While (tmpOptions.MoveToNext)
```

The bolded code in Listing 8-13 will now use the new process property to store the name of the process—in our case, Notepad.exe—that we want to monitor for. Now that we have our process name we need to update our worker threads to query the processes and then shut down any Notepad.exe instances.

Updating the *<Query>* Configuration Value

Aside from adding in the appropriate process element, we also need to update our *<Query>* element to reflect the new dynamic WMI query. Listing 8-14 shows the update.

Listing 8-14   New WMI *<Query>* element value.
```
<Query>Select * from Win32_Process Where Name = 'Notepad.exe'</Query>
```

The new *<Query>* element value will allow us to simplify the resources required to perform the work that we want to do. Because we only care about the *Win32_Process* class—and more specifically, the Notepad.exe process—we will use the following query only to validate against our desired process. If you want to use this same query for another process, just change the process name from Notepad.exe to whatever you want to search for.

Updating the *<WMI.ProcessWMIRequest>* Method

We need to modify the *<ProcessWMIRequest>* method to reflect our required change to shut down any process called Notepad.exe. Listing 8-15 shows the modifications.

Listing 8-15   Updated *<ProcessWMIRequest>* method.
```
Private Sub ProcessWMIRequest()
  While Not m_ThreadAction.StopThread
    If Not m_ThreadAction.Pause Then
      Try
          'Now process the file
          Connect(m_WMIWorkerOptions.Server, m_WMIWorkerOptions.WMIRoot)
          Dim pMOC As ManagementObjectCollection
          pMOC = Query(m_WMIWorkerOptions.Query)
          If Not pMOC Is Nothing Then
              Dim Name As String = Nothing
              Dim ProcessId As String = Nothing
              Dim pMO As ManagementObject
              For Each pMO In pMOC
                  Try
                      ReadProperty(pMO, "Name", Name)
                      ReadProperty(pMO, "ProcessId", ProcessId)
                  Catch ex As Exception
                      Exit For
                  End Try
                  'Lets Log This Information
                  Dim pszOut As String
                  'terminate the process
                  If Name.Trim = "Notepad.exe" Then
                      pMO.InvokeMethod("Terminate", Nothing)
                  End If
                  pszOut = "Shut down of process Name: " + Name.Trim + vbCrLf
                      + "Process ID: " + ProcessId
                  WriteLogEvent(pszOut, WMI_INFO,
          EventLogEntryType.Information, "Tutorials")
                  pMO.Dispose()
              Next
          Else
```

```
            WriteLogEvent("Thread WMI query Error - " + GetError(),
        WMI_ERROR, EventLogEntryType.Error, "Tutorials")
          End If
          pMOC.Dispose()
      Catch tab As ThreadAbortException
          'Clean up the thread here
          WriteLogEvent("Thread Function Abort Error - " + Now.ToString,
        WMI_ERROR, EventLogEntryType.Error, "Tutorials")
      Catch ex As Exception
          WriteLogEvent("Thread Function Error - " + Now.ToString, WMI_ERROR,
        EventLogEntryType.Error, "Tutorials")
      End Try
    End If

    If Not m_ThreadAction.StopThread Then
        Thread.Sleep(THREAD_WAIT)
    End If
  End While
End Sub
```

The bolded code shows that we have modified the code to read the Name and ProcessId properties. In reality, because we only queried processes named Notepad.exe, we don't really need to read the Name property, but it is always better to be safe and validate a process before you terminate it.

After we validate that we are looking at an instance of our queried process, Notepad.exe, we invoke the *Terminate* method of the *WMI Win32_Process* class to shut down the process. The last thing we do is write an event into the Application log to show that we accomplished our goal.

Service Function Validation

To ensure that the service is working properly, configure and install the service to monitor for required processes. For each process, add a new entry in the configuration file. Even if the process is on the same computer, you must add one entry per process. For each process that your service finds, you should see the process disappear and then an event appear in the Application log.

You will notice that if a process requires user interaction, such as saving the current file in Notepad, you may be requested to do so before the process shuts down.

Service Notification

Although putting an entry in the Application log may suffice, you might be required at times to also send a notification when a problem is found and a process has been terminated. In this last section we will implement the code necessary to send an e-mail alert when a process is terminated.

Updating the Configuration.xml File

Listing 8-16 represents the changes required to our configuration file so that the code will send an administrative alert.

Listing 8-16   E-mail configuration elements.
```
<SmtpServer>smtpserver</SmtpServer>
<Subject>Test Subject</Subject>
<Message>Found Message</Message>
<Sender>Michael.E.Gernaey@test.com</Sender>
<Recipient>Michael.E.Gernaey@test.com</Recipient>
<SmtpPort>25</SmtpPort>
<MailEnabled>true</MailEnabled>
```

The changes shown in Listing 8-16 are identical to our previous *FileWorker* chapters. The information you place here will be used to send the alert. Now we need to tie together these changes with the service.

Updating the WMI Class

We have to update the WMI class to enable e-mail notifications. We will add the code shown in Listing 8-17 to our WMI class to reflect these changes. You can add them to any section of your WMI class.

Listing 8-17   WMI e-mail notification changes.
```
Private m_SmtpClient As New SMTP
Private m_MailEnabled As Boolean
Public Property MailEnabled() As Boolean
  Get
      Return m_MailEnabled
  End Get
  Set(ByVal value As Boolean)
      m_MailEnabled = value
  End Set
End Property

Public ReadOnly Property SmtpClient() As SMTP
  Get
      Return m_SmtpClient
  End Get
End Property
```

As with the *FileWorker* class, these properties will be used to implement e-mail notifications in the WMI class.

Updating the *WMIWorkerOptions* Class

Now that we have the WMI changes made, we need to update the *WMIWorkerOptions* class to store the properties required to send the e-mail notification. Listing 8-18 shows the required changes. You will also notice that we need to update the *<Copy>* method to reflect these additional properties.

Listing 8-18   *WMIWorkerOptions* e-mail notification property changes.

```
Private m_MailDetail As New EmailDetail

Public Property EmailProperties() As EmailDetail
    Get
        Return m_MailDetail
    End Get
    Set(ByVal value As EmailDetail)
        m_MailDetail = EmailDetail.Copy(value)
    End Set
End Property

Public Shared Sub Copy(ByVal wwo1 As WMIWorkerOptions, _
                ByVal wwo2 As WMIWorkerOptions)
    wwo1.Query = wwo2.Query
    wwo1.Server = wwo2.Server
    wwo1.WMIRoot = wwo2.WMIRoot
    wwo1.EmailProperties.Message = wwo2.EmailProperties.Message
    wwo1.EmailProperties.Recipient = wwo2.EmailProperties.Recipient
    wwo1.EmailProperties.Sender = wwo2.EmailProperties.Sender
    wwo1.EmailProperties.SmtpPort = wwo2.EmailProperties.SmtpPort
    wwo1.EmailProperties.SmtpServer = wwo2.EmailProperties.SmtpServer
    wwo1.EmailProperties.Subject = wwo2.EmailProperties.Subject
End Sub
```

The changes shown in Listing 8-18 reflect not only the implementation of the e-mail properties, but also the initialization of the e-mail properties in our *<Copy>* method.

Updating the *<Tutorials.ThreadFunc>* Method

Now that we have our new configuration elements and a place to store the properties in the *WMIWorkerOptions* class, we need to implement the changes required to read and assign these values. This will happen in our *<ThreadFunc>* method, as shown in Listing 8-19.

Listing 8-19   *<ThreadFunc>* e-mail notification changes.

```
If (Not tmpOptions Is Nothing) Then
  Dim WWOptions As New WMIWorkerOptions
  Dim children As System.Xml.XPath.XPathNavigator
  Do
      Try
          children = tmpOptions.SelectSingleNode("Query")
          WWOptions.Query = children.Value

          children = tmpOptions.SelectSingleNode("Server")
          WWOptions.Server = children.Value

          children = tmpOptions.SelectSingleNode("WMIRoot")
          WWOptions.WMIRoot = children.Value

          children = tmpOptions.SelectSingleNode("Process")
          WWOptions.Process = children.Value

      Dim tmpDetail As New EmailDetail
```

```
        children = tmpOptions.SelectSingleNode("Message")
        tmpDetail.Message = children.Value

        children = tmpOptions.SelectSingleNode("Subject")
        tmpDetail.Subject = children.Value

        children = tmpOptions.SelectSingleNode("Sender")
        tmpDetail.Sender = children.Value

        children = tmpOptions.SelectSingleNode("Recipient")
        tmpDetail.Recipient = children.Value

        children = tmpOptions.SelectSingleNode("SmtpPort")
        tmpDetail.SmtpPort = children.Value

        children = tmpOptions.SelectSingleNode("SmtpServer")
        tmpDetail.SmtpServer = children.Value

        WWOptions.EmailProperties = tmpDetail
    Dim tmpWW As New WMI(m_ThreadAction, WWOptions)
        children = tmpOptions.SelectSingleNode("MailEnabled")
        tmpWW.MailEnabled = Convert.ToBoolean(children.Value)
        m_WorkerThreads.Add(tmpWW)
        tmpWW.Start()
    Catch ex As Exception
        WriteLogEvent(ex.ToString(), CONFIG_READ_ERROR,
            EventLogEntryType.Error, My.Resources.Source)
    End Try
  Loop While (tmpOptions.MoveToNext)
  End If
End If
```

The code in Listing 8-19 reads the values of our e-mail properties from the configuration file and then populates the EmailDetail property of our *WMIWorkerOptions* class instance for each monitored process. Then it enables or disables e-mail notifications based on the Mail-Enabled element in our configuration file.

Updating the *<WMI.ProcessWMIRequest>* Method

Now we need to update the worker thread to send the e-mail notification when we terminate a process. Listing 8-20 shows these updates.

Listing 8-20   *<ProcessWMIRequest>* e-mail notification code.

```
'terminate the process
If Name.Trim = "Notepad.exe" Then
    pMO.InvokeMethod("Terminate", Nothing)
    If (Me.MailEnabled) Then
'        Send the Email and then move it again to the processed Folder
        m_WMIWorkerOptions.EmailProperties.Message = pszOut
        m_SmtpClient.QueueMail(m_WMIWorkerOptions.EmailProperties)
    End If
End If
```

The code in Listing 8-20 will validate that we have terminated a process and then place an e-mail notification in our SMTP mail queue. When the mail queue has been processed, the administrator or mail recipient will receive the notification.

Service Validation

When the code is installed and started, make sure that you create instances of the process that you want to not only terminate, but also receive notifications for. After the process has been terminated, you should see an Application log entry and also receive an e-mail notification about the termination.

Summary

- WMI is a powerful set of interfaces and classes that allow for applications and services.

- Microsoft Visual Basic 2008 implements support for these classes and interfaces through COM or through the System.Management namespace.

- Take care to consider security when using WMI objects because they can produce unexpected results. Not all properties or methods noted on MSDN are supported by all WMI Objects. Some properties or methods listed in MSDN for WMI Objects do not return any data.

Chapter 9
Talking to the Internet

One of the most powerful features built into .NET is the ability to use different Internet protocols. In many cases you can write your own classes to communicate with TCP/UDP-based streams, as we did for our SMTP class. We could have used other Microsoft technologies, such as Collaboration Data Objects (CDO) or the Messaging API (MAPI), but writing our own SMTP wrapper was easier than adding the overhead into our service. Microsoft Visual Basic 2008 using version 3.5 of the .NET Framework has introduced new ways to talk to Web services or Internet protocols such as HTTP, SMTP, and FTP. In this chapter we'll use the updated *System.NET* class to use ASP.NET Web Services and to upload and download FTP files.

Note   Chapter 9 will be extending the code from Chapter 7, "Data Logging: Processing and Storing Data in SQL Server 2005", so you'll want to close down your Chapter 8, "Monitoring and Reporting with WMI" code and reload your Chapter 7 code.

Reading and Parsing ASP Pages

In this section we'll receive ASP pages from a Web server and then validate the content of the message and the response from the Web server. We will use the WebClient classes in the .NET 3.5 Framework to download ASP content, parse that content, and then call a LINQ To SQL class to update a status table with the status of the servers. This information will then be displayed on a dynamically updated ASPX page. This gives us the ability to monitor a specific page or set of pages, look for a predefined response in the HTML page, and then log the status. We will combine what we've learned from previous chapters as we extend each section to include WebClient, SQL, and once again LINQ to dynamically view changes to our Web server(s) and ASP content.

Creating the ASP Master Page

I use Microsoft Internet Information System (IIS) for this book—and for this chapter specifically. You can use any Web server that you like; however, I'll use both ASP and APSX pages, which are directly compatible with Microsoft IIS. You can create a standard HTML page to monitor if you like and still have the same outcome. I have created an ASP page called status.asp, shown in Listing 9-1.

Listing 9-1   A simple ASP monitoring page.

```
<% Response.Write("OK") %>
```

This page contains a single line of code. This page merely returns the content *OK* to the caller. ASP monitoring pages can be as simple or complex as necessary, but in this case we only want to validate the content within the page and the status of the page from the Web server's perspective. For these tasks, this page will suffice.

Calling the ASP Master Page

We need to find a class that we can use to monitor our Web pages and update the status table for each class instance and URL pass we make. Listing 9-2 shows the class definition we'll use.

Listing 9-2   The HTTP class definition.

```
Imports System.Net
Imports System.IO
Imports System.Threading

Public Class HTTP
    Public m_Error As String = Nothing
    Private m_Url As String
    Public m_Incoming As Thread
    Private m_ThreadAction As ThreadActionState

    Public Sub New(ByRef threadaction As ThreadActionState)
        m_ThreadAction = threadaction
    End Sub

    Public Sub Start()
        m_Incoming = New Thread(AddressOf MonitorUrl)
        m_Incoming.Priority = ThreadPriority.Normal
        m_Incoming.IsBackground = True
        m_Incoming.Start()
    End Sub

    Private Sub MonitorUrl()
        Dim Linq As New LINQSQL(My.Settings.TutorialsConnectionString)

        While Not m_ThreadAction.StopThread
            If Not m_ThreadAction.Pause Then
                Try
                    'Check the Web Status URL here
                    Dim bCheck = CheckStatus(Me.URL)
```

```vbnet
                          'Log the Status Here
                          If (bCheck) Then
                              Linq.InsertRecord(Me.URL, "Success", _
                                  System.DateTime.Now)
                          Else
                              Linq.InsertRecord(Me.URL, "Failed", _
                                  System.DateTime.Now)
                          End If
                      Catch tab As ThreadAbortException
                          WriteLogEvent(My.Resources.ThreadAbortMessage + "_" + _
                          tab.ToString + "_" + Now.ToString, THREAD_ABORT_ERROR, _
                          EventLogEntryType.Error, My.Resources.Source)
                      Catch ex As Exception
                          WriteLogEvent(My.Resources.ThreadErrorMessage + "_" + _
                          ex.ToString + "_" + Now.ToString, THREAD_ERROR, _
                            EventLogEntryType.Error, My.Resources.Source)
                      End Try
              End If

              If Not m_ThreadAction.StopThread Then
                  Thread.Sleep(THREAD_WAIT)
              End If
          End While

      End Sub

      Private Function CheckStatus(ByVal URL As String) As Boolean
          Try
              Dim tmpRequest As WebRequest = WebRequest.Create(URL)
              Dim tmpResponse As HttpWebResponse = _
                          CType(tmpRequest.GetResponse(), HttpWebResponse)

              Dim pszServerStatus As String = tmpResponse.StatusDescription
              Dim tmpStream As Stream = tmpResponse.GetResponseStream()
              Dim tmpReader As New StreamReader(tmpStream)
              Dim pszContent As String = tmpReader.ReadToEnd

              Try
                  tmpReader.Close()
                  tmpStream.Close()
                  tmpResponse.Close()
              Catch ex As Exception
                  tmpReader = Nothing
                  tmpStream = Nothing
                  tmpResponse = Nothing
              End Try

              'Now parse the Status
              'In our example we are only returning back OK in our response
              If ((pszContent.Trim.ToUpper = "OK") And _
                  (pszServerStatus.Trim.ToUpper = "OK")) Then
                  Return True
              Else
                  m_Error = "Server Status: #" + pszServerStatus + "# - Content:#"
+ pszContent + "#"
```

```vb
                Return False
            End If
        Catch wex As WebException
            WriteLogEvent("Error Retrieving Status for URL: " + URL + vbCrLf + _
                wex.ToString + vbCrLf + System.DateTime.Now.ToString, WEB_ERROR, _
                EventLogEntryType.Error, My.Resources.Source)
            m_Error = wex.ToString
            Return False
        Catch ex As Exception
            WriteLogEvent("Error Retrieving Status for URL: " + URL + vbCrLf + _
                ex.ToString + vbCrLf + System.DateTime.Now.ToString, WEB_ERROR, _
                EventLogEntryType.Error, My.Resources.Source)
            m_Error = ex.ToString
            Return False
        End Try
    End Function


    Public Function GetError() As String
        Try
            Return m_Error
        Catch ex As Exception
            Return ex.ToString
        End Try
    End Function


    Private Shared Sub WriteLogEvent(ByVal pszMessage As String, _
            ByVal dwID As Long, ByVal iType As EventLogEntryType, _
            ByVal pszSource As String)
        Try
            Dim eLog As EventLog = New EventLog("Application")
            eLog.Source = pszSource

            Dim eInstance As EventInstance = New EventInstance(dwID, 0, iType)
            Dim strArray() As String

            ReDim strArray(1)
            strArray(0) = pszMessage
            eLog.WriteEvent(eInstance, strArray)

            eLog.Dispose()
        Catch ex As Exception
            'Do not Catch here as it doesn't do any good for now
        End Try
    End Sub


    Public Property URL() As String
        Get
            Return m_Url
        End Get
        Set(ByVal value As String)
            m_Url = value
        End Set
    End Property


    Public ReadOnly Property Incoming() As Thread
```

```
      Get
          Return m_Incoming
      End Get
   End Property
End Class
```

The HTTP class is fairly straightforward. Its constructor takes in a pointer to the *threadaction* variable used by the service to control the state of any class instance threads.

The URL property is used by the class instance for the monitoring thread to do its job of validating the server and the content of the master ASP page.

The service also has two primary methods, <*MonitorUrl*> and <*CheckStatus*>. We need to examine these methods more closely to understand what the class is doing.

The <*MonitorUrl*> Method

The <*Start*> method of our HTTP class instance uses <*MonitorUrl*> to begin the monitoring of our request URL. This method has two important jobs: To call our secondary function <*CheckStatus*> and then, depending on the Boolean result of that call, to update our status table in Microsoft SQL Server. This method will run continuously until the service is told to shut down or to pause, in which case this method will react to either of these requests.

This method uses Microsoft LINQ to talk to Microsoft SQL Server. I have created a specific LINQ To SQL set of source files that I'll discuss shortly.

The <*CheckStatus*> Method

This method does the work of downloading the Web server page and then parsing the content, validating both the server response and the content itself. Let's review the code, which is shown in Listing 9-3.

Listing 9-3   The <*CheckStatus*> method code.

```
    Private Function CheckStatus(ByVal URL As String) As Boolean
        Try
            Dim tmpRequest As WebRequest = WebRequest.Create(URL)
            Dim tmpResponse As HttpWebResponse = _
                        CType(tmpRequest.GetResponse(), HttpWebResponse)

            Dim pszServerStatus As String = tmpResponse.StatusDescription
            Dim tmpStream As Stream = tmpResponse.GetResponseStream()
            Dim tmpReader As New StreamReader(tmpStream)
            Dim pszContent As String = tmpReader.ReadToEnd

            Try
                tmpReader.Close()
                tmpStream.Close()
                tmpResponse.Close()
            Catch ex As Exception
                tmpReader = Nothing
                tmpStream = Nothing
```

```
                    tmpResponse = Nothing
            End Try


            'Now parse the Status
            'In our example we are only returning back OK in our response
            If ((pszContent.Trim.ToUpper = "OK") And
                (pszServerStatus.Trim.ToUpper = "OK")) Then
                Return True
            Else
                m_Error = "Server Status: #" + pszServerStatus + "# - Content:
                    #" + pszContent + "#"
                Return False
            End If
        Catch wex As WebException
            WriteLogEvent("Error Retrieving Status for URL: " + URL + vbCrLf +
                wex.ToString + vbCrLf + System.DateTime.Now.ToString, WEB_ERROR,
                EventLogEntryType.Error, My.Resources.Source)
            m_Error = wex.ToString
            Return False
        Catch ex As Exception
            WriteLogEvent("Error Retrieving Status for URL: " + URL + vbCrLf +
                ex.ToString + vbCrLf + System.DateTime.Now.ToString, WEB_ERROR,
                EventLogEntryType.Error, My.Resources.Source)
            m_Error = ex.ToString
            Return False
        End Try
    End Function
```

To download the content, we use the *WebRequest* class and the *HttpWebResponse* class.

The *WebRequest* class connects to the server and retrieves the page. In this case we use the URL that was passed into our URL property.

HttpWebResponse stores the response from the *WebRequest* call. This means that the content of the page is stored in this class instance.

Finally, we need to validate both the content and the server status response to complete the process. To do this, we first look at the server status response, which is stored in the *HttpWebResponse.StatusDescription* property. This will tell us whether we received the HTTP 200 status code that we were looking for, which indicates that everything is okay. If the status is not okay, we will return *false* to the caller, which in this case is *<MonitorUrl>*. Then we need to create a *Stream* class instance that we will use to retrieve and store the body content of the *HttpWebResponse.GetResponseStream* method. Then we will take that stream object and create a *StreamReader*. We use the *Stream* object's *ReadToEnd* method to populate our new *StreamReader* object.

After we have fully retrieved the content of the *HttpWebResponse* object, we can validate its content. In our case, we know that content is a string, so we can cast it back into a string and then validate that the content is equal to the word *OK*. If the return server status and the content are what we were looking for, we will return true to the caller; otherwise, we will return false.

Application Log InstanceIds

We once again use the *WriteLogEvent* method to capture any information we want to report to the Application log. We have added two new InstanceId constants, as shown in Listing 9-4.

Listing 9-4   Two new InstanceId constants for the *Http* class.

```
Public Const WEB_ERROR As Integer = 5000
Public Const WEB_INFO As Integer = 5001
```

In the modService.vb file, we want to add these two InstanceId constants to use with the *HTTP* class. As with other classes and code, we could hard-code these values for each call to the *WriteLogEvent*, but this way keeps the code cleaner.

Storing ASP Page URL Monitoring Status

We need to be able to store the results of our monitoring in a SQL table that another ASP page can use to show the status of all servers being monitored. To do this we need to create a few items in Microsoft SQL Server as well as build our LINQ To SQL code in the service.

Creating the URLS Status Table

We'll continue using the currently existing Tutorials database that we created in previous chapters. Using the Enterprise Manager for SQL Server 2000 (or the SQL Server 2005 Management Studio, depending on what version you have), let's connect to the Tutorials database and then execute the SQL script shown in Listing 9-5.

Listing 9-5   Urls table SQL script.

```
/****** Object:  Table [dbo].[Urls]    Script Date: 08/12/2007 07:10:18 ******/
SET ANSI_NULLS ON
GO
SET QUOTED_IDENTIFIER ON
GO
CREATE TABLE [dbo].[Urls](
[URL] [nvarchar](1024) NOT NULL,
[Status] [nvarchar](10) NOT NULL,
[Success] [int] NOT NULL,
[Failures] [int] NOT NULL,
[LastChecked] [datetime] NOT NULL
) ON [PRIMARY]
```

The script in Listing 9-5 generates the table necessary for this chapter's demonstration. It will store the URL, the current status, the number of successful attempts, the number of failed attempts, and the date and time of the last attempt to validate this URL.

Creating the UpdateURLStatus Stored Procedure

Although we could simply insert records directly into this table, I wanted to have some logic around the stored procedure that would take into account any already existing URLs. If the URL being passed in with a new status already exists, it updates the success, failure, and lastchecked columns.

Once again, run the SQL script shown in Listing 9-6 against the Tutorials database to create the stored procedure.

Listing 9-6 The UpdateURLStatus SQL script.

```
SET ANSI_NULLS ON
GO
SET QUOTED_IDENTIFIER ON
GO
CREATE PROCEDURE [dbo].[UPDATEURLSTATUS]
@Url NVARCHAR(1024),
@Status NVARCHAR(10),
@LASTCHECKED DATETIME

AS
BEGIN
  SET NOCOUNT ON;
    IF EXISTS (SELECT URL FROM Urls WHERE URL = @URL)
    BEGIN
      IF (@Status = 'SUCCESS')
      BEGIN
        UPDATE URLS SET SUCCESS = SUCCESS + 1, LASTCHECKED = @LASTCHECKED,
          [STATUS] = @Status WHERE URL = @Url
      END
    ELSE
      BEGIN
        UPDATE URLS SET FAILURES = FAILURES + 1, LASTCHECKED = @LASTCHECKED,
          [STATUS] = @Status WHERE URL = @Url
      END
    END
    ELSE
      BEGIN
        IF (@Status = 'SUCCESS')
        BEGIN
          INSERT INTO DBO.URLS (URL, [STATUS], SUCCESS, FAILURES, LASTCHECKED)
            values (@Url, @Status, 1, 0, @LASTCHECKED)
        END
        ELSE
        BEGIN
          INSERT INTO DBO.URLS (URL, [STATUS], SUCCESS, FAILURES, LASTCHECKED)
            values (@Url, @Status, 0, 1, @LASTCHECKED)
        END
      END
    END
```

The stored procedure takes the URL that is passed in and then checks whether it exists already. If the URL already exists in the database Urls table, the procedure checks whether it was a successful or failed attempt and then updates the success, failure, and lastchecked columns. If the record does not exist, the procedure inserts a new record, first determining whether it was a successful attempt.

Creating LINQ To SQL Dependencies

We have to create the LINQ To SQL classes and code required to connect to the Tutorials database. Once again, you need to add a New Item to the current service class. Select the LINQ To SQL file type and name it **URLS.DBML**. After you create the file, drag both the new Urls table and the new UpdateURLStatus stored procedures onto the canvas.

Adding a Table and Stored Procedure to the Canvas

Return to Server Explorer in Visual Studio 2008 and click Data Connections. When you expand Data Connections, you should see the database server that you connected to in previous chapters. If not, right-click Data Connections and create a connection to the SQL Server where your Urls table and *UpdateURLStatus* stored procedure exists.

Open the data connection to the server where you created these items. Expand the Tables view and drag the Urls table onto the canvas to the left. Then expand the Stored Procedures view and drag the UpdateURLStatus stored procedure into the method pane on the right side of the canvas.

Creating the Wrapper LINQ Class

We want to be able to access the functionality of the URLS.dbml file easily, so we'll create the LINQSQL.vb class file shown in Listing 9-7 and add it to our project.

Listing 9-7   The LINQSQL.vb class definition file.

```vb
Public Class LINQSQL
    Private m_UDC As UrlsDataContext

    Public Sub New(ByVal ConnectionString As String)
        m_UDC = New UrlsDataContext(ConnectionString)
    End Sub

    Public Function InsertRecord( _
                        ByVal Url As String, _
                        ByVal Status As String, _
                        ByVal LastChecked As DateTime _
                        ) As Boolean
        Try
            m_UDC.UPDATEURLSTATUS(Url, Status, LastChecked)
            m_UDC.SubmitChanges()
        Catch ex As Exception
            Throw New Exception(ex.ToString)
        End Try
    End Function

    Public Function GetUrls() As Url()
        Try
            Dim AllUrls = (From aUrls In m_UDC.Urls Select aUrls).ToArray

            Return AllUrls
```

```
        Catch ex As Exception
            Throw New Exception(ex.ToString)
        End Try
    End Function

    Public Sub Dispose()
        Try
            m_UDC.Dispose()
        Catch ex As Exception
            m_UDC = Nothing
        End Try
    End Sub

End Class
```

The *<MonitorUrl>* method in our *Http* class uses the *LINQSQL* class to update the status of any URL being monitored by our service.

The Constructor   The constructor takes in a string that represents the connectionstring that this data connector should use. The connectionstring is stored as an application setting in the service. If you look at the *<MonitorUrl>* method, you will see that I use the My.Settings. TutorialsConnectionString property, which I defined previously in Chapter 7.

The *<InsertRecord>* Method   We use the *<InsertRecord>* method to insert the record into the database. As in previous chapters, we could create an instance of the *URL LINQTOSQL* class, which would represent a record, but then we would bypass the logic written in the stored procedure. One way to ensure that no one bypasses the stored procedure is to remove insert, delete, and update privileges directly on the table in the SQL Server Management Studio. I take in the values passed into the call and use the *UpdateURLStatus* method to pass that information to SQL Server to update an already existing row or to create a new one.

The *<GetUrls>* Method   We won't use the *<GetUrls>* method in our service. This method is designed to retrieve all the rows from the URLs table and pass them back to the caller. We will use this in the ASPX status page but not in the service that does the monitoring.

Updating the Configuration File

Now that we have the code to monitor the URLs that we want monitored, we need to pass in those URLs to the service. Unlike updates in previous chapters, this update to the configuration file will be fairly large because we remove the current nodes and replace them with a very simple structure, as shown in Listing 9-8.

Listing 9-8   The Http configuration file.

```xml
<?xml version="1.0" encoding="utf-8" ?>
<Configuration>
  <HttpUrls>
    <HttpUrl>
      <URL>http://localhost/tutorials/status.asp</URL>
    </HttpUrl>
  </HttpUrls>
</Configuration>
```

The configuration file now contains a new parent node called HttpUrls and a child record called Url. There will only be one parent node, but you can have any number of child records. For each entry or Url child record specified, a new instance of our Http class is created and a new record is stored in the Tutorials.URLS table. Currently a single instance of the *Http* class has no way to validate more than one Url, so we don't need to store multiple Urls per class instance. When and if you decide to do so, you can create a structure such as HttpUrls as the parent, URLs as the child, and URL as a complex type under URLs, where each URLs node represents a set of URL records for each *Http* class instance to monitor.

As in previous chapters, if you want a single class to monitor multiple things, you either have to serialize those actions so that each URL check waits for its turn in line based on the number of URLs passed to the class instance, or you need to code some threading logic to monitor more than one URL per class instance at a time.

Updating the *<Tutorials.TThreadFunc>* Method

Now that we have an updated configuration file, we need to update the method that reads the configuration file again. Listing 9-9 shows the updated method.

Listing 9-9   The updated *<TThreadFunc>* method.

```
Private Sub TThreadFunc()
  Try
    'Load our Configuration File
    Dim Doc As XmlDocument = New XmlDocument()
    Doc.Load(My.Settings.ConfigFile)

    Dim Options As XmlNode
    'Get a pointer to the Outer Node
    Options = Doc.SelectSingleNode("//*[local-name()='HttpUrls']")

    If (Not Options Is Nothing) Then
        Dim tmpOptions As System.Xml.XPath.XPathNavigator =
            Options.FirstChild.CreateNavigator()

      If (Not tmpOptions Is Nothing) Then
          Dim children As System.Xml.XPath.XPathNavigator
          Do
              Try
                  children = tmpOptions.SelectSingleNode("URL")
                  Dim tmpHTTP As New HTTP(m_ThreadAction)
                  tmpHTTP.URL = children.Value
                  m_WorkerThreads.Add(tmpHTTP)
                  tmpHTTP.Start()
              Catch ex As Exception
                  WriteLogEvent(ex.ToString(), CONFIG_READ_ERROR,
                      EventLogEntryType.Error, My.Resources.Source)
              End Try
          Loop While (tmpOptions.MoveToNext)
      End If
    End If
```

```
    Catch ex As Exception
        WriteLogEvent(ex.ToString(), ONSTART_ERROR, EventLogEntryType.Error,
            My.Resources.Source)
        Me.Stop()
    End Try
End Sub
```

We needed our code to reflect the changes in the configuration file. We will open the configuration file and our parent node of HttpUrls. Then we will iterate through all the child records or URL entries. Last, we will create an instance of our Http class, passing in our *threadaction* variable and then setting the URL property on the newly created *Http* class instance to the URL read from the configuration file.

After we create the instance and set the URL property, we call the *<Start>* method, which in turn causes the *Http* class instance to start the *<MonitorUrl>* method.

Updating the Tutorials *<OnStop>* Method

We need to update *<OnStop>* to clean up the service threads for each class instance created, as displayed in Listing 9-10.

Listing 9-10   The updated *<OnStop>* service method.

```
Protected Overrides Sub OnStop()
    ' Add code here to perform any tear-down necessary to stop your service.
    Try
        If (Not m_WorkerThread Is Nothing) Then
            Try
                WriteLogEvent(My.Resources.ServiceStopping, ONSTOP_INFO, _
                    EventLogEntryType.Information, My.Resources.Source)

                m_ThreadAction.StopThread = True

                For Each http As HTTP In m_WorkerThreads
                    Me.RequestAdditionalTime(THIRTY_SECONDS)
                    http.Incoming.Join(TIME_OUT)
                Next
            Catch ex As Exception
                m_WorkerThread = Nothing
            End Try
        End If
    Catch ex As Exception
        'We Catch the Exception
        'to avoid any unhandled errors
        'since we are stopping and
        'logging an event is what failed
        'we will merely write the output
        'to the debug window
        m_WorkerThread = Nothing
        Debug.WriteLine("Error stopping service: " + ex.ToString())
    End Try
End Sub
```

Service Validation

To validate the service, make sure to complete the following tasks:

- Create a Web page to monitor.
- Modify the code to validate the specific page content that you want to validate (if it isn't the OK response I created in my status.asp page).
- Be sure that you have Microsoft IIS or another Web server service running.
- Configure the Tutorials database.
- Update your configuration file with the new schema and at least one URL to monitor.

After you complete these tasks and the service is installed, you'll see in the URLS table that one record is created for each URL that you want to monitor. You'll also notice that your failure and success values should increase by 1 for each monitoring cycle. In this chapter, I set my monitoring poll, or thread wait, to 15-second intervals, although in your code you can configure the thread wait timing.

Adding a Dynamic Status ASPX Page

Now that the service is running and monitoring URLs, we want to make it easy for people to view the status of each URL being monitored. We'll add another project to our current service solution that will do this.

Creating a New ASP .NET Web Application

Right-click the solution, select Add New Web Site, and then select ASP.NET Web Site from the Project Template Wizard. Select File for the Web site type and then browse to where you want to save the new application.

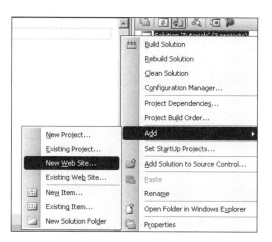

Creating the SQL Datasource

We need to be able to retrieve the information easily from SQL Server, so we'll use a *SQLDataSource* object on the ASPX page. When we created our new project, a default page was created for us called Default.Aspx. Double-click the Default.Aspx page and then select the Design view.

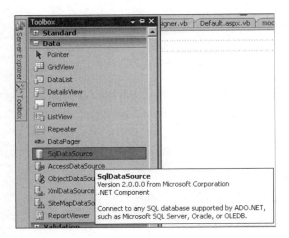

From the ToolBox, select the Data category of tools and then drag a *SqlDataSource* object onto the design canvas. Click Configure DataSource on the control. By default, the new datasource can use the available Data Connection that you created earlier in the drop-down box. If you can't see the existing Data Connection, create a new one and name it **TutorialsConnectionString**.

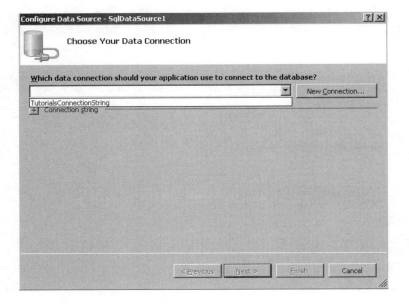

After you select (or create) the new Data Connection, you will be prompted to either write a custom query yourself or select a table. Select the Urls table, and then select the columns you want to include in the query. In this solution, we'll use Select *, which means all columns. Select OrderBy, select the LastChecked column from the first drop-down list, and leave the rest blank.

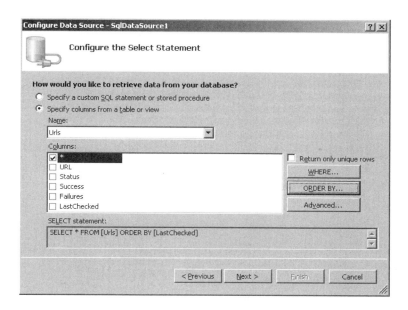

Adding a GridView Control

After configuring *SqlDataSource*, we want to be able to view the data on the page.

Select the ToolBox, select the Data category of tools, and then drag a GridView control onto the design canvas. Select the GridView and then select the arrow on the top right corner of the GridView control. In the DataSource drop-down list, you should see the SqlDataSource1 control listed. You should see this name because we did not rename the control when we dragged it onto the design canvas.

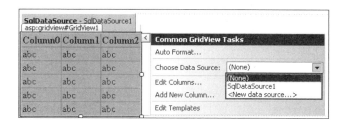

We don't need to set any of the other options in GridView for now because we don't yet have many records. If you have run the service once and records are available, we can use them to ensure that the site is working.

Validating the Web Site

Save and then build the Web site. After it is compiled, we want to make sure that it is the default startup project for our solution. Right-click the Web site project and select Set As StartUp Project. Right-click the Default.Aspx page and select Set As Start Page.

Press F5 and run the Web site. When prompted, select the Run With Debugging Enabled option. You should see the grid control on the screen filled with data based on your data-source query selection criteria, sorted by the LastChecked column.

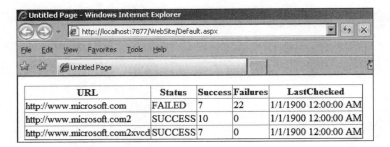

Add new URL entries into the configuration file of the service and then restart your service. While the service runs, refresh your Web site page. The grid should reflect any updates made to the table, including updates and new inserted records.

Monitoring Web services is standard practice for many companies. In many cases, these companies run many Web sites on a single server or a set of clustered servers. IT departments will develop a single HTML, ASP, or ASPX page that will do server or service validation and return those results to the caller.

You can code your service to monitor these status pages and then raise alerts or log event log informational or error events for issues that it finds.

FTP and Your Service

One way that businesses pass information around is through the FTP protocol. This can be internal, external, secured, unsecured, and many other variations. Using a service to pick up files that have been sent via FTP between customers or groups within a company can be a useful way to move data between data stores. You can do a number of things using FTP or a service that supports the FTP protocol, including picking up files from one location and moving them to a secure internal location using an internally authenticated procedure, or processing a data dump from one data store to another data store. With version 3.5 of the .NET Framework we no longer need a large amount of TCP–specific coding. With built-in classes to support FTP, HTTP, and SMTP we can quickly, easily, and efficiently develop services that provide much greater functionality than that of simple batch jobs or scheduled tasks.

Using FTP in the Service

In this section we will set up a Microsoft FTP site with an upload and a download folder with the appropriate read/write privileges. Using these directories, we can read and write files that we'll use to pass data between data stores such as SQL Server 2005. I'm using the Microsoft FTP Publishing Service on Windows Server 2003; however, this process will work on Windows XP, Windows 2000, and most other FTP Servers.

Creating FTP Directories

I have created an upload and download directory beneath the FTP Home Directory, which in my case is c:\inetpub\ftproot. I have assigned write privileges to the upload directory and read privileges to the download directory, and set the anonymous logons to true. Microsoft FTP Publishing Service does not support authentication over secured sockets, so we will use anonymous logons.

Adding an FTP Class

Our FTP class is very simple. It allows for uploading and downloading files, but it lacks more in-depth features, such as listing directories locally or remotely. For our purposes, though, it will be sufficient. In this section, we'll simulate downloading and processing files from one FTP folder that can exist anywhere in the world. This could mean moving the file from its current location to another intranet or extranet location where a predefined process such as a SQL Task, Web Service, or other mechanism is in place to process the file further. This procedure works well for moving data from one data store to another, where a process specific to that data store has been created to export data to a flat file. In many cases the systems that create these files have no access to other intranet or extranet sites and thus have no ability themselves to directly or indirectly move or process this data on behalf of the remote data store. Imagine that you have a small Web store application that uses SQL Server as its back-end data store. Your shipping and receiving, purchase order information, and customer database is stored in your back-end mainframe or other secondary centralized SQL Server. If the two databases can't communicate—whether because of security issues or network limitations—you can use an intermediate process, such as a service that sits on both subnets and has the proper authority to move the data between network segments or data stores.

We'll use the FTP class to read data files from our download directory and store it in our locally defined folder. In this section, we will do no other processing because the service will only simulate moving data between network subnets, allowing a predefined process running on the upload directory's subnet, or with access to that subnet, to capture that file and process it. Let's review the FTP class, shown in Listing 9-11.

Listing 9-11 FTP class implementation.

```
Imports System.Net
Imports System.IO
Imports System.Text
Imports System.Threading

Public Class FTP
    Public m_Error As String = Nothing
    Private m_Uri As String
    Private m_User As String
    Private m_Pwd As String
    Private m_Port As Integer
    Private m_LocalFolder As String
    Private m_File As String
    Private m_Files() As String
    Public m_Incoming As Thread
    Private m_ThreadAction As Thread_Action_State

    Public Sub New(ByRef threadaction As Thread_Action_State)
        m_ThreadAction = threadaction
    End Sub

    Public Sub Start()
        m_Incoming = New Thread(AddressOf DownloadFiles)
        m_Incoming.Priority = ThreadPriority.Normal
        m_Incoming.IsBackground = True
        m_Incoming.Start()
    End Sub

    Public Function GetError() As String
        Try
            Return m_Error
        Catch ex As Exception
            Return ex.ToString
        End Try
    End Function

    Private Sub DownloadFiles()
        While Not m_ThreadAction.StopThread
            If Not m_ThreadAction.Pause Then
                Try
                    Dim bDownload As Boolean
                    bDownload = GetFile(Me.URI, Me.File, Me.User, Me.Pwd, _
                        Me.Port, Me.LocalFolder)

                    If Not (bDownload) Then
                        Throw New Exception("Failed to Download File: " + _
                            Me.File)
                    End If
                Catch tab As ThreadAbortException
                    WriteLogEvent(My.Resources.ThreadAbortMessage + "_" + _
                        tab.ToString + "_" + Now.ToString, THREAD_ABORT_ERROR, _
                        EventLogEntryType.Error, My.Resources.Source)
                Catch ex As Exception
                    WriteLogEvent(My.Resources.ThreadErrorMessage + "_" +
```

```vb
                    ex.ToString + "_" + Now.ToString, THREAD_ERROR, _
                    EventLogEntryType.Error, My.Resources.Source)
                End Try
            End If

            If Not m_ThreadAction.StopThread Then
                Thread.Sleep(THREAD_WAIT)
            End If
        End While

    End Sub

    Private Shared Sub WriteLogEvent(ByVal pszMessage As String, _
                ByVal dwID As Long, ByVal iType As EventLogEntryType, _
                ByVal pszSource As String)
        Try
            Dim eLog As EventLog = New EventLog("Application")
            eLog.Source = pszSource

            Dim eInstance As EventInstance = New EventInstance(dwID, 0, iType)
            Dim strArray() As String

            ReDim strArray(1)
            strArray(0) = pszMessage
            eLog.WriteEvent(eInstance, strArray)

            eLog.Dispose()
        Catch ex As Exception
            'Do not Catch here as it doesn't do any good for now
        End Try
    End Sub

    Public Property URI() As String
        Get
            Return m_Uri
        End Get
        Set(ByVal value As String)
            m_Uri = value
        End Set
    End Property

    Public Property LocalFolder() As String
        Get
            Return m_LocalFolder
        End Get
        Set(ByVal value As String)
            m_LocalFolder = value
        End Set
    End Property

    Public Property User() As String
        Get
            Return m_User
        End Get
        Set(ByVal value As String)
```

```vb
                m_User = value
        End Set
End Property

Public Property Pwd() As String
    Get
        Return m_Pwd
    End Get
    Set(ByVal value As String)
        m_Pwd = value
    End Set
End Property

Public Property Port() As Integer
    Get
        Return m_Port
    End Get
    Set(ByVal value As Integer)
        m_Port = value
    End Set
End Property

Public Property File() As String
    Get
        Return m_File
    End Get
    Set(ByVal value As String)
        m_File = value
    End Set
End Property

Public Property Files() As String()
    Get
        Return m_Files
    End Get
    Set(ByVal value As String())
        Array.Copy(value, m_Files, value.Length)
    End Set
End Property

Public Function GetFile( _
                    ByVal pszUri As String, _
                    ByVal pszFile As String, _
                    ByVal pszUser As String, _
                    ByVal pszPWD As String, _
                    ByVal dwPort As Integer, _
                    ByVal pszLocalDir As String) _
                    As Boolean
    Try
        ' Set up the request
        Dim ftpURI As New Uri(pszUri + "/" + pszFile)

        Dim ftpRequest As FtpWebRequest = _
                        CType(FtpWebRequest.Create(ftpURI), _
                            FtpWebRequest)
```

```vbnet
        'Setup the Credentials
        If pszUser.ToUpper <> "ANONYMOUS" Then
            ftpRequest.Credentials = New NetworkCredential(pszUser, pszPWD)
        End If

        'Download a file.
        ftpRequest.Method = WebRequestMethods.Ftp.DownloadFile

        ' get the response object
        Dim ftpResponse As FtpWebResponse = _
                    CType(ftpRequest.GetResponse, FtpWebResponse)

        Dim tmpStream As Stream = Nothing
        Dim tmpReader As StreamReader = Nothing
        Dim tmpWriter As StreamWriter = Nothing

        'Read the Stream from the Response and Save the File Locally
        Try
            tmpStream = ftpResponse.GetResponseStream
            tmpReader = New StreamReader(tmpStream, Encoding.UTF8)
            tmpWriter = New StreamWriter(pszLocalDir + "\" + pszFile, _
                                         False)
            tmpWriter.Write(tmpReader.ReadToEnd)
        Finally
            tmpStream.Close()
            tmpReader.Close()
            tmpWriter.Close()
        End Try

        Return True
    Catch ex As Exception
        m_Error = ex.ToString
        Return False
    End Try

End Function

Public Function GetFiles( _
                ByVal pszUri As String, _
                ByVal pszFiles() As String, _
                ByVal pszUser As String, _
                ByVal pszPWD As String, _
                ByVal dwPort As Integer, _
                ByVal pszLocalDir As String) _
                As Boolean()
    Try
        'Setup our Return Object
        Dim bRet(pszFiles.Length - 1) As Boolean

        Dim iLoop As Short

        For iLoop = 0 To pszFiles.Length - 1
            Try
                bRet(iLoop) = GetFile( _
                                pszUri, _
```

```vb
                                        pszFiles(iLoop), _
                                        pszUser, _
                                        pszPWD, _
                                        dwPort, _
                                        pszLocalDir _
                                )
                Catch ex As Exception
                    bRet(iLoop) = False
                End Try
            Next

            Return bRet
        Catch ex As Exception
            m_Error = ex.ToString
            Return Nothing
        End Try

    End Function

    Public Function SendFile( _
                        ByVal pszServer As String, _
                        ByVal pszRemoteDir As String, _
                        ByVal pszFile As String, _
                        ByVal pszUser As String, _
                        ByVal pszPWD As String, _
                        ByVal dwPort As Integer, _
                        ByVal pszLocalDir As String) _
                        As Boolean
        Try
            ' Set up the request
            Dim ftpURI As New Uri("FTP://" + pszServer + "/" + pszRemoteDir +
                                "/" + pszFile)

            Dim ftpRequest As FtpWebRequest = _
                            CType(FtpWebRequest.Create(ftpURI),
                                    FtpWebRequest)

            'Setup the Credentials
            ftpRequest.Credentials = New NetworkCredential(pszUser, pszPWD)

            'Upload a file.
            'setup options
            ftpRequest.Method = WebRequestMethods.Ftp.UploadFile
            ftpRequest.UseBinary = False
            '           ftpRequest.UsePassive = True

            'Now we have to read the local file into a stream
            Dim pFile As New FileInfo(pszLocalDir + pszFile)
            Dim bData(pFile.Length) As Byte
            Dim fStream As FileStream = pFile.OpenRead

            fStream.Read(bData, 0, pFile.Length)
            fStream.Close()

            ftpRequest.ContentLength = bData.Length
```

```
            Dim tmpStream As Stream = Nothing

            'Read the Stream from the Response and Save the File Locally
            Try
                tmpStream = ftpRequest.GetRequestStream
                tmpStream.Write(bData, 0, bData.Length)
            Finally
                tmpStream.Close()
            End Try

            'Whats the Response
            Dim ftpResponse As FtpWebResponse = _
                                    CType(ftpRequest.GetResponse, _
                                        FtpWebResponse)
        Return True
    Catch ex As Exception
        m_Error = ex.ToString
        Return False
    End Try
End Function


Public Function SendFiles( _
                    ByVal pszServer As String, _
                    ByVal pszRemoteDir As String, _
                    ByVal pszFiles() As String, _
                    ByVal pszUser As String, _
                    ByVal pszPWD As String, _
                    ByVal dwPort As Integer, _
                    ByVal pszLocalDir As String) _
                    As Boolean()
    Try
        Dim iLoop As Short
        Dim bRet(pszFiles.Length - 1) As Boolean

        For iLoop = 0 To pszFiles.Length - 1
            Try

                bRet(iLoop) = SendFile( _
                                    pszServer, _
                                    pszRemoteDir, _
                                    pszFiles(iLoop), _
                                    pszUser, _
                                    pszPWD, _
                                    dwPort, _
                                    pszLocalDir _
                                    )
            Catch ex As Exception
                bRet(iLoop) = False
            End Try
        Next

        Return bRet
    Catch ex As Exception
        m_Error = ex.ToString
        Return Nothing
```

```
            End Try
        End Function

        Public Sub Dispose()
            Try
                    Return
            Catch ex As Exception
                m_Error = ex.ToString
                Return
            End Try
        End Sub

        Public ReadOnly Property Incoming() As Thread
          Get
             Return m_Incoming
          End Get
        End Property
End Class
```

The *<DownloadFiles>* Method

<DownloadFiles> is our thread method, started by the *<Start>* method. It will use the *<GetFile>* method to download the files that have been specified in our modService.vb file. If the file doesn't download successfully, we will throw a new exception of System.Exception type. Our Try/Catch will catch the exception and then write an event into the Application log. If the file downloads successfully, it will be saved locally in the local folder, which is specified in the LocalFolder property.

FTP Class Properties

The FTP class has several properties that are required to make our *FTP* class work. These properties are outlined in Listing 9-12.

Listing 9-12 FTP class properties.

```
Public Property URI() As String
    Get
        Return m_Uri
    End Get
    Set(ByVal value As String)
        m_Uri = value
    End Set
End Property

Public Property LocalFolder() As String
    Get
        Return m_LocalFolder
    End Get
    Set(ByVal value As String)
        m_LocalFolder = value
    End Set
End Property
```

```
Public Property User() As String
    Get
        Return m_User
    End Get
    Set(ByVal value As String)
        m_User = value
    End Set
End Property

Public Property Pwd() As String
    Get
        Return m_Pwd
    End Get
    Set(ByVal value As String)
        m_Pwd = value
    End Set
End Property

Public Property Port() As Integer
    Get
        Return m_Port
    End Get
    Set(ByVal value As Integer)
        m_Port = value
    End Set
End Property

Public Property File() As String
    Get
        Return m_File
    End Get
    Set(ByVal value As String)
        m_File = value
    End Set
End Property
```

- The Uri property represents the physical path and virtual location of the server and FTP directory where the file that we want to download resides.

- The User property represents the user that we want to log in as. Since we are using anonymous logins, I'll use *anonymous* as my user entry.

- The LocalFolder property represents where we will store the files after downloading them. This can represent a physical local or remote location.

- The Pwd property represents the password used to log on. Since I am using anonymous, any e-mail address will be valid here.

- The Port property represents the port being used by the FTP service. By default this will be 21 on an FTP server, so I'll use 21. The File property represents the name of the file that we want to look for. This is not a very flexible FTP example. We could extend it to use a wild card or use the Files property to allow you to pass in an array of file names to download.

Adding New FTP Constants

As in previous chapters, we need to define the constants we'll use for our service. We'll only use two, which are listed in Listing 9-13.

Listing 9-13   FTP constant declaration.
```
Public Const FTP_ERROR As Integer = 6000
Public Const FTP_INFO As Integer = 6001
```

Modifying the Configuration File

We need to modify the configuration file to represent the changes in our service. We need to be able to store and then retrieve the information about the properties we have defined in our *FTP* class. Listing 9-14 shows the new configuration file.

Listing 9-14   FTP configuration file schema.
```xml
<?xml version="1.0" encoding="utf-8" ?>
<Configuration>
  <FTPUris>
    <FTPUri>
      <URI>FTP://mgern1/download</URI>
      <LocalFolder>c:\temp\ftpsave</LocalFolder>
      <User>anonymous</User>
      <Pwd>anonymous@anon.com</Pwd>
      <Port>21</Port>
      <File>mydata.dat</File>
    </FTPUri>
  </FTPUris>
</Configuration>
```

The configuration file matches all the required property fields that we added to our *FTP* class.

Modifying the <*Tutorials.ThreadFunc*> Method

We once again have to modify the <*ThreadFunc*> method to retrieve and then assign the property values from the configuration file to the correct property of the *FTP* class instance that we created. Listing 9-15 shows the new <*ThreadFunc*> method.

Listing 9-15   The modified <*ThreadFunc*> method.
```
Private Sub ThreadFunc()
    Try
        'Load our Configuration File
        Dim Doc As XmlDocument = New XmlDocument()
        Doc.Load(My.Settings.ConfigFile)

        Dim Options As XmlNode
        'Get a pointer to the Outer Node
        Options = Doc.SelectSingleNode("//*[local-name()=FTPUris]")

        If (Not Options Is Nothing) Then
            Dim tmpOptions As System.Xml.XPath.XPathNavigator =
                        Options.FirstChild.CreateNavigator()
```

```
        If (Not tmpOptions Is Nothing) Then
            Dim children As System.Xml.XPath.XPathNavigator
            Do
                Try
                    Dim tmpFTP As New FTP(m_ThreadAction)

                    children = tmpOptions.SelectSingleNode("URI")
                    tmpFTP.URI = children.Value

                    children = tmpOptions.SelectSingleNode("LocalFolder")
                    tmpFTP.LocalFolder = children.Value

                    children = tmpOptions.SelectSingleNode("File")
                    tmpFTP.File = children.Value

                    children = tmpOptions.SelectSingleNode("Port")
                    tmpFTP.Port = children.Value

                    children = tmpOptions.SelectSingleNode("User")
                    tmpFTP.User = children.Value

                    children = tmpOptions.SelectSingleNode("Pwd")
                    tmpFTP.Pwd = children.Value

                    m_WorkerThreads.Add(tmpFTP)
                    tmpFTP.Start()
                Catch ex As Exception
                    WriteLogEvent(ex.ToString(), CONFIG_READ_ERROR,
                        EventLogEntryType.Error, My.Resources.Source)
                End Try
            Loop While (tmpOptions.MoveToNext)
        End If
    End If
    Catch ex As Exception
        WriteLogEvent(ex.ToString(), ONSTART_ERROR, EventLogEntryType.Error,
                    My.Resources.Source)
        Me.Stop()
    End Try
End Sub
```

This new code will open the configuration file and then navigate to the starting parent node of *FTPWorkerOptions*. When we have a pointer to that node, the code will read through each sibling and populate the appropriate FTP class property with the value read from the configuration file. After all the values have been set, the FTP class *<Start>* method is called, and monitoring for files and downloading of files commences.

Updating the Tutorials *<OnStop>* Method

We need to update the *<OnStop>* method to clean up the service threads for each class instance created. The updated method is displayed in Listing 9-16.

Listing 9-16   The updated *<OnStop>* service method.

```
Protected Overrides Sub OnStop()
    ' Add code here to perform any tear-down necessary to stop your service.
    Try
        If (Not m_WorkerThread Is Nothing) Then
            Try
                WriteLogEvent(My.Resources.ServiceStopping, ONSTOP_INFO, _
                    EventLogEntryType.Information, My.Resources.Source)

                m_ThreadAction.StopThread = True

                For Each ftp As FTP In m_WorkerThreads
                    Me.RequestAdditionalTime(THIRTY_SECONDS)
                    ftp.Incoming.Join(TIME_OUT)
                Next
            Catch ex As Exception
                m_WorkerThread = Nothing
            End Try
        End If
    Catch ex As Exception
        'We Catch the Exception
        'to avoid any unhandled errors
        'since we are stopping and
        'logging an event is what failed
        'we will merely write the output
        'to the debug window
        m_WorkerThread = Nothing
        Debug.WriteLine("Error stopping service: " + ex.ToString())
    End Try
End Sub
```

Service Validation

To test the new functionality, make sure that you have the service installed and the properly formatted configuration.xml file. After you run the service you should copy some files with the names that you wanted to download into the folder. You will notice a few things immediately.

First, you have no way to delete the remote file, so once you download it locally it is there forever, and you will start to see errors the next time you try to download the file because it can't be saved again locally. Because I have not written my code to append to any already existing file, you should modify the code to either delete any existing file locally, delete the file remotely, or name the file something unique. If you choose this last option, I suggest that you use a GUID, because it is possible for two threads to try to write a file with the same name at the same time. If you try to do this, the file will overwrite itself.

The second thing you'll notice is that the service only allows you to specify a single file to download, even though the service itself—or more specifically the FTP class—has the ability to download an array of passed-in file names. You can modify the service configuration file to pass in more than one file, and then have the *<ThreadFunc>* supply the FTP.Files property instead with an array of file names.

The last thing you'll notice is that you cannot pass in a wildcard. You can allow for wildcards by querying the remote directory for the files in advance and then using the <GetFiles> method to download all the queried files.

The next section will demonstrate how to upload files using the FTP protocol. This is an important concept because many people need to move files back and forth between servers and between companies.

Uploading Data Using FTP

In the previous section, we used the FTP class to download files from our local FTP server and store them locally. It would have been just as easy to download the files from a remote FTP Server and store them on any network-reachable server share.

Another situation that might arise is where files that are accessible by a service are required on a remote server that is only accessible through the FTP protocol. Files stored on the FTP server might have been generated by our service, a database server that exports data, or another process capable of generating file output.

Updating the FTP Class

The nice thing is that our FTP class already has the ability to send files via FTP to a local or remote server. However, it currently only supports anonymous use of FTP, which is fine for demonstration purposes, though not always useful for more secured FTP requirements. We'll use the <SendFile> or the <SendFiles> method, shown in Listing 9-17.

Listing 9-17   FTP upload support methods.

```
Public Function SendFile( _
                    ByVal pszUri As String, _
                    ByVal pszFile As String, _
                    ByVal pszUser As String, _
                    ByVal pszPWD As String, _
                    ByVal dwPort As Integer, _
                    ByVal pszLocalDir As String) _
                    As Boolean
    Try
        ' Set up the request
        Dim ftpURI As New Uri(pszUri + "/" + pszFile)
        Dim ftpRequest As FtpWebRequest = _
                        CType(FtpWebRequest.Create(ftpURI), FtpWebRequest)
        'Setup the Credentials
        ftpRequest.Credentials = New NetworkCredential(pszUser, pszPWD)
        'Upload a file.
        'setup options
        ftpRequest.Method = WebRequestMethods.Ftp.UploadFile
        ftpRequest.UseBinary = False
        'Now we have to read the local file into a stream
        Dim pFile As New FileInfo(pszLocalDir + "\" + pszFile)
        Dim bData(pFile.Length) As Byte
```

```vbnet
        Dim fStream As FileStream = pFile.OpenRead
        fStream.Read(bData, 0, pFile.Length)
        fStream.Close()
        ftpRequest.ContentLength = bData.Length

        Dim tmpStream As Stream = Nothing
        'Read the Stream from the Response and Save the File Locally
        Try
            tmpStream = ftpRequest.GetRequestStream
            tmpStream.Write(bData, 0, bData.Length)
        Catch ex As Exception
            m_Error = ex.ToString
            Return False
        Finally
            If (Not tmpStream Is Nothing) Then
                tmpStream.Close()
            End If
        End Try
        'Whats the Response
        Dim ftpResponse As FtpWebResponse = _
                            CType(ftpRequest.GetResponse,  _
                                FtpWebResponse)


        Return True
    Catch ex As Exception
        m_Error = ex.ToString
        Return False
    End Try
End Function

Public Function SendFiles( _
                    ByVal pszUri As String, _
                    ByVal pszFiles() As String, _
                    ByVal pszUser As String, _
                    ByVal pszPWD As String, _
                    ByVal dwPort As Integer, _
                    ByVal pszLocalDir As String) _
                    As Boolean()
    Try
        Dim iLoop As Short
        Dim bRet(pszFiles.Length - 1) As Boolean

        For iLoop = 0 To pszFiles.Length - 1
            Try
                bRet(iLoop) = SendFile( _
                                    pszUri, _
                                    pszFiles(iLoop), _
                                    pszUser, _
                                    pszPWD, _
                                    dwPort, _
                                    pszLocalDir _
                                    )

            Catch ex As Exception
                bRet(iLoop) = False
            End Try
```

```
        Next
        Return bRet
    Catch ex As Exception
        m_Error = ex.ToString
        Return Nothing
    End Try
End Function
```

We don't have to make any changes to the *FTP* class and can move to the next section.

Updating the Configuration File

We are lucky that our current configuration file matches the information that we need to extend our service to send files. It already captures the logon information, Uri, LocalFolder, and File properties, which are also required by the *<SendFile>* method. This means that we don't have to make any changes to the configuration file and can move to the next section.

Updating the *<Tutorials.ThreadFunc>* Method

As in the previous two sections, we don't have to make any changes to this method. Instead, we can move to the last section, which does require a change—to the FTP class itself. We need to add a new thread method to perform the work.

Updating the FTP Class

We now need to add a method that will act as our new thread method and move files from our local folder to the local or remote FTP server, as specified in our configuration file. Listing 9-18 shows this method.

Listing 9-18   FTP upload thread method.

```
Private Sub UploadFiles()
    While Not m_ThreadAction.StopThread
        If Not m_ThreadAction.Pause Then
            Try
                If (My.Computer.FileSystem.FileExists(Me.LocalFolder + "\" +
                        Me.File)) Then
                    Dim bUpload As Boolean
                    bUpload = SendFile(Me.URI, Me.File, Me.User, Me.Pwd,
                            Me.Port, Me.LocalFolder)
                    If Not (bUpload) Then
                        Throw New Exception("Failed to Upload File: " +
                                    Me.File)
                    End If

                    My.Computer.FileSystem.DeleteFile(Me.LocalFolder + "\" +
                                    Me.File)
                End If
            Catch tab As ThreadAbortException
                WriteLogEvent(My.Resources.ThreadAbortMessage + "_" +
                        tab.ToString + "_" + Now.ToString,
                        THREAD_ABORT_ERROR, EventLogEntryType.Error,
```

```
                                  My.Resources.Source)
            Catch ex As Exception
                WriteLogEvent(My.Resources.ThreadErrorMessage + "_" +
                                  ex.ToString + "_" + Now.ToString, THREAD_ERROR,
                              EventLogEntryType.Error, My.Resources.Source)
            End Try
        End If

        If Not m_ThreadAction.StopThread Then
            Thread.Sleep(THREAD_WAIT)
        End If
    End While
End Sub
```

The method shown in Listing 9-18 first checks whether the file listed in our configuration file and assigned to our File property exists. If so, the method sends the file to the FTP server. If the file is successfully uploaded, it is deleted locally.

You'll notice again that we can only upload one file per FTP class instance. However, it would be simple to add a delimited list of files, a wildcard set of files, or even another complex type in our configuration file for a set of files. You simply have to change this method to be able to iterate through those files or possibly create a queue that allows you to upload multiple files at a time.

Updating the *<Start>* Method

The last step we need to take is to update the *<FTP.Start>* method so that it will start the *<UploadFiles>* method instead of the *<DownloadFiles>* method, as shown in Listing 9-19.

Listing 9-19   *<Start>* method changes.

```
Public Sub Start()
    m_Incoming = New Thread(AddressOf UploadFiles)
    m_Incoming.Priority = ThreadPriority.Normal
    m_Incoming.IsBackground = True
    m_Incoming.Start()
End Sub
```

Service Validation

Compile and install the service. Create a directory or two on the local system and then place some files into those directories. Add some of these files and local folders into your configuration file. Then make sure you have a preconfigured FTP server service running, such as Microsoft FTP Service, with a folder that is able to receive files. Be sure to configure the Uri of each configuration file entry to this Uri. When you have placed some files into your local directories and run the service, you should see these files being sent to the FTP server and then deleted from the local directory.

As in the previous section, an important thing to note is that each FTP class is only looking for a single file to send to the service. Because of this, you have to keep recreating the local file to have it sent again. The issue is that the FTP server won't be able to automatically overwrite the copy of the file that is created when it is sent to the FTP service. You will need to consider this when writing your code. My recommendation again is to use a GUID before the file is sent so that it is unique each time.

Summary

- Microsoft Visual Basic 2008 has an extensive capability using the Microsoft .NET namespace to utilize *FTPWebResponse*, *HTTPWebResponse*, *HTTPWebRequest*, and many other classes that can communicate easily, securely, and directly with FTP or HTTP servers to read and write files.

- Uploading and downloading data is a simple process of creating the specified request class object, setting security, and opening the URL.

- Microsoft FTP Service and Microsoft IIS are two scaleable Enterprise solutions used by businesses around the world. You can use Visual Basic 2008 to write internal and external applications and services to talk to these services.

Chapter 10
Services That Listen

Sometimes you need your service to be triggered by more than the generation of external data. Services also have the ability to wait for direct input, whether by listening on a Transmission Control Protocol (TCP), User Datagram Protocol (UDP), Simple Network Management Protocols (SNMP), Named Pipes, MailSlots, or any other mechanism that allows for direct one-to-one or one-to-many communications.

You can design your service for more than just processing data. In some cases an end user or even another process needs to request data in real time. To do this, we have to design how the service will process incoming requests or monitor for incoming requests. Depending on how the request or connection is made, we need to set up our service listening protocols appropriate to that communication method. You'll need to decide whether to use static connections—such as a TCP connection—or a call/caller/callback method. For example, when a UDP request comes in, an acknowledgement might be sent, the data gathered, and then a call made from the service to the requester with either a static connection request or with a request for the original caller. Sometimes a request can come in that defines the information being requested and where and how it should be returned to the requester. Your service might be designed to accept a set of parameters from the caller that will determine the information requested, as well as the directory to store the data when the processing is completed. You can also provide security credentials, logon information, IP addresses, and any other information required to process the caller's request.

Listening with TCP/IP

When using TCP/IP to accept incoming connections and requests, you must account for several things before designing your service. These depend on the solution you are trying to build or the problem you are trying to resolve.

Design Points for Service Listeners

Many different types of service listeners are available. Whether the protocol is TCP, HTTP, UDP, FTP, or some custom variation, you need to consider some important questions before you start coding your service, including the following:

- Which server port (or list of ports) will requests come in on?

- How many active connections will you allow at one time?

- What type of security will you implement? Will you use network authentication, implied security, or clear-text authentication with user names and passwords stored in a secured place such as Microsoft SQL Server?

- If your service must perform actions on behalf of that caller, will it do so in the context of the caller, or in its own security context? Will your service have more or less security authorization than the caller?

- Will the connections be synchronous or asynchronous?

- Will connections have a time limit?

- Will each request from a caller require a new connection or can connections be static after a user is connected successfully?

- How will the service handle invalid connection attempts?

- In what format does the service expect the requests?

- What format will you use for communications between the service and the client?

Creating the First Listener Service

The preceding list shows some important characteristics of a service that you must carefully consider before design. In this section, we'll use a single server port to listen for connections. When connections arrive, they will be authenticated using a very simple, basic text authentication scheme. The user name and password will be hard-coded for now. When the connection is authenticated and a secondary socket has been created to service clients' requests, we'll wait for requests to come in from the client. All of these requests will be standard text-based requests with a standard delimiter. When the request comes in, the service will process the request and then return the information to the caller. After the caller acknowledges receipt of the information or the request times out, the connection will be dropped and the resources for that connection and any work it did will be cleaned up.

Coding the Service Listener

We'll continue with the code in Chapter 9, "Talking to the Internet." The code base gives us our standard service framework with the ability to start, stop, pause, continue, and shut down the service.

Adding a Configuration File

We need to add a configuration file that our application can use to create single or multiple listeners. In the first example, shown in Listing 10-1, we'll only use a single listener.

Listing 10-1   Configuration file schema.

```xml
<?xml version="1.0" encoding="utf-8" ?>
<Configuration>
  <Listeners>
    <Listener>
      <Port>15000</Port>
      <MaxConnections>1</MaxConnections>
    </Listener>
  </Listeners>
</Configuration>
```

The configuration file will allow us to have as many listeners as we want. The listeners themselves consist of the following two properties:

- *Port* represents the server side port to listen on. For most systems this is a number between 1 and 65,000. Ensure that the port you want to listen on is not already in use.

- *MaxConnections* represents how many client connections you can have at one time. Remember that connections do not stay connected on the server port that the client initially connected to. You have to create a server-side socket to hold the client's connection.

Creating a Listener Class

We need to create a class that can support multiple listeners. Although we won't be creating multiple services, we will be creating the ability for multiple entry points into this service. We could also extend our configuration file to include information that would tell the *Listener* class instance to do a specific task. If a single service could have multiple actions, you would want to have separate server ports, threads, and worker data for each possible action. You could optimize your service even more by separating the workload of each task that your service is capable of. Let's review our *Listener* class, shown in Listing 10-2.

Listing 10-2   The *Listener* class.

```vb
Imports System.Threading
Imports System.IO
Imports System.Text
Imports System.Net.Sockets
Imports System.Net
Imports System.ServiceProcess

Public Class Listener
    Public m_Incoming As Thread
    Private m_ThreadAction As ThreadActionState
    Private m_Listener As Socket = Nothing
    Private m_ClientSocket As Socket = Nothing
```

```
Private m_MaxConnections As Integer
Private m_Port As Integer

Public Sub New(ByRef threadaction As ThreadActionState)
    m_ThreadAction = threadaction
End Sub

Public Sub Start()
    m_Incoming = New Thread(AddressOf StartListener)
    m_Incoming.Priority = ThreadPriority.Normal
    m_Incoming.IsBackground = True
    m_Incoming.Start()
End Sub

Private Sub StartListener()
    While Not m_ThreadAction.StopThread
        If Not m_ThreadAction.Pause Then
            Try
                'We need to set up our Port listener and the ability
                'to accept an incoming call.
                Dim localEndPoint As IPEndPoint = Nothing

                m_Listener = New Socket(AddressFamily.InterNetwork, _
                            SocketType.Stream, ProtocolType.Tcp)

                Dim ipHostInfo As IPHostEntry = Dns.GetHostEntry(Dns.GetHostName())
                Dim ipAddress As IPAddress = ipHostInfo.AddressList(0)

                localEndPoint = New IPEndPoint(ipAddress.Any, Me.Port)

                m_Listener.Bind(localEndPoint)
                m_Listener.Listen(Me.MaxConnections)

                Dim bytes() As Byte = New [Byte](1024) {}

                While True
' Program is suspended while waiting for an incoming connection.
                    m_ClientSocket = m_Listener.Accept

                    Dim Data As String = Nothing
                    Dim bError As Boolean = False
                    ' An incoming connection needs to be processed.
                    While True
                        Dim iStart As Long = Now.Ticks
                        'Create a Byte Buffer to receive data on.
                        bytes = New Byte(1024) {}

                        Dim bytesRec As Integer = _
                        m_ClientSocket.Receive(bytes)
                        Data += Encoding.ASCII.GetString(bytes, 0, _
                                                    bytesRec)

                        If ((Now.Ticks - iStart) / 10000000) > 30 Then
'We have timed out based on a 30 second timeout
                            Try
```

```vbnet
                        m_ClientSocket.Shutdown(SocketShutdown.Both)
                    Catch ex As Exception
                        'do nothing
                    End Try

                    Try
                        m_ClientSocket.Close()
                    Catch ex As Exception
                        'do nothing
                    End Try

                    Exit While
                End If
'if we have not timed out yet then let us    see if a command
                'has come in and process it
                If Data.IndexOf("<EOF>") > -1 Then
'If we have found an EOF then we need to process that information
'we could reset our timeout variable also if we have a command so it
                    'does not time out falsely
                    'Process the Command
                    Dim pszOut As String = Nothing

                    Try
                        WriteLogEvent(Data, 15, _
            EventLogEntryType.Information, My.Resources.Source)
                        Call ProcessCommand(Data, pszOut)
                        m_ClientSocket.Send(Encoding.ASCII.GetBytes(pszOut), _
            Encoding.ASCII.GetBytes(pszOut).Length, SocketFlags.None)
                    Catch ex As Exception
                        Exit While
                    End Try
                    'clean up
                    Try
m_ClientSocket.Shutdown(SocketShutdown.Both)
                    Catch ex As Exception
                    End Try

                    Try
                        m_ClientSocket.Close()
                    Catch ex As Exception
                    End Try
                End If

                Exit While
            End While
        End While
    Catch nex As SocketException
    WriteLogEvent(My.Resources.ThreadErrorMessage + "_" + _
    nex.ToString + "_" + Now.ToString, THREAD_ERROR, _
                EventLogEntryType.Error, My.Resources.Source)
    Catch tab As ThreadAbortException
    WriteLogEvent(My.Resources.ThreadAbortMessage + "_" + _
    tab.ToString + "_" + Now.ToString, THREAD_ABORT_ERROR, _
            EventLogEntryType.Error, My.Resources.Source)
```

```
                Catch ex As Exception
                WriteLogEvent(My.Resources.ThreadErrorMessage + "_" + _
                    ex.ToString + "_" + Now.ToString, THREAD_ERROR, _
                    EventLogEntryType.Error, My.Resources.Source)
                End Try
            End If

            If Not m_ThreadAction.StopThread Then
                Thread.Sleep(THREAD_WAIT)
            End If
        End While

    End Sub

    Private Shared Sub WriteLogEvent(ByVal pszMessage As String, _
        ByVal dwID As Long, ByVal iType As EventLogEntryType, _
        ByVal pszSource As String)
        Try
            Dim eLog As EventLog = New EventLog("Application")
            eLog.Source = pszSource

Dim eInstance As EventInstance = New EventInstance(dwID, 0, iType)
            Dim strArray() As String

            ReDim strArray(1)
            strArray(0) = pszMessage
            eLog.WriteEvent(eInstance, strArray)

            eLog.Dispose()
        Catch ex As Exception
            'Do not Catch here as it doesn't do any good for now
        End Try
    End Sub

    Private Function ProcessCommand(ByVal pszCommand As String, _
                ByRef pszOut As String) As Boolean
        Try
            If pszCommand Is Nothing Then
                Return False
            End If

            'Get the Data and clear out our ending delimiter
            Try
                pszCommand = pszCommand.Remove(pszCommand.Length - 5, _
                    "<EOF>".Length)
            Catch ex As Exception
                Return False
            End Try

            'Split the Command and find out which one we are doing
            Dim pszArray() As String = Split(pszCommand, "##")

            Select Case UCase(pszArray(0))
                Case "GETDATETIME"
                    pszOut = GetDateTime()
```

```vbnet
                Case "GETSERVICESTATUS"
                    pszOut = GetServiceStatus(pszArray(1))
                Case "GETPROCESSLIST"
                    pszOut = GetProcessList()
                Case Else
                    pszOut = Nothing
                    Return False
            End Select


        Return True
    Catch ex As Exception
        Return False
    End Try
End Function

Private Function GetDateTime() As String
    Try
        Return Now.ToString
    Catch ex As Exception
        Return Nothing
    End Try
End Function

Private Function GetServiceStatus(ByVal pszService As String) As String
    Try
        Dim tmpService As New ServiceController(pszService)
        Dim pszOut As String = Nothing

        Select Case tmpService.Status
            Case ServiceControllerStatus.ContinuePending
                pszOut = "ContinuePending"
            Case ServiceControllerStatus.Paused
                pszOut = "Paused"
            Case ServiceControllerStatus.PausePending
                pszOut = "PausePending"
            Case ServiceControllerStatus.Running
                pszOut = "Running"
            Case ServiceControllerStatus.StartPending
                pszOut = "StartPending"
            Case ServiceControllerStatus.Stopped
                pszOut = "Stopped"
            Case ServiceControllerStatus.StopPending
                pszOut = "StopPending"
            Case Else
                pszOut = "Unknown"
        End Select

        Try
            tmpService.Close()
            tmpService.Dispose()
            tmpService = Nothing
        Catch ex As Exception
            'Do nothing
        End Try
```

```
                Return pszOut
        Catch ex As Exception
                Return "Unknown"
        End Try
    End Function

    Private Function GetProcessList() As String
        Try
            Dim pszOut As String = Nothing
            Dim tmpProcesses() As Process = Process.GetProcesses
            Dim objProcess As Process
            For Each objProcess In tmpProcesses
                If pszOut Is Nothing Then
                    pszOut = objProcess.ProcessName
                Else
                    pszOut += "##" + objProcess.ProcessName
                End If
            Next

            objProcess = Nothing
            tmpProcesses = Nothing

            Return pszOut
        Catch ex As Exception
            Return Nothing
        End Try
    End Function

    Public Property Port() As Integer
        Get
            Return m_Port
        End Get
        Set(ByVal value As Integer)
            m_Port = value
        End Set
    End Property

    Public Property MaxConnections() As Integer
        Get
            Return m_MaxConnections
        End Get
        Set(ByVal value As Integer)
            m_MaxConnections = value
        End Set
    End Property

    Public ReadOnly Property Incoming() As Thread
        Get
            Return m_Incoming
        End Get
    End Property
End Class
```

The following sections review this code.

Listener Class Properties

Listener has two properties that we read from our configuration file. First is the *Port* property, which tells us which server port to use for this instance. Second is the *MaxConnections* property, which tells us how many clients can connect to this instance at one time. Each property must be set before the *<Start>* method of the class instance is called.

The *<StartListener>* Method

If you've never worked with sockets and TCP/IP before, it's especially important that you review this code.

The first thing I do is create an endpoint, shown in Listing 10-3. An endpoint defines the binding information used by the socket to bind to the local server and socket instance based on the port and server IP address.

Listing 10-3   Define local endpoint used by listener socket.
```
Dim localEndPoint As IPEndPoint = Nothing
```

Next I create a listener socket, shown in Listing 10-4. The listener socket waits on the endpoint for incoming requests.

Listing 10-4   Define listener socket used by service.
```
m_Listener = New Socket(AddressFamily.InterNetwork, _
                    SocketType.Stream, ProtocolType.Tcp)
```

I am using the standard TCP protocol. This indicates that I want to create a connection-based socket.

Next, as shown in Listing 10-5, I create the required *IPHostEntry* and *IPAddress* instances that are used by *IPEndPoint* to create the binding information for the listener socket. I use the *Dns.GetHostName* method to get the list of IP addresses of the local computer. I actually get back a list of IP addresses, but I only care about the first one. I could, of course, iterate through the list if I had multiple adapters and wanted to bind to a specific adapter.

Listing 10-5   Define listener socket attributes used to bind to server local port.
```
Dim ipHostInfo As IPHostEntry = Dns.GetHostEntry(Dns.GetHostName())
Dim ipAddress As IPAddress = ipHostInfo.AddressList(0)
localEndPoint = New IPEndPoint(ipAddress, Me.Port)
m_Listener.Bind(localEndPoint)
m_Listener.Listen(Me.MaxConnections)
```

Last, you will see that I use *IPEndPoint* to bind the listener socket, and then I use the *Socket.Listen* method to start listening for incoming connections. You should also notice that I am using the *MaxConnections* property from the configuration file to tell the listener how many client sockets can be connected at any time before it will return an unavailable connection error to the clients.

The *<StartListener>* Processing Loop

Once we have the service listener socket running, we are waiting for a client connection request. When a request comes in, we want to process that request. Let's review the code that does this, shown in Listing 10-6.

Listing 10-6 The *<StartListener>* processing loop.

```
Dim bytes() As Byte = New [Byte](1024) {}
While True
' Program is suspended while waiting for an incoming connection.
    m_ClientSocket = m_Listener.Accept

Dim Data As String = Nothing
Dim bError As Boolean = False
' An incoming connection needs to be processed.
    While True
Dim iStart As Long = Now.Ticks
'Create a Byte Buffer to receive data on.
        bytes = New Byte(1024) {}
Dim bytesRec As Integer = m_ClientSocket.Receive(bytes)
        Data += Encoding.ASCII.GetString(bytes, 0, bytesRec)
        If ((Now.Ticks - iStart) / 10000000) > 30 Then
'We have timed out based on a 30 second timeout
            Try
                m_ClientSocket.Shutdown(SocketShutdown.Both)
            Catch ex As Exception
            End Try

            Try
                m_ClientSocket.Close()
            Catch ex As Exception
            End Try
            Exit While
        End If
        If Data.IndexOf("<EOF>") > -1 Then
Dim pszOut As String = Nothing

            Try
                WriteLogEvent(Data, 15, EventLogEntryType.Information, _
                        My.Resources.Source)
                Call ProcessCommand(Data, pszOut)
                m_ClientSocket.Send(Encoding.ASCII.GetBytes(pszOut), _
                            Encoding.ASCII.GetBytes(pszOut).Length, _
                            SocketFlags.None)
            Catch ex As Exception
                Exit While
            End Try
'clean up
            Try
                m_ClientSocket.Shutdown(SocketShutdown.Both)
            Catch ex As Exception
            End Try

            Try
                m_ClientSocket.Close()
```

```
            Catch ex As Exception
            End Try
        End If

        Exit While
    End While
End While
```

When a client connection request comes in, we use our single client socket and then use the listener socket's *accept* method to assign the client to the client socket. Then we begin an inner loop to receive the request from the client. In this case I am requiring a 30-second window for the client to send its request. If the request doesn't come within the allotted time, I consider a time-out has occurred, and then exit the loop and disconnect the client.

If the client does send its request in the time period allotted, I begin to peek the data and look for the <EOF>, which is required based on the communication specification for this client-server pair.

When I find the <EOF>, the data is read off into the allocated buffer and then sent to the <ProcessCommand> method. (I will go over this method shortly.) If the <ProcessCommand> call has no errors or issues, I use the client socket to send the response to the client, shut down the socket, close the socket, and then go back to listening for another connection request.

Listener Processing Methods

The *Listener* class has several processing methods that are used to parse, process, and respond to clients' requests. In our service, we support three separate requests. Each request is covered by a separate processing method. Each processing method is wrapped around the <ProcessCommand> function, which takes the request from the client, parses it, calls the processing method, and then returns the data to the <StartListener> thread.

The <ProcessCommand> Method

<ProcessCommand> is the main method used by our service. The service will use this wrapper method to determine the type of client request and then call the appropriate method to handle the gathering of the client's request. After the request is complete, the <ProcessCommand> method will return the data via a reference pointer to a string passed to it from the <StartListener> thread method. Each processing method will return back the appropriate string to <ProcessCommand>.

The <GetDateTime> Method

<GetDateTime> will return the current date and time of the local server. Although not an incredibly useful method, <GetDateTime> is good for demonstration purposes.

The *<GetServiceStatus>* Method

When *<GetServiceStatus>* is called, the user will pass in the short name of any service whose status it wants to validate. After this method is called, it will return the state of the requested service. In the case of an error, or if no service is found, *<GetServiceStatus>* will return an unknown status to the caller.

The *<GetProcessList>* Method

<GetProcessList> will return a comma-delimited list to the client of currently running processes on the server. The client can then parse the processes and get an alphabetized list of server processes.

Updating the *<Tutorials.ThreadFunc>* Method

We need to update the *<ThreadFunc>* method (as shown in Listing 10-7) so that we can read in the values from our configuration file.

Listing 10-7   The *<ThreadFunc>* method configuration code.

```vb
Private Sub ThreadFunc()
    Try
        'Load our Configuration File
        Dim Doc As XmlDocument = New XmlDocument()
        Doc.Load(My.Settings.ConfigFile)

        Dim Options As XmlNode
        'Get a pointer to the Outer Node
        Options = Doc.SelectSingleNode("//*[local-name()='Listeners']")

        If (Not Options Is Nothing) Then
            Dim tmpOptions As System.Xml.XPath.XPathNavigator = _
                        Options.FirstChild.CreateNavigator()

            If (Not tmpOptions Is Nothing) Then
                Dim children As System.Xml.XPath.XPathNavigator
                Do
                    Try
                        Dim tmpListener As New Listener(m_ThreadAction)

                        children = tmpOptions.SelectSingleNode("MaxConnections")
                        tmpListener.MaxConnections = Int32.Parse(children.Value)

                        children = tmpOptions.SelectSingleNode("Port")
                        tmpListener.Port = Int32.Parse(children.Value)

                        m_WorkerThreads.Add(tmpListener)
                        tmpListener.Start()
                    Catch ex As Exception
                        WriteLogEvent(ex.ToString(), CONFIG_READ_ERROR, _
                                    EventLogEntryType.Error, My.Resources.Source)
                    End Try
                Loop While (tmpOptions.MoveToNext)
```

```
            End If
        End If

    Catch ex As Exception
        WriteLogEvent(ex.ToString(), ONSTART_ERROR, _
                    EventLogEntryType.Error, My.Resources.Source)
        Me.Stop()
    End Try
End Sub
```

As with all our previous services, we need to be able to read in the values from the configuration file and then assign them to the properties of the class instance. In this case, we are assigning both the *MaxConnections* and *Port* properties to the *Listener* class instance. We can have as many instances as we want, and we can listen on practically an unlimited number of ports. I would recommend, however, that you don't use any ports below 1024 because these are usually associated with already existing applications or standards.

Updating the Tutorials *<OnStop>* Method

The service *<OnStop>* method needs to be updated to clean up the service threads properly for each class instance created, which is displayed in Listing 10-8.

Listing 10-8   The updated *<OnStop>* service method.

```
Protected Overrides Sub OnStop()
    ' Add code here to perform any tear-down necessary to stop your service.
    Try
        If (Not m_WorkerThread Is Nothing) Then
            Try
                WriteLogEvent(My.Resources.ServiceStopping, ONSTOP_INFO, _
                EventLogEntryType.Information, My.Resources.Source)

                m_ThreadAction.StopThread = True

                For Each listener As Listener In m_WorkerThreads
                    Me.RequestAdditionalTime(THIRTY_SECONDS)
                    Listener.Incoming.Join(TIME_OUT)
                Next
            Catch ex As Exception
                m_WorkerThread = Nothing
            End Try
        End If
    Catch ex As Exception
        'We Catch the Exception
        'to avoid any unhandled errors
        'since we are stopping and
        'logging an event is what failed
        'we will merely write the output
        'to the debug window
        m_WorkerThread = Nothing
        Debug.WriteLine("Error stopping service: " + ex.ToString())
    End Try
End Sub
```

Service Validation

To test the service, we need to connect to the service and call each of the processing methods to see what we get back. For this reason, I have created a client that can use the functionality of the service, whether it is remote or local. The important thing to realize is that we haven't yet implemented any type of authentication in the service, which means that anyone who has access to the server remotely would have access to call the functionality of the service. We will work on this in later chapters.

The Test Client

I have created a test client that looks like this and can be used to demonstrate the functionality of the service on any given port.

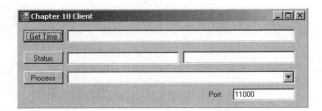

The code, which appears in Listing 10-9, is very simple, but shows how easily you can use your service. The three buttons do three different things: Each creates a Socket, calls *<GetDateTime>*, *<GetProcessList>*, or *<GetServiceStatus>*, and fills in the appropriate box with the response from the server. For the status, the first text box represents the service name, such as w3svc, and the second text box represents its status after you click the button and a response returns from the server.

Listing 10-9   Chapter 10 test client code.

```
Imports System.Text
Imports System.Net
Imports System.Net.Sockets

Public Class frmClient

    Private Sub Button1_Click(ByVal sender As System.Object, _
ByVal e As System.EventArgs) Handles getTime.Click
        Try
            Dim bytes(1024) As Byte
            Dim ipHostInfo As IPHostEntry = Dns.GetHostEntry(Dns.GetHostName())

            Dim ipAddress As IPAddress

            Dim sendersocket As New Socket(AddressFamily.InterNetwork, _
                SocketType.Stream, ProtocolType.Tcp)
            Dim remoteEP As IPEndPoint

            For Each ipAddress In ipHostInfo.AddressList
                Debug.WriteLine(ipAddress.ToString + "-" +
```

```vb
ipAddress.AddressFamily.ToString)
            If ipAddress.AddressFamily = AddressFamily.InterNetwork Then
                remoteEP = New IPEndPoint(ipAddress, CInt(txtPort.Text))

                Try
                    sendersocket.Connect(remoteEP)
                    Exit For
                Catch ex As Exception
                    Debug.WriteLine(ex.ToString())
                End Try
            End If
        Next

        Dim msg As Byte() = _
            Encoding.ASCII.GetBytes("GETDATETIME##<EOF>")
        Dim bytesSent As Integer = sendersocket.Send(msg)
        Dim bytesRec As Integer = sendersocket.Receive(bytes)
        txtTime.Text = Encoding.ASCII.GetString(bytes, 0, bytesRec)

        sendersocket.Shutdown(SocketShutdown.Both)
        sendersocket.Close()
    Catch ex As Exception
    End Try
End Sub

Private Sub Button1_Click_1(ByVal sender As System.Object, _
ByVal e As System.EventArgs) Handles Button1.Click
    Try
        cmbProcessList.Items.Clear()
        Dim bytes(1024) As Byte
        Dim ipHostInfo As IPHostEntry = Dns.GetHostEntry(Dns.GetHostName())

        Dim ipAddress As IPAddress = ipHostInfo.AddressList(0)
        Dim remoteEP As New IPEndPoint(ipAddress, CInt(txtPort.Text))
        Dim sendersocket As New Socket(AddressFamily.InterNetwork, _
            SocketType.Stream, ProtocolType.Tcp)

        For Each ipAddress In ipHostInfo.AddressList
            Debug.WriteLine(ipAddress.ToString + "-" +
ipAddress.AddressFamily.ToString)
            If ipAddress.AddressFamily = AddressFamily.InterNetwork Then
                remoteEP = New IPEndPoint(ipAddress, CInt(txtPort.Text))

                Try
                    sendersocket.Connect(remoteEP)
                    Exit For
                Catch ex As Exception
                    Debug.WriteLine(ex.ToString())
                End Try
            End If
        Next

        Dim msg As Byte() = _
            Encoding.ASCII.GetBytes("GETPROCESSLIST##<EOF>")
```

```vbnet
            Dim bytesSent As Integer = sendersocket.Send(msg)
            Dim bytesRec As Integer = sendersocket.Receive(bytes)
            Dim tmpArray() As String = Split((Encoding.ASCII.GetString(bytes, 0, bytesRec)),
  "##", , CompareMethod.Text)
            Dim iLoop As Integer

            For iLoop = 0 To tmpArray.Length - 1
                cmbProcessList.Items.Add(tmpArray(iLoop))
            Next
            sendersocket.Shutdown(SocketShutdown.Both)
            sendersocket.Close()
        Catch ex As Exception
        End Try
    End Sub

    Private Sub Button2_Click(ByVal sender As System.Object, _
ByVal e As System.EventArgs) Handles Button2.Click
        Try
            Dim bytes(1024) As Byte
            Dim ipHostInfo As IPHostEntry = Dns.GetHostEntry(Dns.GetHostName())
            Dim ipAddress As IPAddress = ipHostInfo.AddressList(0)
            Dim remoteEP As New IPEndPoint(IPAddress, CInt(txtPort.Text))
            Dim sendersocket As New Socket(AddressFamily.InterNetwork, _
                SocketType.Stream, ProtocolType.Tcp)

            For Each ipAddress In ipHostInfo.AddressList
                Debug.WriteLine(ipAddress.ToString + "-" +
ipAddress.AddressFamily.ToString)
                If ipAddress.AddressFamily = AddressFamily.InterNetwork Then
                    remoteEP = New IPEndPoint(ipAddress, CInt(txtPort.Text))

                    Try
                        sendersocket.Connect(remoteEP)
                        Exit For
                    Catch ex As Exception
                        Debug.WriteLine(ex.ToString())
                    End Try
                End If
            Next

            Dim msg As Byte() = _
                Encoding.ASCII.GetBytes("GETSERVICESTATUS##" +
txtService.Text + "<EOF>")
            Dim bytesSent As Integer = sendersocket.Send(msg)
            Dim bytesRec As Integer = sendersocket.Receive(bytes)
            txtServiceStatus.Text =
                Encoding.ASCII.GetString(bytes, 0, bytesRec)

            sendersocket.Shutdown(SocketShutdown.Both)
            sendersocket.Close()
        Catch ex As Exception
        End Try
    End Sub
End Class
```

The code in Listing 10-9 is fast and reliable, and you can click the buttons repeatedly. This is neither a complicated process nor a robust one, but you can use this same client to test the code we created previously in this chapter, as we extend the service to allow more than one connection at a time.

If you click one of the buttons, the client utility will connect to the local server and try to run one of the commands. Because it is intended only for demonstration purposes, the error handling is not robust. If you wanted to test it against a remote server, you will need to modify the code to use the name of the server you want to connect to in place of the *Dns.GetHostName()* method used in conjunction with the *Dns.GetHostEntry()* method.

Allowing Multiple Connections

Allowing only a single connection might work, especially in cases where the requests come from either a single source or at intervals that help ensure that two resources cannot compete for a connection at the same time. However, in some circumstances a single instance of a service could be used to generate requests for multiple resources. A good example of this is when you have a server that is multi-homed for several subnets, and receives requests for data from any or all of these subnets—and possibly from multiple computers or processes on each subnet. In this case, a single point connection would not be beneficial; however, you still want to limit how many connections you allow for performance reasons.

Extending the *Listener* Class

We are going to modify the code in Listing 10-9 to allow for up to 10 simultaneous connections to our service. This will require us to create up to 10 client sockets to accept the incoming requests, as well as telling our listener socket to accept up to 10 client requests before it returns an error to the client stating that it is unable to connect. Listener sockets only accept one socket at a time. Our code uses synchronous sockets with a backlog of up to 10 socket requests. Remember, though, that our configuration file allows us to specify the maximum number of sockets at any given time. Therefore, it is not a hard-coded value.

We'll use *ThreadPool* to take care of the multiple connections that our class will now be able to accept. Let's review the new modifications.

The *<SocketThread>* Method

We need to create a secondary thread method that will act as our socket processing thread. Since we will allow more than one connection at a time, having only a single thread won't work. Listing 10-10 shows the newly created thread method.

Listing 10-10   The *<SocketThread>* thread method.

```
Private Sub SocketThread(ByVal args As Object)
    Dim lSocket As Socket = CType(args, Socket)
```

```
Try
    Dim bytes() As Byte = New [Byte](1024) {}
    Dim Data As String = Nothing
    Dim bError As Boolean = False

    While Not m_ThreadAction.StopThread
        If Not m_ThreadAction.Pause Then
            Dim iStart As Long = Now.Ticks
            bytes = New Byte(1024) {}
            Dim bytesRec As Integer = lSocket.Receive(bytes)
            Data += Encoding.ASCII.GetString(bytes, 0, bytesRec)

            If ((Now.Ticks - iStart) / 10000000) > 30 Then
                Try
                    lSocket.Shutdown(SocketShutdown.Both)
                Catch ex As Exception
                End Try

                Try
                    lSocket.Close()
                Catch ex As Exception
                End Try

                lSocket = Nothing
                Exit Sub
            End If
            If Data.IndexOf("<EOF>") > -1 Then
                Dim pszOut As String = Nothing
                Try
                    Call ProcessCommand(Data, pszOut)
                    lSocket.Send(Encoding.ASCII.GetBytes(pszOut),
        Encoding.ASCII.GetBytes(pszOut).Length, SocketFlags.None)
                Catch ex As Exception
                    'clean up
                    lSocket.Shutdown(SocketShutdown.Both)
                    lSocket.Close()
                    lSocket = Nothing
                    Return
                End Try
            End If

            Exit While
        End If
    End While
Catch ex As Exception
    lSocket = Nothing
Finally
    'clean up
    Try
        lSocket.Shutdown(SocketShutdown.Both)
        lSocket.Close()
        lSocket = Nothing
    Catch ex As Exception
        lSocket = Nothing
```

```
            Finally
                lSocket = Nothing
            End Try
        End Try
    End Sub
```

The method shown in the preceding listing will be created as a temporary thread by our *<StartListener>* method, which will listen for incoming connections and then create a temporary thread to process the request. The temporary thread accepts a socket as a parameter.

Next, we call the *<ProcessCommand>* method, just as we did earlier, and then send the response to the caller. Last, we close the socket and consider the communication closed. Although this requires us to continually recreate new sockets for the same client calling many different methods, or calling the same method many times, it is for demonstration purposes only. We are not required to drop this socket at all. We could simply make the temporary thread go back into a receive blocking state waiting for a new command from the client.

We could also consider using asynchronous sockets instead of synchronous sockets; however, depending on the workload required, synchronous sockets work for a fast, small service that has limited functional requirements and connections.

Updating the *<StartListener>* Method

We need to update our primary thread method because we only want it to listen for incoming connections now and not process them. Let's review the new code, shown in Listing 10-11.

Listing 10-11   The new *<StartListener>* method.

```
Private Sub StartListener()
    While Not m_ThreadAction.StopThread
        If Not m_ThreadAction.Pause Then
            Try
                Dim localEndPoint As IPEndPoint = Nothing

                m_Listener = New Socket(AddressFamily.InterNetwork, _
                        SocketType.Stream, ProtocolType.Tcp)

                Dim ipHostInfo As IPHostEntry =
                        Dns.GetHostEntry(Dns.GetHostName())
                Dim ipAddress As IPAddress = ipHostInfo.AddressList(0)

                localEndPoint = New IPEndPoint(ipAddress.Any, Me.Port)

                m_Listener.Bind(localEndPoint)
                m_Listener.Listen(Me.MaxConnections)

                While Not m_ThreadAction.StopThread
                    Dim tmpSocket As Socket
                    tmpSocket = m_Listener.Accept

                    Dim tmpThread As New Thread(AddressOf SocketThread)
```

```
                    tmpThread.IsBackground = True
                    tmpThread.Name = "Socket Thread"
                    tmpThread.Start(tmpSocket)
                End While
            Catch nex As SocketException
                WriteLogEvent(My.Resources.ThreadErrorMessage + "_" +
                        nex.ToString + "_" + Now.ToString, THREAD_ERROR,
                        EventLogEntryType.Error, My.Resources.Source)
            Catch tab As ThreadAbortException
                WriteLogEvent(My.Resources.ThreadAbortMessage + "_" +
                        tab.ToString + "_" + Now.ToString, THREAD_ABORT_ERROR,
                        EventLogEntryType.Error, My.Resources.Source)
            Catch ex As Exception
                WriteLogEvent(My.Resources.ThreadErrorMessage + "_" +
                        ex.ToString + "_" + Now.ToString, THREAD_ERROR,
                        EventLogEntryType.Error, My.Resources.Source)
            End Try
        End If

        If Not m_ThreadAction.StopThread Then
            Thread.Sleep(THREAD_WAIT)
        End If
    End While
End Sub
```

Now that we have our processing thread, this code just needs to wait for an incoming socket connection and then hand that socket off to our processing thread. It simply creates a local background thread and then passes it the socket that it just accepted from the client. Notice that our error handling is not as exhaustive as it could or should be. You should be very careful when deciding to run any type of service, especially when it comes to error handling and resources.

Service Validation

Install the new service and make sure that your configuration file has at least two separate entries for ports to listen on, with more than a single connection as its *MaxConnections* property.

Run multiple instances of the test client, assigning different ports to the test client to cover all possible listening server ports you configured. For each client you should receive a response from the server on the specified port. You can even run multiple instances of the client against the same port and each client will still receive its own response. Remember that the *accept* method can only accept one socket connection at a time per server port, so you won't be able to receive a response at the same instant that you do on another—the server has to process the incoming connection and hand it off to the processing thread. Also, remember that your *MaxConnections* property specifies how many connections can wait in the backlog of queued requests to the server. So if you launch, for example, 11 or more clients and expect them all to work at the same time, you'll be disappointed. When more than 10 clients are queued, client connections will start to fail.

Summary

- Microsoft Visual Basic 2008 has built-in support for sockets that allows for creation of services that can act as a client or a server answering to incoming requests.

- Services written in Visual Basic 2008 can support secured or unsecured socket protocols.

- Microsoft Visual Basic 2008 *System.NET* and *System.NET.Sockets* classes provide a vast amount of support for traditional and nontraditional connection and connectionless protocols.

- To interact properly, client-server applications must be written to a standard understood by both the client and the server.

- The number of sockets within a client or server is limited by several factors, but revolves around system resources such as memory, network hardware, virtual memory, and CPU. You should write applications to scale with worker threads and sockets, not on an unlimited one-to-one basis with simultaneous connection requests.

Chapter 11
Advanced Security Considerations and Communications

Throughout the previous chapters we have dealt with different communication protocols without focusing directly on the type of security that you can use for each type of protocol. This chapter is going to focus on securing your service both from a communication and configuration perspective. We'll look at both the client and the server, because sometimes your service acts as a client and sometimes it acts as a server. Although these are sometimes equivalent, when they are not, it is important to understand the differences and properly secure your code and your service.

What Does Securing the Service Mean?

There are many important security issues, but depending on the level of security you require, you may not need to take all of them into account. Remember that any interaction that your service has should occur in a secure fashion. Let's review a list of security issues that you should consider. I'll cover each of these as the chapter progresses, breaking down some of them based on server and client:

- Service logon privileges
- Securing your services configuration
- Ensuring that your code is well protected internally
- Making sure that your code captures all exceptions properly
- Validating that your code follows Microsoft security best practices
- In-memory data protection
- On-disk data protection
- Data storage protection when using SQL data stores
- Client authentication

- Impersonation requirements

- Protocol layer encryption and security

- Authentication types (NTLM, Kerberos, Basic)

- Creating, installing, and using certificates

- Remote access

Each of these represents a core feature that you must take into account each time you begin designing a service, and most certainly before deployment. Let's look at some of these features and see how to ensure the security of our service, its functionality, and its data.

Note This book covers only issues regarding services. For a broader look at security, please see *Security for Microsoft Visual Basic .NET* by Ed Robinson and Michael James Bond (Microsoft Press, 2003).

Service Logon Privileges

In Chapter 3, "Services and Security," we already covered logon privileges, so I won't go over them again in detail. However, remember that when it comes to the security of your service, you must make sure that the account that your service runs under has only the required privileges necessary. Giving your service account too much authority can jeopardize not only your service and the computer it runs on, but also your network. Take care to change the services account password frequently and share it only as necessary.

Securing Your Service's Configuration

When you create services, you usually need to store some configuration information that the service will use. Let's review the types of information that we might store and how to protect this information.

SQL Server Logon Information

Your service might need to connect to a Microsoft SQL Server data store. You may need the data stored in Microsoft SQL Server database to be encrypted, the connection to be encrypted, such as with SSL, or both. I will describe some of the options in the following sections.

Remote File Locations

Services are often required to retrieve or store information from remote locations that are not sent to it by a client but instead are configured before the service is run. Any remote file locations should be kept secret so that users cannot attempt to access them. It is always possible that these locations were not properly secured. Hiding their identity helps to ensure that they stay secure.

Remote Server Identities

Your service will often need access to remote servers. This access can be through any protocol or transport available to the service. When this is required you should protect those servers' identities by not allowing their IP addresses, host names, or FDQNs to become publicly available. Unsecured configuration data can hamper your ability to keep your servers and your data safe.

File or Data Attributes

In previous chapters, we stored attributes related to the data that we wanted to poll for. Whether this is data from a data store or a filename, we need to make sure that these items are kept safe. Imagine that you have an FTP server that doesn't allow viewing of remote files, but does allow downloading of remote files. Now imagine that it allows anonymous access, and by just knowing the remote filenames or types, users can access these files. Protecting this information would be crucial.

No matter what information you need to store, it is imperative to keep that data safe. You can store configuration data both locally and remotely. Let's review some of the data configuration options briefly:

- Microsoft SQL Server
- Microsoft Access
- The registry
- The local file system
- A remote file share

Any of these choices requires you to use the most appropriate means to protect configuration data. In the next section we'll review some of our options.

Options for Securing Configuration Data

The options that you choose for storing configuration data don't always have to be the same for each service. In fact, a combination of these options may be required to create a robust, flexible, secure service. Let's review some of our options and then look at the pros and cons of each.

Hash Values

You can use hash values to authenticate and protect data. The issue with hash values is that many of the schemes using hashes are susceptible to dictionary attempts by unauthorized users to gain access to the data. This doesn't make using hash values unfeasible. In fact this option is part of the NTLM challenge-and-response mechanism of Microsoft Windows. We'll use a hash value to validate access to a service as well as to a resource in code shortly.

Private and Public Keys

Using keys gives us a greater security level, but also gives us a more complex solution. Depending on your requirements, you will need to generate client, server, or bidirectional keys. You will also need a deployment strategy and a certificate storage location on each server and client that wants to participate in certificate validation. I will cover how to use keys and certificates in a moment.

Impersonation

Using impersonation requires that you accept the clients' credentials, authenticate them, and then run processes or threads available to that remote user under her own security context. We can also use the built-in capabilities of Windows to validate the credentials of a user by attempting to run our process or threads as the credentials that were passed in. We will look at this option shortly.

Restricting Access and ACLs

Restricted access doesn't refer only to the ability to validate users' credentials, or a hash, but also to using Microsoft Windows and Active Directory directory service to restrict access to only specific user accounts. Access Control Lists (ACLs) allow you to define levels of access and then restrict access to only those who are allowed to view the protected information. This doesn't require the service developer to store any user names or passwords directly. You can pass the information collected either from the service or from the service account to Windows or Active Directory to validate not only access to the resource, but also the level of that access.

Using Windows Authentication for SQL Server

When you use SQL Server to store configuration data, you have to make sure that the service—and only the service—has access to your data. You should use parameterized stored procedures and then grant execute privileges only to the accounts—specifically your service account that requires the retrieval of the configuration data. Although you could use direct table access, that would allow too much direct access to your data and should be avoided. Stored procedures allow you to secure your data while locking down access to the table itself.

A Closer Look at Security Options

Let's take a closer look at each configuration security option, including exactly how we implement and use it to help secure a service.

Restricted Access and ACLs

Using the built-in capabilities of Windows to secure access to configuration data allows you to configure your service to run under an account that only has access to your data. When you grant access to a resource on the Windows platform, the steps are very similar. The following areas use ACLs for access.

The Registry   The registry provides a storage location for the operating system, Microsoft-specific applications, and customer applications. The registry stores information in branches and key value pairs. If, for instance, you store an ODBC connection string, you want to make sure that access is only granted to the accounts that should have privileges to view the data in the database. In some cases this may also require you to grant access to some administrators or possibly SQL administrators to ensure that the data is not lost forever if the users with access to the registry key leave the company or are unable to access the system for any reason. To set the permissions, click Start, click Run, type **regedit** at the command line, and press Enter or click OK. Find the registry key that you want to secure either by using the Find feature or by opening the appropriate registry key. In this example, I created a key called HKEY_LOCAL_MACHINE\Software\Tutorials. Under this key I created a string value called TutorialString. I set the value to *TestString*. Now I need to modify the permissions so that only my service account and local administrators have access. To do so, I right-click the Tutorial-String key and select Permissions.

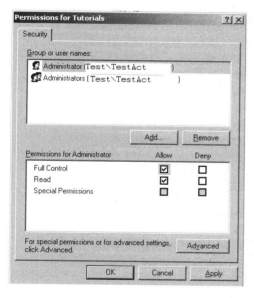

After I set the ACLs in the registry, I only need to set the service to run as the user account that has access. As with any service, the account's information must be known to someone, which means the information will never be 100 percent secure; however, limiting the administrators who have access to the account information helps to ensure that the data is secure.

File Folders   File folders provide a secure way to store configuration data with at least two important configurations:

■ **Encryption** allows each document created in a given folder to be encrypted automatically. Access to the files is specific to the user who created the file and to the recovery agents. To turn on encryption for a given folder, open Windows Explorer and right-click the folder that you want to encrypt. Select Properties and then click the General tab. Select Advanced and then select the Encrypt Content To Secure Data check box.

I created a folder called Test and enabled the encryption bit. Make sure that the folder is empty before you turn on encryption—otherwise all files within the folder will get encrypted with the current users' private keys and will not allow the original creators of the documents to view them. This could cause the files to be lost forever.

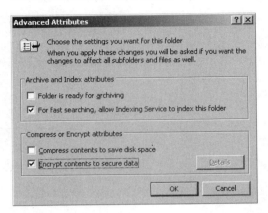

■ **Restricted Access** through the settings of ACLs will also prevent unwanted users from gaining access to the files within the folders. In the following graphic, I have removed everyone from the ACL list who does not need access to the folder. At this point, I need to make sure that only the account the service runs as has access to the folder. Because administrators can recover security access to the folder at a later time, you don't need to even list the administrators here.

Note You aren't required to share a folder before using it to store documents. If you do share the folder, you must make sure to set the appropriate access privileges to the folder as well. Full control of the share does not overwrite the local ACL privileges on the folder.

> **Tip**   You can use both security ACLs and encryption to enhance your data configuration file. Set the folder to only allow the account of the service and then enable encryption before the security file is added to the folder.

Windows SQL Server Authentication   When you use SQL Server authentication, it is recommended that you set the server to use Windows Authentication Mode only. Allowing SQL Server authentication requires that you pass a user name and password with the connection string to the server. This information can be more easily stolen and requires that you store the information somewhere in your configuration file directly. Open SQL Server 2005 Manager, right-click the server, click the Security tab, select the Windows Authentication Mode, and then click OK. Make sure that you have enabled Failed Logins Only for auditing—this is very important in catching potential security risks.

To enable Failed Logins Only for Microsoft SQL Server, follow these steps:

1. Start SQL Server Management Studio.

2. Log on into the Database Engine Services of your database server.

3. Right-click the database server name, and then select Properties.

4. Select Security.

5. Under Login Auditing, select Failure Logins Only, and then click OK.

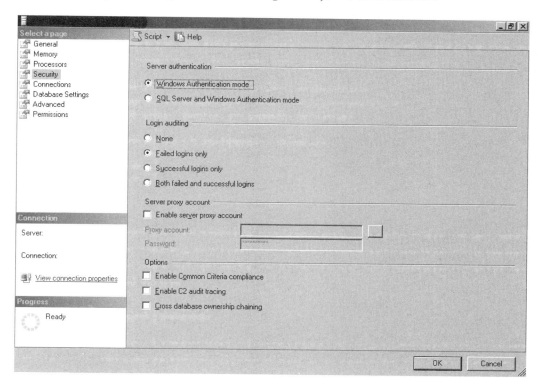

Certificates, Impersonation, and Configuration Access   Configuration data comes in two different types. *Application-specific* configuration data represents information that only the service needs. This could include information such as ports to listen on, whether it is a server application, or the maximum number of users that should be able to connect to your service simultaneously. Store this information in the application-specific configuration file, which would be named after your service, such as service.exe.config. You should also protect this data from outside interference because the service may very well store database access information that only allows it to connect as the context of the user the service is running under. When this is the case you end up with a second set of configuration data.

User-specific configuration data represents data that end users use to make the service perform the way they need it to. The service might run in a multi-threaded context and perform the same or different sets of actions on a per-user basis. Some users may have access to certain parts of the configuration data but not other users. This type of authentication might require the end user to provide a user name and password, a hash, or a public or private key to validate who he is before the service will interact with his configuration data. Because the user-specific data has an impact on the server that the service runs on, as well as any other servers that the service interacts with, making this information as secure as possible is very important. For example, if you're storing configuration data for users in a database table, because the service may not be running as the user who request the data, it must validate who the user requesting the data is, and then retrieve the user's information from the database table. This user would not have access to other users' configuration data unless given explicitly by the administrator of the data.

Using Hash Values   It is possible that all users will use the service in the same way. Imagine a service that merely returns information from the same data store but the results are different based only on the user's request. If you take this a step further, it is possible that the user information is not stored, but that a hash is used to determine what data will be returned to the user.

When you combine multiple configuration security models, your data is even safer. After a hash is generated, you can assign that hash to a given command for the service. A user could attempt to log on to your service where a challenge response occurs. The following steps can occur before the data is returned and validated by both the server and the client:

1. The client connects to the server.

2. The server authenticates the client.

3. The client authenticates the server.

4. The client sends a hash representing the request it has made.

5. The server responds to the client.

6. The client disconnects from the server.

You can use hash values for both authentication-specific and configuration-specific detail access.

If you combine encryption, restricted folder access, database server restricted access, and hash values, you can create a secured method of storing both application-specific and user-specific information. Securing application and user configuration data is a very important part of securing your service. If information about your service is readily available to anyone, everyone will be able to easily manipulate and attack your entire application, from the file system to remote systems and even your data stores.

Services as Clients

Some servers act as a client to other services, servers, and applications. Even in listening services, or server services, parts of the service can act as a client. In this section we'll look at some of the ways in which a service acts as a client using standard Internet protocols and how you can help ensure that your services use secure communications. The code for this demonstration is quite simple—we're simply extending code from previous chapters to include secured communications.

Securing the HTTP Client Service

In Chapter 9, "Talking to the Internet," we created an Http client service that allowed us to gather status information from a Web page and then have the results stored in a database. In this section, we'll take the existing service and extend it to use a more secure authentication channel through SSL and configurable authentication types. Let's review how to extend a service to support both SSL and configurable authentication types.

Updating the Configuration File

We know that we want to support SSL, but we need several pieces of information to properly support SSL and configurable authentication. Let's look at the properties that we need to store.

The URL Property   We are already storing the *Url* element in our configuration file, so we don't need to add it; however, we do need to update this property in the configuration file to reflect that we want to use *https* instead of *http*. Using SSL is not a requirement for using different types of authentication, so we do not need a specific SSL switch as we do with some other protocols. The *WebRequest* method can handle any number of authentication protocols over SSL or non-SSL connections.

The AuthType Property   The AuthType property is used to determine the Authentication-Level that our request requires. This property has three different options:

- **MutualAuthRequest**   This option makes the client request—but not require—that client and server mutually authenticate. If this option is not available, the developer must decide what to do if it is unsupported.

- **MutualAuthRequired**   This option tells the client to require mutual authentication with the server before communication will continue. If the server is unable to process the request, the client should disconnect from the server until such a request can be made.

- **None**   With this option the client neither requests nor requires any type of authentication or impersonation.

We will store one of these possible choices: request, required, or none in our configuration file. In my case I will use request.

The AuthMethod Property   We'll use the AuthMethod property to dictate which authentication method we want to use in our service. I'll define one of two types of authentication:

- **NTLM**   This authentication method will be used to pass the logon information of the service to the remote Web server.

- **Basic**   This authentication method will be used to pass the user name and password of the account that we want to use to log on to the remote Web server.

> **Note**   The authentication type does not have anything to do with the protocol or port, but only the way in which the user will be authenticated to validate access to the URL requested from the server.

The UserName Property   If the authentication method is Basic, we will provide the user name for the *WebRequest* call to download the content from the Web server. If this property is not defined but the authentication type is Basic, the service should throw an error in the event log and the service should stop.

The Password Property   If the authentication method is Basic, we need to supply a password to send to the remote server for validation. If this property is not defined, an error should be thrown in the service to stop the service from continuing until the required password issue has been resolved. Although a password is never required on a user account, you should not leave it blank.

> **Note**   You should never use Basic authentication without using SSL.

Sample Configuration File

Now that we have the properties that we need to store, let's take a look at a sample configuration file, shown in Listing 11-1.

Listing 11-1   Sample configuration file.

```xml
<?xml version="1.0" encoding="utf-8" ?>
<Configuration>
  <HttpUrls>
    <Url>https://testserver/httpchapter/asp/status.asp</Url>
    <AuthType>Request</AuthType>
    <AuthMethod>NTLM</AuthMethod>
    <UserName></UserName>
    <Password></Password>
  </HttpUrls></Configuration>
```

The sample allows us to see that we are requesting an SSL connection with a mutual authentication and impersonation level and the use of NTLM authentication scheme. If any of these things were to fail on the server, we would get an IOException or SecurityException, which the service needs to handle.

Updating the *Http* Class

We need to add two properties to our existing *Http* class to support the values that we are storing in our configuration file. These properties will be used by our <*CheckStatus*> method, which we will update shortly.

Adding New Properties   We need to store our newly created properties, as shown in Listing 11-2.

Listing 11-2   New *Http* class properties.

```vb
Private m_AuthType As String
Private m_AuthMethod As String
Private m_UserName As String
Private m_Password As String

Public Property AuthType() As String
    Get
        Return m_AuthType
    End Get
    Set(ByVal value As String)
        m_AuthType = value
    End Set
End Property

Public Property AuthMethod() As String
    Get
        Return m_AuthMethod
    End Get
    Set(ByVal value As String)
        m_AuthMethod = value
    End Set
End Property

Public Property UserName() As String
    Get
        Return m_UserName
    End Get
```

```
        Set(ByVal value As String)
            m_UserName = value
        End Set
End Property

Public Property Password() As String
    Get
            Return m_Password
    End Get
        Set(ByVal value As String)
            m_Password = value
        End Set
End Property
```

The properties shown in Listing 11-2 are required if we want to support SSL and configurable authentication types. We will store each property as a string, although we could use an enumerator. Even with an enumerator we need to convert from the string we are storing into the property type we want to store in the *Http* class, so leaving it as a string is easier for now.

Once again the AuthType will specify the authentication and impersonation level while the AuthMethod represents the authentication type.

> **Note**   Remember UserName and Password are only used if you use Basic authentication and should never be used without SSL and file encryption to store your user name and password.

Updating the <*CheckStatus*> Method   With the new properties, we need to update the <*CheckStatus*> method so that it can use them. Listing 11-3 shows the updated method. Note that I am not adding any new error handling because it does not help enhance the service for demonstration purposes.

Listing 11-3   The updated <*CheckStatus*> method.

```
Private Function CheckStatus(ByVal URL As String) As Boolean
    Try
        Dim tmpRequest As WebRequest = WebRequest.Create(URL)
          Select Case Me.AuthType.ToUpper
            Case "REQUEST"
                tmpRequest.AuthenticationLevel =
                Security.AuthenticationLevel.MutualAuthRequested
            Case "REQUIRE"
                tmpRequest.AuthenticationLevel =
                Security.AuthenticationLevel.MutualAuthRequired
            Case "NONE"
                tmpRequest.AuthenticationLevel = Security.AuthenticationLevel.None
            Case Else
                tmpRequest.AuthenticationLevel =
                Security.AuthenticationLevel.MutualAuthRequested
        End Select

        Select Case Me.AuthMethod.ToUpper
            Case "NTLM"
                tmpRequest.Credentials = CredentialCache.DefaultCredentials
```

```
            Case "BASIC"
                tmpRequest.Credentials = New NetworkCredential(Me.UserName,
                                                                Me.Password)
            Case Else
                tmpRequest.Credentials = CredentialCache.DefaultCredentials
        End Select

        Dim tmpResponse As HttpWebResponse = _
                    C Type(tmpRequest.GetResponse(), HttpWebResponse)

        Dim pszServerStatus As String = tmpResponse.StatusDescription

        Dim tmpStream As Stream = tmpResponse.GetResponseStream()
        Dim tmpReader As New StreamReader(tmpStream)
        Dim pszContent As String = tmpReader.ReadToEnd

        Try
            tmpReader.Close()
            tmpStream.Close()
            tmpResponse.Close()
        Catch ex As Exception
            tmpReader = Nothing
            tmpStream = Nothing
            tmpResponse = Nothing
        End Try

        If ((pszContent.Trim.ToUpper = "OK") And (pszServerStatus.Trim.ToUpper =
                                                            "OK")) Then
            Return True
        Else
            m_Error = "Server Status: #" + pszServerStatus + "# - Content: #" +
                                                    pszContent + "#"
            Return False
        End If
    Catch wex As WebException
        WriteLogEvent("Error Retrieving Status for URL: " + URL + vbCrLf +
                    wex.ToString + vbCrLf + System.DateTime.Now.ToString,
                    WEB_ERROR, EventLogEntryType.Error, My.Resources.Source)
        m_Error = wex.ToString
        Return False
    Catch ex As Exception
        WriteLogEvent("Error Retrieving Status for URL: " + URL + vbCrLf +
                    ex.ToString + vbCrLf + System.DateTime.Now.ToString,
                    WEB_ERROR, EventLogEntryType.Error, My.Resources.Source)
        m_Error = ex.ToString
        Return False
    End Try
End Function
```

The bolded code in Listing 11-3 shows that we are attempting to read the property values that have been set and associating them to a WebRequest object instance. Then the authentication and impersonation level, the authentication type, and the user name and password are all set. Each property has a default value.

You may notice that when the authentication type is Basic, I create a new NetworkCredential instance and then pass in the user name and password. This method is not only used for

Basic, but you can also use it for Kerberos and NTLM. However, in Basic I do not provide the domain, as I would with NTLM and Kerberos.

Updating the *<Tutorials.ThreadFunc>* Method

We have updated both our configuration file and our Http class; we still need to update *<ThreadFunc>* to read in these properties and set them on the Http class instance. Listing 11-4 shows the updated code.

Listing 11-4 The updated *<ThreadFunc>* method.

```
Private Sub ThreadFunc()
    Try
        'Load our Configuration File
        Dim Doc As XmlDocument = New XmlDocument()
        Doc.Load(My.Settings.ConfigFile)

        Dim Options As XmlNode
        'Get a pointer to the Outer Node
        Options = Doc.SelectSingleNode("//*[local-name()='HttpUrls']")

        If (Not Options Is Nothing) Then
            Dim tmpOptions As System.Xml.XPath.XPathNavigator =
                        Options.FirstChild.CreateNavigator()

            If (Not tmpOptions Is Nothing) Then
                Dim children As System.Xml.XPath.XPathNavigator
                Do
                    Try
                        Dim tmpHTTP As New HTTP(m_ThreadAction)

                        children = tmpOptions.SelectSingleNode("URL")
                        tmpHTTP.URL = children.Value
                        children = tmpOptions.SelectSingleNode("AuthType")
                        tmpHTTP.AuthType = children.Value
                        children = tmpOptions.SelectSingleNode("AuthMethod")
                        tmpHTTP.AuthMethod = children.Value

                        Try
                            children = tmpOptions.SelectSingleNode("UserName")
                            tmpHTTP.UserName = children.Value
                        Catch ex As Exception
                        End Try
                        Try
                            children = tmpOptions.SelectSingleNode("Password")
                            tmpHTTP.Password = children.Value
                        Catch ex As Exception
                        End Try

                        m_WorkerThreads.Add(tmpHTTP)
                        tmpHTTP.Start()
                    Catch ex As Exception
                        WriteLogEvent(ex.ToString(), CONFIG_READ_ERROR,
                            EventLogEntryType.Error, My.Resources.Source)
                    End Try
```

```
                    Loop While (tmpOptions.MoveToNext)
              End If
         End If

    Catch ex As Exception
        WriteLogEvent(ex.ToString(), ONSTART_ERROR, EventLogEntryType.Error,
                     My.Resources.Source)
        Me.Stop()
    End Try
End Sub
```

In the updated *<ThreadFunc>* method I read in the AuthType and the AuthMethod, which are required, and set those properties on the Http class instance. However, you will notice that I wrap the UserName and Password properties in a try-catch block. This is because these properties are not required, and I don't want the service to fail if they aren't set. I could validate the authentication type to check whether it is Basic, but that would not guarantee that the properties were filled in. Using a try-catch block provides some protection against the null values that would be present if they were not populated. If the properties are not populated, but were required in the class instance because of a Basic authentication setting, an error would be thrown in the *<CheckStatus>* method when it attempted to create the *NetworkCredential* instance.

We have now successfully added the ability to use both SSL-encrypted connections and programmable authentication. Although this is not an all-encompassing Security Support Provider Interface (SSPI)-supported service, you do get an idea of how to create a more secure and robust Http client service.

Configuring the Web Server   Before the code in Listing 11-4 will work against the Web server, you have to make sure that a few things are completed on the server and on any firewalls in between.

■ Create or purchase and install an SSL certificate for your Web server. You can purchase a third-party certificate or create one using Microsoft Certificate Server. If you are using Microsoft IIS, use the Certificate Wizard to install the new certificate.

■ Configure your Web service to use SSL and apply a port to it. By default SSL uses port 443.

■ Make sure that any firewalls between the client and the server allow for your configured SSL port.

Now that the server is configured and the code deployed, you can test your ability to download a secured and authenticated version of your Web page.

Securing the FTP Service

To secure our FTP client service, we need to focus on three areas, each representing a specific security enhancement we need to make to ensure that our service and data are secured:

■ Securing the transport using SSL and encrypted authentication

■ Securing access to the configuration data that stores user name and password

■ Securing access to the remote FTP folders and server using ACLs

After covering these topics, you'll be better prepared to host an FTP solution.

Securing the Transport Channel and Authentication Method

As with the Http client service, we need to update the FTP client service to use SSL and secure authentication. The *FtpWebRequest* class supports using secured authentication and communication using SSL and configurable authentication.

> **Note**   If you are using Microsoft FTP Service, you cannot configure the service to use SSL and can use only anonymous or clear-text authentication.

We need to update the FTP client service starting with the configuration file.

Updating the Configuration File   We need to add two properties to the configuration file that will tell us what type of authentication we want to use and whether we want to use SSL. Unlike the Http client service, simply changing the Uri will not have the same effect because the *FtpWebRequest* object has a specific attribute for SSL connections.

We need to add two properties. The AuthMethod property represents either Basic or NTLM. Although Basic can also represent anonymous authentication, we will not specifically state anonymous here as a type and require instead that users state their user names and passwords.

The UseSSL property represents whether this Uri request is to be made over SSL. It can only be set to true or false and will have a default value of false.

Listing 11-5 is a sample of our new configuration file.

Listing 11-5   The sample FTP service configuration file.

```xml
<?xml version="1.0" encoding="utf-8" ?>
<Configuration>
  <FTPUris>
    <FTPWorkerOptions>
      <Uri>FTP://testserver/download</Uri>
      <LocalFolder>c:\temp\ftpsave</LocalFolder>
      <User>anonymous</User>
      <Pwd>anonymous@anon.com</Pwd>
      <Port>21</Port>
      <File>mydata.dat</File>
      <UseSSL>true</UseSSL>
      <AuthMethod>Basic</AuthMethod>
    </FTPWOrkerOptions>
  </FTPUris>
</Configuration>
```

In this sample, I configured the Uri to use Basic authentication, anonymous access over an SSL connection. Remember that the AuthMethod has nothing to do with the transport channel used. SSL is used to create an encrypted channel, not a specific type of authentication.

Now that we have our configuration file updated, we can continue to update our service.

Updating the FTP Class

We need to update two separate items in the FTP class. First, we need to update the properties that we are using in our class; second, we need to update our *get* and *send* file methods so that they support the new properties that we have created.

Updating FTP Class Properties   We have to update the FTP class to support additional properties, just as we did with the Http class. Listing 11-6 shows the new properties.

Listing 11-6   The new FTP class properties.

```
Private m_AuthMethod As String
Private m_UseSSL As Boolean

Public Property UseSSL() As Boolean
    Get
        Return m_UseSSL
    End Get
    Set(ByVal value As Boolean)
        m_UseSSL = value
    End Set
End Property

Public Property AuthMethod() As String
    Get
        Return m_AuthMethod
    End Get
    Set(ByVal value As String)
        m_AuthMethod = value
    End Set
End Property
```

As noted earlier, we need to add both a set of private member variables and two public properties that represent the *AuthMethod*. After we add these properties, we can continue with the update.

Updating the *<SendFile>* Method   The *<SendFile>* method represents how we send files to a remote or local FTP server. We need to update this method to use the proper transport and authentication based on the user's configuration. Listing 11-7 shows the required changes.

Listing 11-7   The updated *<SendFile>* method.

```
Public Function SendFile( _
                ByVal pszUri As String, _
                ByVal pszFile As String, _
                ByVal pszUser As String, _
                ByVal pszPWD As String, _
                ByVal dwPort As Integer, _
                ByVal pszLocalDir As String) _
                As Boolean
    Try
        ' Set up the request
        Dim ftpURI As New Uri(pszUri + "/" + pszFile)
```

```vb
Dim ftpRequest As FtpWebRequest = _
                    CType(FtpWebRequest.Create(ftpURI), FtpWebRequest)
'Setup the Credentials
Select Case Me.AuthMethod.ToUpper
    Case "BASIC"
        ftpRequest.Credentials = New NetworkCredential(pszUser, pszPWD)
    Case "NTLM"
        ftpRequest.Credentials = CredentialCache.DefaultCredentials
    Case Else
        ftpRequest.Credentials = New NetworkCredential(pszUser, pszPWD)
End Select
ftpRequest.EnableSsl = Me.UseSSL
ftpRequest.Method = WebRequestMethods.Ftp.UploadFile
ftpRequest.UseBinary = False

'Now we have to read the local file into a stream
Dim pFile As New FileInfo(pszLocalDir + pszFile)
Dim bData(pFile.Length) As Byte
Dim fStream As FileStream = pFile.OpenRead

fStream.Read(bData, 0, pFile.Length)
fStream.Close()

ftpRequest.ContentLength = bData.Length

Dim tmpStream As Stream = Nothing

'Read the Stream from the Response and Save the File Locally
Try
    tmpStream = ftpRequest.GetRequestStream
    tmpStream.Write(bData, 0, bData.Length)
Finally
    tmpStream.Close()
End Try

'Whats the Response
Dim ftpResponse As FtpWebResponse = _
                    CType(ftpRequest.GetResponse, FtpWebResponse)


    Return True
Catch ex As Exception
    m_Error = ex.ToString
    Return False
End Try
End Function
```

The bolded code in Listing 11-7 represents the changes required for us to create an SSL-encrypted connection as well as specifying whether we use Basic or NTLM authentication. Remember that you should never use anything other than Anonymous unless you are using SSL. Using real user credentials with clear text is an unsafe practice even if the service is running internally and is not available to extranet or Internet sources.

Updating the *<GetFile>* **Method**   As with *<SendFile>*, we need to update the *<GetFile>* method. Listing 11-8 shows the required changes.

Listing 11-8   The updated *<GetFile>* method.

```vb
Public Function GetFile( _
                    ByVal pszUri As String, _
                    ByVal pszFile As String, _
                    ByVal pszUser As String, _
                    ByVal pszPWD As String, _
                    ByVal dwPort As Integer, _
                    ByVal pszLocalDir As String) _
                    As Boolean
    Try
        ' Set up the request
        Dim ftpURI As New Uri(pszUri + "/" + pszFile)

        Dim ftpRequest As FtpWebRequest = _
                        CType(FtpWebRequest.Create(ftpURI), FtpWebRequest)

        'Setup the Credentials
        Select Case Me.AuthMethod.ToUpper
            Case "BASIC"
                ftpRequest.Credentials = New NetworkCredential(pszUser, pszPWD)
            Case "NTLM"
                ftpRequest.Credentials = CredentialCache.DefaultCredentials
            Case Else
                ftpRequest.Credentials = New NetworkCredential(pszUser, pszPWD)
        End Select

        ftpRequest.EnableSsl = Me.UseSSL
        ftpRequest.Method = WebRequestMethods.Ftp.DownloadFile

        Dim ftpResponse As FtpWebResponse = _
                    CType(ftpRequest.GetResponse, FtpWebResponse)

        Dim tmpStream As Stream = Nothing
        Dim tmpReader As StreamReader = Nothing
        Dim tmpWriter As StreamWriter = Nothing

        'Read the Stream from the Response and Save the File Locally
        Try
            tmpStream = ftpResponse.GetResponseStream
            tmpReader = New StreamReader(tmpStream, Encoding.UTF8)
            tmpWriter = New StreamWriter(pszLocalDir + "\" + pszFile, False)
            tmpWriter.Write(tmpReader.ReadToEnd)
        Finally
            tmpStream.Close()
            tmpReader.Close()
            tmpWriter.Close()
        End Try

        Return True
    Catch ex As Exception
        m_Error = ex.ToString
        Return False
    End Try
End Function
```

You will notice that the changes made in Listing 11-8 are identical to the changes made in the *<SendFile>* method. It would be sensible at this point to create a single method that connects to the remote server and passes a pointer to *FtpWebRequest* so that you don't have to duplicate this code. Listing 11-9 shows a pseudo-method that you could use to accomplish this.

Listing 11-9 A sample FTP connection method.

```
Private Function Connect() As FtpWebRequest
    Try
        Dim ftpURI As New Uri(Me.URI)

        Dim ftpRequest As FtpWebRequest = _
                        CType(FtpWebRequest.Create(ftpURI), FtpWebRequest)

        Select Case Me.AuthMethod.ToUpper
            Case "BASIC"
                ftpRequest.Credentials = New NetworkCredential(Me.User, Me.Pwd)
            Case "NTLM"
                ftpRequest.Credentials = CredentialCache.DefaultCredentials
            Case Else
                ftpRequest.Credentials = New NetworkCredential(Me.User, Me.Pwd)
        End Select

        ftpRequest.EnableSsl = Me.UseSSL

        Return ftpRequest
    Catch ex As Exception
        Return Nothing
    End Try
End Function
```

With this change, you can easily update your *send* and *get* methods so that you no longer have to duplicate this code in each method that requires a connection to the server. Remember to validate in your client whether you are returned a request or *Nothing*.

Updating the *<Tutorials.ThreadFunc>* Method Now let's update the *<ThreadFunc>* method, as shown in Listing 11-10, to tie the properties that we have added to the configuration file to the properties in the FTP class.

Listing 11-10 The updated *<ThreadFunc>* method.

```
If (Not tmpOptions Is Nothing) Then
Dim children As System.Xml.XPath.XPathNavigator
    Do
        Try

Dim tmpFTP As New FTP(m_ThreadAction)

            children = tmpOptions.SelectSingleNode("URI")
            tmpFTP.URI = children.Value

            children = tmpOptions.SelectSingleNode("LocalFolder")
            tmpFTP.LocalFolder = children.Value
```

```
            children = tmpOptions.SelectSingleNode("File")
            tmpFTP.File = children.Value

            children = tmpOptions.SelectSingleNode("Port")
            tmpFTP.Port = children.Value

            children = tmpOptions.SelectSingleNode("User")
            tmpFTP.User = children.Value

            children = tmpOptions.SelectSingleNode("Pwd")
            tmpFTP.Pwd = children.Value
             children = tmpOptions.SelectSingleNode("AuthMethod")
            tmpFTP.AuthMethod = children.Value
            children = tmpOptions.SelectSingleNode("UseSSL")
            tmpFTP.UseSSL = Boolean.Parse(children.Value)
            m_WorkerThreads.Add(tmpFTP)
            tmpFTP.Start()
        Catch ex As Exception
            WriteLogEvent(ex.ToString(), CONFIG_READ_ERROR, EventLogEntryType.Error,
                       My.Resources.Source)
        End Try
    Loop While (tmpOptions.MoveToNext)
End If
```

As with previous sections, we've added the two new properties: AuthMethod and UseSSL. When these properties are enabled you are ready to test the service. Remember that you must configure the server based on the authentication method and transport you want to use.

Securing the SMTP Client Class

Let's return to the SMTP class from Chapter 5, "Processing and Notification." We need to enable SSL and configurable authentication by making changes similar to those we made to the FTP and Http classes. Let's review the required changes based on our current SMTP class.

Securing the Transport Channel and Authentication Method

The *SmtpClient* class supports using secured authentication and communication using SSL and configurable authentication.

Updating the Configuration File   As shown in Listing 11-11, let's add the required properties to the configuration file. Notice that each of these protocols uses the same information for authentication and transport security.

Listing 11-11   The updated configuration file properties.

```
<?xml version="1.0" encoding="utf-8" ?>
<Configuration>
  <FileWorkerOptions>
    <FileWorkerProperties>
      <SmtpServer>smtptestserver</SmtpServer>
      <Subject>Test Subject</Subject>
      <Message>Found Message</Message>
```

```
    <Sender>Michael@test.com</Sender>
    <Recipient>Michael@test.com</Recipient>
    <SmtpPort>25</SmtpPort>
    <AuthMethod>NTLM</AuthMethod>
    <User></User>
    <Password></Password>
    <UseSSL>true</UseSSL>
    <MailEnabled>true</MailEnabled>
  </FileWorkerProperties>
 </FileWorkerOptions>
</Configuration>
```

I have removed some of the properties because we don't need them for the demonstration. I have added the bolded properties so that the configuration file includes all the required properties.

Updating the *EmailDetail* Properties   Remember that in our SMTP notification we store all properties in the *EmailDetail* class. We need to update this class, as shown in Listing 11-12, to reflect the new properties that we want to support.

Listing 11-12   The updated *EmailDetail* class properties.

```
Private m_AuthMethod As String
Private m_UseSSL As Boolean
Private m_User As String
Private m_Pwd As String

Public Property UseSSL() As Boolean
    Get
        Return m_UseSSL
    End Get
    Set(ByVal value As Boolean)
        m_UseSSL = value
    End Set
End Property

Public Property AuthMethod() As String
    Get
        Return m_AuthMethod
    End Get
    Set(ByVal value As String)
        m_AuthMethod = value
    End Set
End Property

Public Property User() As String
    Get
        Return m_User
    End Get
    Set(ByVal value As String)
        m_User = value
    End Set
End Property
```

```
Public Property Pwd() As String
    Get
        Return m_Pwd
    End Get
    Set(ByVal value As String)
        m_Pwd = value
    End Set
End Property
```

Just as with the Http and FTP classes, we need to be able to pass in the authentication method, the credentials to use, and whether we will use SSL.

Updating the SMTP Class Methods   We have to make several changes to the SMTP class methods for the service to work, as shown in Listing 11-13.

Listing 11-13   The updated *<SendMail>* method.

```
Public Function SendMail(ByVal emaildetail As EmailDetail) As Boolean
    Try
        Return Send(emaildetail.Sender, _
                    emaildetail.Recipient, _
                    emaildetail.SmtpServer, _
                    emaildetail.SmtpPort, _
                    emaildetail.Subject, _
                    emaildetail.Message, _
                    emaildetail.UseSSL, _
                    emaildetail.User, _
                    emaildetail.Pwd, _
                    emaildetail.AuthMethod)
    Catch ex As Exception
        System.Diagnostics.EventLog.WriteEntry("SMTP Tutorials Class", ex.ToString(),
                    EventLogEntryType.Error, SMTP_ERROR)
        Return False
    End Try
End Function
```

You can see in the bolded section of code that I have added the authentication and transport properties to the *<Send>* method (shown in Listing 11-14) being called by the wrapper *<SendMail>* method.

Listing 11-14   The updated *<Send>* method.

```
Private Function Send( _
                ByVal sender As String, _
                ByVal rcpt As String, _
                ByVal server As String, _
                ByVal port As Integer, _
                ByVal subject As String, _
                ByVal message As String, _
                ByVal usessl As Boolean, _
                ByVal user As String, _
                ByVal pwd As String, _
                ByVal authmethod As String) As Boolean
    Try
        If ((String.IsNullOrEmpty(sender)) Or _
            (String.IsNullOrEmpty(rcpt)) Or _
```

```
                (String.IsNullOrEmpty(server)) Or _
                (port <= 0 Or port >= 65000) Or _
                (String.IsNullOrEmpty(subject)) Or _
                (String.IsNullOrEmpty(message))) Then

            System.Diagnostics.EventLog.WriteEntry("Tutorials SMTP Class", _
                            "Error sending Email - Invalid Parameters", _
                            EventLogEntryType.Error, _
                            SMTP_ERROR)
            Return False
        End If

        Dim bSent As Boolean

        SyncLock (m_SmtpClient)
            Try
                Select Case authmethod
                    Case "BASIC"
                        m_SmtpClient.Credentials = New NetworkCredential(user, pwd)
                    Case "NTLM"
                        m_SmtpClient.Credentials = CredentialCache.DefaultCredentials
                    Case Else
                        m_SmtpClient.Credentials = New NetworkCredential(user, pwd)
                End Select

                m_SmtpClient.EnableSsl = usessl
                m_SmtpClient.Host = server
                m_SmtpClient.DeliveryMethod = SmtpDeliveryMethod.Network
                m_SmtpClient.Port = port

                m_SmtpClient.Send(sender, rcpt, subject, message)
                bSent = True
            Catch ex As Exception
                bSent = False
                System.Diagnostics.EventLog.WriteEntry("Tutorials SMTP Class",
                "Error Sending Email - " + ex.ToString, EventLogEntryType.Error,
                SMTP_ERROR)
            End Try
        End SyncLock

        Return bSent
    Catch ex As Exception
        System.Diagnostics.EventLog.WriteEntry("Tutorials SMTP Class",
                "Error Sending Email - " + ex.ToString,
                EventLogEntryType.Error, SMTP_ERROR)
        Return False
    End Try
End Function
```

Once again we use the new properties to set our authentication and transport channel properties on the *SmtpClient* class instance. You will notice that Basic or Anonymous is the default authentication method; however, you must supply the user as anonymous if you want the service to run as anonymous.

Updating the *<Tutorials.ThreadFunc>* **Method**   We need to update the *<ThreadFunc>* method, shown in Listing 11-15, to link the newly created properties.

Listing 11-15   The updated *<ThreadFunc>* method.

```
If (Not tmpOptions Is Nothing) Then
Dim FWOptions As New FileWorkerOptions
Dim children As System.Xml.XPath.XPathNavigator
    Do
        Try
'Other Properties Have been removed to save space
            children = tmpOptions.SelectSingleNode("AuthMethod")
            tmpDetail.AuthMethod = children.Value

            children = tmpOptions.SelectSingleNode("UseSSL")
            tmpDetail.UseSSL = Boolean.Parse(children.Value)

            Try
                children = tmpOptions.SelectSingleNode("User")
                tmpDetail.User = Boolean.Parse(children.Value)
            Catch ex As Exception
            End Try

            Try
                children = tmpOptions.SelectSingleNode("Password")
                tmpDetail.Pwd = Boolean.Parse(children.Value)
            Catch ex As Exception
            End Try

            FWOptions.EmailProperties = tmpDetail

Dim tmpFW As New FileWorker(m_ThreadAction, FWOptions)

            children = tmpOptions.SelectSingleNode("MailEnabled")
            tmpFW.MailEnabled = Convert.ToBoolean(children.Value)

            m_WorkerThreads.Add(tmpFW)
            tmpFW.Start()
        Catch ex As Exception
            WriteLogEvent(ex.ToString(), CONFIG_READ_ERROR, EventLogEntryType.Error,
                    My.Resources.Source)
        End Try
    Loop While (tmpOptions.MoveToNext)
End If
```

I have removed the previously required properties to remove extra code and added the bolded code, which now ties together all our properties and the *EmailDetail* class instance. We have now completed the changes required to secure our SMTP client service. Be sure that you've properly configured the server before you test the service.

Writing Secure Code

You can find a number of books about writing secure code. Covering this large topic is beyond the scope of this book. However, a few things are important to note, and I'd like to point out where you can find help making sure that you are writing secure code.

Exception Handling

One of the most important aspects of coding is error handling. When an error occurs you want to make sure that you accomplish two things: first, capturing the error; second, capturing the error as specifically as possible—in other words, catching an exception in the type that it was thrown.

Catching the Proper Exceptions   Imagine that you are working with Microsoft SQL Server. You try to perform some database actions and an exception is thrown. In most cases this will throw a SqlException, not a standard SystemException. For this reason you should be as specific as possible in your error handling routines to avoid attacks on your code. If you aren't expecting your code to throw or to catch a specific error type, and one occurs, you can more easily track down where the error is in your code and determine whether you have an issue in which your code is being exploited.

Throwing Exceptions   It is very important that the users or callers of your code know exactly when an error occurs so that they can code their methods or applications to react appropriately. In many cases, you may want certain exceptions to be thrown, and these should be passed on to the caller. Although you should never mask exceptions, in many cases you should throw a new exception to the user so that she can see cleaner and less extensive error information. Imagine that you are catching exceptions when trying to make connections to a remote server. You should not present the user with an exception that might display server names or attributes that he could use to exploit your service or your network.

Some exceptions that you capture are unique to the system and should never be rethrown to the user. In these cases you need to create a secondary exception, such as InvalidOperation, and throw that to the user. Provide the user with as little information as required and then log or alert your administrators of the real issue. Exposing too much information to the end user can be confusing and dangerous.

Determining Exceptions   When using .NET classes, it is easy to determine what exceptions, if any, a method or class throws. The following two techniques can help you determine available exceptions:

- **IntelliSense**   If you have IntelliSense enabled, you can hover your mouse over the method you want to use. Any exceptions available should be displayed in a pop-up dialog box. You should capture all of these exceptions and either rethrow them or throw a more user-friendly error to the caller.

- **MSDN Documentation**   If you have the documentation installed for Microsoft Visual Studio, or if you go to *http://msdn.microsoft.com*, you can find all the relevant documentation for a given class, object, property, or method. Use this information to create your error-handling methodology.

> **Note** It is possible a method may not throw an error. In these cases you usually need to make sure that the object is valid before using it. Not validating the object—even with a higher-level exception handler—can cause an unhandled exception. Do not assume that nested exception handlers will always work.

Understanding the Exception Stack   When you look at an exception, the initial level may not be where the exception occurred. You may need to iterate through the InnerException collection to validate where the problem started.

You also have to be careful about using global error handling. When an error handler is not directly found, the .NET runtime will navigate back through the frame stack until it fails to locate a handler, finds a handler, or runs out of frame space to continue backtracking. If it runs out of frames or is unable to find a handler at all, an unhandled exception will occur and data that you don't want the user to see might be displayed.

Microsoft Recommendations   Microsoft has spent a lot of time creating documentation about validating your code to make sure that it is safe. I will not reiterate all of that work. Instead, you can follow this link to find the documentation: *http://msdn2.microsoft.com/ en-us/security/default.aspx.*

A lot of documentation is also written specifically for the Microsoft .NET Framework 2.0. Although this documentation is a bit out of date because the .NET Framework 3.5 is used in Visual Studio 2008, it is very important to review this information, which contains some of the best techniques and procedures for securing your code.

Securing In-Memory and On-Disk Data

Protecting your data—whether it is on the hard drive or in memory—is incredibly important. From a memory perspective, the disk and physical memory can be the same. Each application by default is allotted up to 2 GB of memory. Of course not all applications can have 2 GB of memory at the same time.

Virtual memory is an allocation of hard-disk space to emulate physical memory. When you attempt to write to physical memory, that data might end up cached to the local disk in virtual memory. When this happens, the data is stored in the swap file. If the swap file were exploited—just as if the computer were exploited—you could lose important information.

Physical memory also allows for possible tampering and data loss if a user has the ability to read or write the memory allocated to an application on the fly. Imagine if someone took a memory dump of your application process while it was in use. That memory could be read and used to attempt to exploit your service. For this reason you should encrypt any data that must reside in memory for any period of time, and in most cases you should avoid storing data in memory if it is not needed. Configuration data is one thing that may allow you to read the encrypted data off the disk, configure your service to do what it must, and then release that data from memory. If you cannot do this, encrypting the data when access to the configuration data is not needed can also help protect you from exploits and data loss.

Microsoft .NET provides enhanced protection through its *ProtectedData* class, which allows you to read and create not only memory-protected data, but also to protect file-based data. For examples of how to use *ProtectedData* classes, which were new with .NET Framework 2.0, go to *http://msdn2.microsoft.com/en-us/library/system.security.cryptography.protecteddata.aspx*.

Using SSL with Server Services

In Chapter 10, "Services That Listen," we created a service that allowed for incoming connections and then allowed the client to make certain requests to the service, which the service attempted to fulfill and then respond to. In Chapter 10, we used standard sockets to implement the communication protocol, but we did not provide any security around the service.

In this section, we'll add both transport-level and authentication-level security to the service. We'll modify the Chapter 10 code to reflect the changes required to use SSL as well as different forms of authentication to secure the service.

Using *TcpClient* and *TcpListener* Classes

In our previous code, we used the socket class to create our server. This time we want to use two new classes, *TcpClient* and *TcpListener*, so that we can create a properly secured *SSLStream* instance that we can read and write to the client with.

TcpListener is used to listen for incoming TcpClient requests; we will use it to replace our current listener socket. *TcpClient* is used to make requests to a listening *TcpListener*; we will use it in our testing client to connect to our new service and validate the server certificate over SSL.

Using the *TcpClient*, *TcpListener*, and *SSLStream* classes, we can create a secure channel to communicate with. However, we have a few initial tasks.

Creating a Certificate   Before you can use an SSL stream, you need to create a certificate. Microsoft provides the MakeCert utility to allow users to create certificates and use them for testing purposes. If you are unfamiliar with this utility, please see the following Web site: *http://msdn2.microsoft.com/en-us/library/bfsktky3(vs.90).aspx*.

After you create a certificate, you can import it into any store you want on the local computer; however, you should store certificates in the appropriate store based on the user or computer that they are relevant to.

Using Certificates in Code   There are different ways to access certificates that are required by our server. The System.Security.Cryptography namespace provides access to other classes such as X.509 Certificates and methods that are able to read certificates from certificate stores or from disk. For examples on reading certificates, go to: *http://msdn2.microsoft.com/en-us/ library/system.security.cryptography.x509certificates(vs.90).aspx.*

In our code, we'll load our certificate from the disk after it has either been created with the MakeCert utility, purchased from a third-party, or exported to disk from a local certificate store.

Updating the Configuration File

We need to allow for the configuration of the certificate location. Each Listener instance can use its own certificate, so we have to update the configuration file to support it. Listing 11-16 shows the updated configuration file.

Listing 11-16   The updated configuration file.

```xml
<?xml version="1.0" encoding="utf-8" ?>
<Configuration>
  <Listeners>
    <Listener>
      <Port>15000</Port>
      <MaxConnections>1</MaxConnections>
      <Cert>MyCertPath</Cert>
    </Listener>
  </Listeners>
</Configuration>
```

As you can see, I added a *<Cert>* element that will be used to configure each listener to have its own certificate.

Updating the *Listener* Class

We need to modify the *Listener* class so that we can use a locally stored certificate on the hard disk. The certificate can be returned from the certificate store as well. Once you have it loaded, you can easily create a *TcpListener* class and use the *SSLStream* class.

Adding the Proper Imports   We need to add imports to our *Listener* class so that we can use the new Tcp classes and *SSLStream* class. Listing 11-17 shows the required imports.

Listing 11-17   Required server service imports statements.

```
Imports System.Net
Imports System.Net.Sockets
Imports System.Net.Security
Imports System.Security.Authentication
Imports System.Text
Imports System.Security.Cryptography.X509Certificates
```

Adding New Listener Properties   We need to add a new property to our class that will represent our X.509 certificate that we need to pass in the physical location of the file. Because the service can support multiple listeners on multiple ports, we will configure it to allow loading multiple certificates. Listing 11-18 shows the newly required properties.

Listing 11-18   The updated *Listener* class properties.

```
Private m_Certificate As X509Certificate = Nothing
Private m_Cert As String

Public Property Certificate() As String
    Get
        Return m_Cert
    End Get
    Set(ByVal value As String)
        m_Cert = value
    End Set
End Property
```

Our certificate location is represented by the Certificate property and our certificate is stored in our new data member, m_Certificate.

Creating the *ClientStream* Class   Because we're using multiple threads to represent separate listeners, we need to make sure that each thread can use its own client socket and client SSL stream. To make this easy, I created the *ClientStream* class shown in Listing 11-19. This will allow us to set, store, and pass an instance of our client-required stream and socket to our client processing thread.

Listing 11-19   The *ClientStream* class.

```
Imports System.Threading
Imports System.IO
Imports System.ServiceProcess
Imports System
Imports System.Collections
Imports System.Net
Imports System.Net.Sockets
Imports System.Net.Security
Imports System.Security.Authentication
Imports System.Text
Imports System.Security.Cryptography.X509Certificates

Public Class ClientStream
    Private m_Stream As SslStream
    Private m_Socket As TcpClient

    Public Sub New()
    End Sub

    Public Property ClientStream() As SslStream
        Get
            Return m_Stream
        End Get
        Set(ByVal value As SslStream)
            m_Stream = value
        End Set
    End Property
```

```
Public Property ClientSocket() As TcpClient
    Get
        Return m_Socket
    End Get
    Set(ByVal value As TcpClient)
        m_Socket = value
    End Set
End Property

Public Sub Dispose()
    Try
        m_Stream.Close()
        m_Socket.Close()
    Catch ex As Exception
    End Try
End Sub
End Class
```

This class shown in Listing 11-19 represents our client connection and underlying server-authenticated stream to which we will read and write. We also need to add an instance of this class to our *Listener* class.

Adding the *ClientStream* Class to the *Listener* Class   Before we can use the *ClientStream* class, we need to add and create an instance. I added an instance to the class, and I instantiated it in the Listener *New()* method. Listing 11-20 shows the code.

Listing 11-20   Adding a *ClientStream* class instance.
```
Private m_ClientStream As ClientStream

Private m_Port As Integer

Public Sub New(ByRef threadaction As Thread_Action_State)
    m_ThreadAction = threadaction
    m_ClientStream = New ClientStream()
End Sub
```

Now that we have an instance of our *ClientStream* class, we can update the remaining class methods to use the class for sending and receiving data based on client requests.

Updating the *<StartListener>* Method   *<StartListener>* represents the startup of our server listening service. Listing 11-21 shows the newly created code.

Listing 11-21   The updated *<StartListener>* code.
```
Private Sub StartListener()
    While Not m_ThreadAction.StopThread
        If Not m_ThreadAction.Pause Then
            Try
                'Load our certificate. Each listener can use it's own.
                Try
                    m_Certificate = X509Certificate.CreateFromCertFile(Certificate)
                Catch ex As Exception
```

```vbnet
                    WriteLogEvent(My.Resources.ThreadErrorMessage + "_" + ex.ToString
                        + "_" + Now.ToString, THREAD_ERROR,
                        EventLogEntryType.Error, My.Resources.Source)
                Return
            End Try

            Dim localEndPoint As IPEndPoint = Nothing
            Dim ipHostInfo As IPHostEntry = Dns.GetHostEntry(Dns.GetHostName())
            Dim ipAddress As IPAddress = ipHostInfo.AddressList(0)

            localEndPoint = New IPEndPoint(ipAddress, Me.Port)
            m_Listener = New TcpListener(localEndPoint)
            m_Listener.Start(Me.MaxConnections)

            While Not m_ThreadAction.StopThread
                Dim tmpSocket As TcpClient
                tmpSocket = m_Listener.AcceptTcpClient()
                'Now Authenticate Yourself
                Dim clientstream As SslStream = New
                    SslStream(tmpSocket.GetStream(), False)

                Try
                    clientstream.AuthenticateAsServer(m_Certificate, False,
                                        SslProtocols.Tls, True)
                Catch ex As AuthenticationException
                    clientstream.Close()
                    tmpSocket.Close()
                End Try

                m_ClientStream.ClientSocket = tmpSocket
                m_ClientStream.ClientStream = clientstream
                Dim tmpThread As New Thread(AddressOf SocketThread)
                tmpThread.IsBackground = True
                tmpThread.Name = "Socket Thread"
                tmpThread.Start(m_ClientStream)
            End While
        Catch nex As SocketException
            WriteLogEvent(My.Resources.ThreadErrorMessage + "_" + nex.ToString +
                    "_" + Now.ToString, THREAD_ERROR,
                    EventLogEntryType.Error, My.Resources.Source)
        Catch tab As ThreadAbortException
            WriteLogEvent(My.Resources.ThreadAbortMessage + "_" + tab.ToString +
                    "_" + Now.ToString, THREAD_ABORT_ERROR,
                    EventLogEntryType.Error, My.Resources.Source)
        Catch ex As Exception
            WriteLogEvent(My.Resources.ThreadErrorMessage + "_" + ex.ToString +
                    "_" + Now.ToString, THREAD_ERROR,
                    EventLogEntryType.Error, My.Resources.Source)
        End Try
    End If

    If Not m_ThreadAction.StopThread Then
        Thread.Sleep(THREAD_WAIT)
    End If
    End While
End Sub
```

I changed the m_Listener member of the *Listener* class from a socket to a *TcpListener*. The *<StartListener>* method starts by loading the certificate from the file location that was passed into the class instance from the *<ThreadFunc>* method. After the certificate is loaded, we begin to listen for new client requests.

When a client request comes in, we assume that it is a TcpClient connection request, but we could also have validated a regular socket connection and then attempted to create a server-side *SSLStream* instance based on the client stream. After we have a stream, we attempt to authenticate the server to the client using the server certificate. When the authentication is successful, we set the properties on our *ClientStream* class instance to the newly created and authenticated *TcpClient* and *SSLStream* instances. Finally, we create a thread and pass it the newly created *ClientStream* instance. It will use that instance to send and receive data from the client.

Updating *<SocketThread>* Method   *<SocketThread>* represents a client connection to our service and uses the *ClientStream* instance passed to it to respond to client requests. Listing 11-22 shows the changes required based on our new TcpClient usage.

Listing 11-22   The updated *<SocketThread>* method.

```
Private Sub SocketThread(ByVal args As Object)
    Dim lstream As ClientStream = CType(args, ClientStream)

    Try
        Dim bytes() As Byte = New [Byte](1024) {}
        Dim Data As String = Nothing
        Dim bError As Boolean = False

        While Not m_ThreadAction.StopThread
            If Not m_ThreadAction.Pause Then
                Dim iStart As Long = Now.Ticks
                bytes = New Byte(1024) {}
                    lstream.ClientStream.ReadTimeout = THREAD_WAIT

                Dim bytesRec As Integer = lstream.ClientStream.Read(bytes, 0, _
                                                    bytes.Length)

                Data += Encoding.ASCII.GetString(bytes, 0, bytesRec)

                If ((Now.Ticks - iStart) / 10000000) > 30 Then
                    Try
                        lstream.Dispose()
                        Return
                    Catch ex As Exception
                    End Try

                    Exit Sub
                End If
                If Data.IndexOf("<EOF>") > -1 Then
                    Dim pszOut As String = Nothing
```

```
                    Try
                        Call ProcessCommand(Data, pszOut)
                        lstream.ClientStream.Write(Encoding.ASCII.GetBytes(pszOut),
                                        0, Encoding.ASCII.GetBytes(pszOut).Length)
                    Catch ex As Exception
                        'clean up
                        lstream.Dispose()
                        Return
                    End Try
                End If

                Exit While
            End If
        End While
    Catch ex As Exception
        lstream.Dispose()
    Finally
        lstream.Dispose()
    End Try
End Sub
```

As in Chapter 10, we'll use our socket to send and receive data from the client; however, this time we'll use an SSL encrypted socket to send and receive the data. The service will read from the buffer until it either times out or the client sends it a valid request.

> **Tip** You should use the *ReadByte* method instead of the *Read* method so that you do not accidentally read more bytes than the End of File (EOF) terminator. In cases where your service does not shut down after one request, you could lose data if you read all the data off the buffer each time.

Another important thing to remember is that, like the socket class, the *Read* method blocks processing. If you want the method to only block for a limited amount of time, you must set the Send and Receive timeout properties so that it will not block forever. I use the THREAD_WAIT value to block for a certain amount of time before allowing the loop to continue or reach the time-out value. Now we can complete the changes to the new SSL-supported service.

Updating the *<Tutorials.ThreadFunc>* Method   The last step is to change the *<ThreadFunc>* method to pass in the new properties to the *Listener* class instance. Listing 11-23 shows the code.

Listing 11-23   The updated *<ThreadFunc>* method.

```
If (Not Options Is Nothing) Then
Dim tmpOptions As System.Xml.XPath.XPathNavigator =
                Options.FirstChild.CreateNavigator()

    If (Not tmpOptions Is Nothing) Then
Dim children As System.Xml.XPath.XPathNavigator
        Do
            Try
```

```
Dim tmpListener As New Listener(m_ThreadAction)

                children = tmpOptions.SelectSingleNode("MaxConnections")
                tmpListener.MaxConnections = Int32.Parse(children.Value)

                children = tmpOptions.SelectSingleNode("Port")
                tmpListener.Port = Int32.Parse(children.Value)

                children = tmpOptions.SelectSingleNode("Cert")
                tmpListener.Certificate = children.Value

                m_WorkerThreads.Add(tmpListener)
                tmpListener.Start()
            Catch ex As Exception
                WriteLogEvent(ex.ToString(), CONFIG_READ_ERROR,
                    EventLogEntryType.Error, My.Resources.Source)
            End Try
        Loop While (tmpOptions.MoveToNext)
    End If
End If
```

We need to update our startup thread to pass the newly created properties, or in this case the new *<Cert>* property. When this code is in place and you have created a certificate, you can start listening for secured, SSL-encrypted connections. We now need to update the test client so that it can communicate with the new server.

Updating the Test Client to Use SSL

Now that we have a server that uses—or in our case requires—SSL, we need a client that can also use SSL. In Chapter 10 I created a test client that used sockets to send requests to the server to get the time, a status of a service, or the current process list on the server. Now we want to use SSL to do the same thing.

Using *TcpClient* with SSL

We'll use the *TcpClient* class to represent our connection to the server and an *SSLStream* class instance to read and write to when the server has been authenticated. To do this we'll modify and add several pieces of code.

Adding the Imports   As with the server service, we need to add the appropriate imports to our client so that we can communicate with the server. Listing 11-24 shows the imports.

Listing 11-24   Client import statements.

```
Imports System.Net
Imports System.Net.Sockets
Imports System.Net.Security
Imports System.Security.Authentication
Imports System.Text
Imports System.Security.Cryptography.X509Certificates
```

When these imports are in place, we are ready to create the rest of the code necessary to use SSL and communicate with the server.

Adding the Server SSL Certificate Validation Callback Method   When the client attempts to create a local *SSLStream* instance, it needs to validate the server's certificate. To do this, we need to create the code shown in Listing 11-25.

Listing 11-25   SSL server certificate validation code.
```
Private Function ValidateServerSSLCertificate( _
          ByVal sslsender As Object, _
          ByVal sslcertificate As X509Certificate, _
          ByVal sslchain As X509Chain, _
          ByVal sslerrors As SslPolicyErrors) As Boolean
    If (sslerrors = Net.Security.SslPolicyErrors.None) Then
        Return True
    End If

    'since it failed to authenticate we need to disconnect
    Return False
End Function
```

Because this method is run under a delegate call, if it fails the client should disconnect from the server and do nothing else, otherwise it risks being connected to the wrong server and transmitting data to an inappropriate listener.

Updating the Client Request Code   We need to update the client to connect using a TcpClient, create an *SSLStream*, and then authenticate the server before sending a request and reading the response. I won't modify the entire client project to do this; instead, I'll modify one of the currently implemented server methods. Recall that you can make three possible requests to the server. I'm going to update the call to request the current time from the server. When this code has been changed, it will also work for all of the other methods, so I don't need to modify them all. Listing 11-26 shows the updated code.

Listing 11-26   Updated client request method to request the remote server time.
```
Private Sub GetTime_Click(ByVal sender As System.Object, ByVal e As System.EventArgs)
              Handles getTime.Click
    Try
        Dim bytes(1024) As Byte
        Dim clientsocket As TcpClient = New TcpClient(Dns.GetHostName(),
              CInt(txtPort.Text))

        Dim clientStream As SslStream = New SslStream( _
              clientsocket.GetStream(), _
              False, _
              New RemoteCertificateValidationCallback(AddressOf
                ValidateServerSSLCertificate), _
              Nothing)

        Try
            clientStream.AuthenticateAsClient(Dns.GetHostName())
```

```
        Catch ex As Exception
            MsgBox(ex.ToString())
            Return
        End Try

        Dim msg As Byte() = _
            Encoding.ASCII.GetBytes("GETDATETIME##<EOF>")

        clientStream.Write(msg)
        Dim bytesRec As Integer = clientStream.Read(bytes, 0, bytes.Length)

        txtTime.Text = Encoding.ASCII.GetString(bytes, 0, bytesRec)

        clientStream.Close()
        clientsocket.Close()
    Catch ex As Exception
    End Try
End Sub
```

The client method starts by creating a TcpClient and connecting to the remote server. Once the connection is established—but before any real communication can occur—the client attempts to authenticate the server. If the authentication is successful, the client sends its request to the server and displays the output of the response. If the authentication fails, the client does not continue the communication process and exits the method, closing the connection attempt to the server.

Note   Make sure that the name you pass into the *AuthenticateAsUser* method matches the name of the remote server and the certificate used—if it does not, the authentication will fail.

You can modify the rest of the client code to use this same methodology if you want to test the rest of the functionality.

Summary

- Security is important in building services with Microsoft Windows and Microsoft Visual Studio 2008. Microsoft provides a large number of documented patterns and best practices that you should follow when developing not only services but also applications in general.

- Whether you require internal communication or external communication, security will always be an issue. You need to make sure that your data is secured in both memory and on the disk and across the network of the Internet.

- Using secured transports and authentication both from a client and server perspective ensures the security of your data. Microsoft Visual Studio provides tools and built-in classes for encryption-level, authentication-level, and transport-level security.

Part IV
Advanced Windows Services Topics

Chapter 12

Scheduling, Configuring, Administering, and Setting Up Windows Services

A service would have little benefit if you had no way to schedule or control the timing of the tasks it needed to perform. In the previous chapter, "Advanced Security Considerations and Communications," the service waited on incoming connections, so scheduling was not a problem. In many cases, services will perform one or more tasks not based on a request but instead based on a polling action—the service waits for something to occur and then reacts. Examples include waiting for a data file or an NT event, reading a Web page, or any other situation that allows the service to poll before firing whatever task it is coded to perform.

What Does Scheduling Mean?

Scheduling a service does not refer to the kind of scheduling you do with the operating system's built-in Task Scheduler. Instead, I'm referring to scheduling a service's polling or administrative functionality. If you're building a service for gathering Web logs from a set of Web servers, or data files from an FTP server, designing the service to monitor the servers nonstop would be impractical. This nonstop monitoring could cause congestion not only on the server you are monitoring, but also on the server that runs your service. Nonstop logging on and off of a remote server is a costly procedure that can make the local system run at a high rate of CPU utilization, causing any other applications that are running to perform poorly. Network administrators might also complain about the constant network chatter. And you could also affect the performance of a remote server being used as a production or business internal server.

Scheduling Options

You don't have many options for scheduling a service to perform its tasks. One solution is to set up a thread to monitor for what you are looking for and then have it kick off the code needed to perform the service's functionality. You can either set up this thread to check for its startup signal and then sleep for a designated time period, or set up a socket to wait for incoming requests.

Another option is to set up a profile for your service. A profile is an integration or configuration data set used to tell the service what to do and when to do it. You can store this information in an XML file, a text file, a back-end or local database server instance, or any storage type you choose. You can administer the data from Control Panel, a custom UI, an XML editor, or again, any other modifiable interface you want to use or create.

Permission Requirements

The most important detail to remember is that however you schedule your service, if you use a datastore or configuration file, the service will need permission for the directory and the file itself. If you use Microsoft SQL Server, you will need to log on to SQL Server or to run the service in the context of a user who has access to query its configuration information.

Determining the Type of Scheduling to Use

There isn't one perfect way to have your service perform its requested actions when you want. This depends on the requirements for the service. If your service isn't looking to react to something, it doesn't really require polling or scheduling. Scheduling is appropriate when you want to perform an action based on another set of factors.

Whether you are considering polling because you are waiting for another system to do something, or you merely want to limit the impact of your service on the local system, you must consider the network or remote systems that it might interact with.

There are other important things to consider each time your service performs its polling or scheduled tasks. Do you want it to remember anything about the previous time? Do you need it to keep a log of each time it runs and the outcome?

Whatever your needs are, your service will either need to be poll-driven, configuration-driven, or event-driven. I have demonstrated both event- and poll-driven services throughout this book.

The Event-Driven Model

An event-driven service is defined by some reaction to a given performed routine or set of routines that the service notices. Whether the service reacts because it was actively looking for the routine—such as looking for a given file using the *FileSystemWatcher* object—or because a connection request comes in over a blocking synchronous socket, the service is not required to poll.

The Poll-Driven Model

The polling model requires that a thread actively monitor something that it will react to when that certain something happens. Monitoring a folder using a thread and then putting that thread to sleep for a given period of time between validation of the files is an example of polling. Although Microsoft provides programming models that support pure event-driven service notifications that the service will react to, being able to poll for something is still important.

Polling when a specific set of actions occurs may be the only way your service can validate when it should perform the preconfigured reactionary routines. Another important thing to note is that if you require simultaneous validation of multiple things before performing your intended routines, you may find yourself mixing the event-driven and poll-driven models. Imagine that you are monitoring for a given file using a *FileSystemWatcher* object. After this file is found, you want to validate that an entry has been placed in a remote data store for that file. You'd use the event-driven model to first trigger your service, but then you would poll the remote data store for more information. If the information isn't there, you could perform any number of actions, including exiting the active thread and waiting for the *FileSystemWatcher* events to fire again.

Administration of Services

Services usually require some sort of configuration to make them do what you have coded them to do, which will vary from service to service. You will seldom see—and you should never create—services that require recoding each time you want to modify something that should have been configurable.

You can configure a service in several ways. You are only limited by being able to expose that administrative capability to external users. Imagine you wrote a service that downloaded files from different sources and placed them in a different location. This type of activity is quite common, especially between the extranet and the intranet.

When writing such a service, you should take into account whether it should be single-threaded and only able to download one file from one source at a time, or multithreaded and able to download one or more files from one or more sources at a time. With either service, you would need to know the following information to make the service perform. Although this is not an exhaustive list, it demonstrates that you should always consider some important information when deciding how to best administer and configure your service.

- Uri of the remote server
- Port to connect on
- File or files to download

- Location to copy files to after downloading
- Logon information

Types of Configuration Data

I always consider two main types of configuration data when I write a service: configuration information about how the service should run, and the configuration data used by the service to perform the tasks it was written to do. Let's take a closer look at the difference between these two types of data.

Service Configuration Data

The difference between service and user configuration data is that the service relies upon its data to determine how it will run, not what it will do. Although this may seem like a fine distinction, a few items, which I'll cover in the next sections, are specific to the service itself.

Number of Active Threads   Imagine that your service can create multiple instances of a particular class and have that class perform some work. Now imagine that the service itself starts each class instance on its own thread. The number of threads that the service is allowed to create would be specific to the service and how it runs, not to how it does the work.

Global Configuration Data   In many cases your service will need to do things such as send e-mail notifications or raise alerts to a central location. Because this information can be user-specific or globally used by the service, you should determine the granularity of the data itself. If appropriate, you should then place the data in the configuration file that is automatically associated to your application.

Location of User Configuration Data   The user-specific data location is another example of service-specific information. It would do no good for the class instances in our previous example to know where the data is if the service can't first retrieve it to even start the class instances.

Storing Service-Specific Configuration Data   When you use the Microsoft .NET Framework, any application that you write has a default location for service-specific data in a file that follows this format: *applicationname*.exe.config. You can store all of your information in this one place, but usually it is better to separate application data from user data.

This file is available directly from your code at run time and design time; you should use it to store information that your service needs to run.

Creating Application Settings

Creating application settings is quite simple in Microsoft Visual Studio 2008. Create a sample project or open a project that you have already created. I have created a sample project called AppConfigSample and configured it to be a console application.

Right-click the project name and choose Properties. In the Properties window, click the Settings tab.

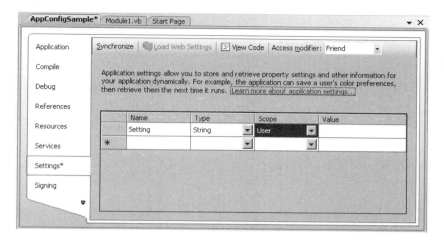

You need to configure the following four pieces of data for each setting:

- **Name**   This setting represents the name used by your application to retrieve the value that you assign to this setting.

- **Type**   This setting represents the type of information that you are storing. You are able to store any type of information that can be represented by a value in the configuration file.

- **Scope**   This setting represents whether this is a user- or application-level setting. User settings are updatable by the user during run time; application-level settings are not modifiable.

- **Value**   This setting represents the data that you want to retrieve while your application is running. This data should represent the internal .NET Framework object type you have associated to the setting so that it can be easily recast into that type when used by your application.

In previous chapters we created connection strings as application settings and used them to access our tutorials data stores that we created in Microsoft SQL Server.

Accessing Application Settings

In my sample application I created a user-level setting called testsetting, of type *string*, and assigned it the value of *teststring*. The following graphic demonstrates what the setting looks like after I add it to my AppConfigSample console application.

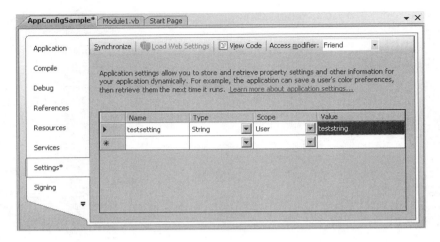

When the application user setting is in place, we can write the code to access the value and use it in our code. Currently the value is not very useful—we're using it for demonstration purposes only.

In my sample application, I use the *Main* method to read the value from the configuration file appconfigsample.exe.config and write it to the console. Listing 12-1 shows this code.

Listing 12-1 Sample user setting access.

```
Module Module1
    Sub Main()
        Console.WriteLine( _
            "The User Setting Value is: " + _
            My.Settings.testsetting + _
            System.DateTime.Now.ToString())
    End Sub
End Module
```

You can see that I use the *My* object to access the Settings instances for this sample application and then access the *testsetting* setting. Any setting that you create will be accessible through this same method. When I run this code I get the following output.

The sample application demonstrates the ability to use application-level settings that can affect both the application and the user. Application settings represent changes to how the application runs, not how it does the tasks at hand, which are usually more user-level settings.

In this case, I used a user scope setting. However, from a service perspective, I do not consider this to be a good configuration model because in this scope, user-level settings are defined for how they affect the appearance or use of that specific user on a specific system, not how a single instance of an application in a central location treats the requirements of each user. Therefore, putting every possible user setting in the application-level configuration file really isn't the best option.

Each time your application runs, it will have access to this file directly. You can update this file while in run-time mode so that in the future you can access any new attributes or settings that you define. Now let's look at the user configuration.

User Configuration Data

Users aren't the only ones that need to connect to services. Services could be automated and not require any user interaction.

When a service is automated with no user interaction, it still may allow users to configure for themselves how it does the work it is programmed to do on their behalf. For instance, if you create a service that downloads files from different locations, each location can be owned by a different user, or each file type that you download can be owned by a different group of users. For each of these users you need a way to configure the service to know how and what to do specifically for them.

User data is information required by a service to perform the same tasks in a different way for a different user. For that reason, user data is used to explain to the service how a particular user expects something to happen. Aside from explaining how things are done, user data explains how that user wants to be notified of specific errors or successes that occur within the service.

Going back to my previous example of a service creating instances of a class that does the work on separate threads, this definition of user data would mean that each class instance needs to receive its particular configuration data so that it can run properly.

From a service perspective, we should use a service-level, application-specific setting to tell us where the configuration data resides. From a storage perspective, we can keep this information anywhere. Let's look at several options.

- **Microsoft SQL Server**   This option is used by larger services to store both user-specific and application-specific configuration data. In many cases an entry or entries in the application-specific configuration file stores the connection settings required to connect to SQL Server and gather the configuration information. When user information is stored here, it is up to the developers to create the tables and stored procedures required to store and retrieve the data.

- **Microsoft Access or FoxPro**   These options are used to create localized data stores that act similarly to Microsoft SQL Server but are much smaller and less scalable.

- **Flat files**   These files are used to store configuration data, but they require developers to create parsing, reading, and writing routines so that information can be properly read. You can use the service-level application log to store the location of this file for later retrieval.

- **XML files**   These files are similar to flat files except that they already have built-in classes in .NET to read from and write to them. The developer still needs to create the schema for the file, but after that, reading and writing are easy. This is the method that I have chosen for this book.

If you look at the configuration files in previous chapters, you will see an example of using XML files to contain your user configuration data. Each time you had the option of creating multiple nodes of the same type, you were representing user configuration data that described how many instances would be created by the service and how they would run.

Advanced Service Administration

The general steps taken by a service are to start, read the application-specific file, load the user configuration data, and then begin performing the tasks it is designed to do. The problem is that in many cases you want to be able to change the behavior of your service to perform more tasks, or change how it performs the current tasks. You might change the way the service performs based on user requests or administrative requests.

Imagine that your service is running and you can configure the number of threads it can create or the number of users who connect at the same time. Imagine that you're monitoring your service and notice that although the service is running fine, users are complaining about performance. When users connect, or their specific task begins, things run just fine, but it's taking a while for the service to start performing its task or to get connected.

In this case it might be necessary to reconfigure the service to allow for more threads, more user connections, or new work loads because of new user configuration requests. Restarting the service each time you make a change can become an administrative burden. Not only does this require administrative interaction each time a user requests a change, but it also causes an impact to every other user when the service is stopped.

Dynamic Service Configuration

Let's look at how to make your service dynamically configurable. Three levels of configuration change are possible:

- **Service**   This configuration change reflects, for example, how many threads or connections the service allows at one time. Increasing the number of threads or connections might be easy to code, but you need to take into account some maximum number so that your service doesn't become overloaded.

- **User**   User preferences include pointing to a new file location or new storage location for an existing and already running process. Allowing users to change preferences on the fly requires you to have a way to map the user change request to an already existing class instance and data set. This means you must have a way to uniquely identify users and user configurations.

- **New**   This includes user configuration data where new threads, connections, and processing have to take place. New user configurations are usually the easiest because they only require you to validate that the new configuration won't overload your system in advance. The steps to launch new configuration data should be nearly identical to the steps required to launch data when it was first read as the service started. Therefore it requires only small coding changes.

Each one of these changes can have a different effect on your system, and you have to take that into account when deciding on which changes to make dynamic.

Dynamic File Configurations   If you use files to do your configurations, you need a way to know when the file has been updated so that you can reflect those changes in your service. The great thing is that Microsoft Visual Studio 2008 provides this capability in the *FileSystem-Watcher* class.

The *FileSystemWatcher* class allows us to monitor for new files or changes to existing files. You can use an instance of this class to monitor when your configuration file changes and then reload the file and make the changes where appropriate.

> **Caution**   Be careful when monitoring for new or changed files. The system can report that a file has been created or changed before the locks from the system or modifying application have been released. You will need to take this into account when monitoring for a change.

You have to be able to identify a change and associate it to an already existing instance. This means you need to have code that will identify, shut down, clean up, and restart any instances that are affected by the change. Making sure that the code cleanly shuts down the processing that is already occurring for a given user is important so that you can avoid losing important data or transactions.

If you want to allow for dynamic configuration, be sure to take the following precautions:

- Make sure that all user data is uniquely identifiable—at least at the top root of the information required to run the user request. If you use a name property, make sure that it is unique and enforced. Because you are using a flat file or XML files, you may need to validate the configuration file first by looping through the names. For any duplicates found, throw an error and then ignore that request.

- Make sure that if you are using multiple configuration files and are monitoring for new or updated files, you take into account that the file may still be locked even though you received the event. I recommend making multiple attempts (with some delay between attempts) to access and read the file. If you are still unable to read the file after a specified amount of time and number of tries, throw a final error and then decide to shut down or send out an alert to administrators.

Microsoft Database Dynamic Configuration   Whether you are using Microsoft Access, FoxPro, or SQL Server, you can monitor the data store for any changes. Depending on the data store, you might even be able to create events—such as in Microsoft SQL 2005 stored procedures—that will notify your service when a change occurs.

Your service can use two primary types of monitoring events to create your required reactionary events: data store and code-based monitoring.

- **Data Store**   Data store events are one way to acknowledge changes in the underlying data. There may be requirements for complicated business logic to make sure that the data is completely written or configured properly before letting the service know it is ready to be updated. Stored procedures, Microsoft SQL Server Notification Services, Microsoft SQL Agent, and triggers are some ways to know within the data store itself that a change has occurred. How you get that change to the service depends on the service.

- **Code-based**   For code-based monitoring of the data store, you need a thread or set of threads within the service to monitor for any changes in the data store from the time you load the data to the time it changes. In many cases you can use state columns on the data, which would reflect whether that data is in use and its current state. Imagine that a user disables her data configuration. The state of the use of the data would be inactive even though the data itself could be up to date. Monitoring for activated data sets with states of *new* or *updated* would allow you to properly read configuration data on the fly.

Administrative UI

Previously service developers created a console application that you ran from the control panel to update or modify services. Now Microsoft gives you ways to create Microsoft Management Console (MMC) snap-ins that can provide access to your configuration data.

Whether you are using a data store or a flat file, your administration would be much easier if you created an administrative UI instead of trying to always modify the files in Notepad or directly in the tables using stored procedures that you create. Although an administrative UI is not necessary, it is something you should consider when you develop your service.

Administrative UIs should allow users to view the status of their service and make changes or add new configuration options. This ties in directly with the ability to make dynamic content changes; however, the UI itself is independent from the code that looks for changes, because it merely makes those changes.

If you are using a data store, you may want to consider using a Web-based solution for making changes to your configuration data so that it is more flexible and requires less maintenance when it comes to software updates. Windows-based clients require you to update everyone using the application each time it is changed.

Installing Services

Although you can easily create batch files to install a service, at times you might want to carry out more sophisticated actions than a batch file allows.

Microsoft Visual Studio 2008 provides you with the ability to create a setup project by either using the setup project template or by using the setup project wizard. I'll use the code from Chapter 1, "Writing Your First Service in Visual Basic 2008," to demonstrate how to create a setup project for a service, build it, and then deploy the service to the local computer.

Adding the Setup Project

The first thing we need to do is create the setup project. Open your tutorials Chapter 1 solution. Right-click the solution, choose Add, and then select New Project. From the Project Template dialog box, expand Other Project Types, select Setup And Deployment, and then select Setup Project.

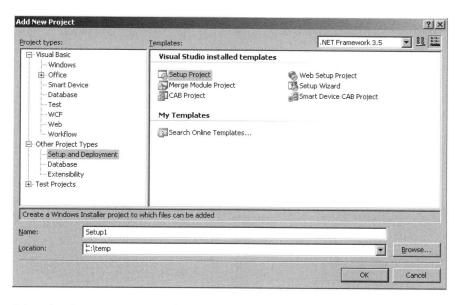

Select the Setup Project, not the Setup Wizard. I have left my setup project named setup1. After we add the setup project to the solution, we need to configure it.

Add the Project Output

Right-click the setup1 project, select Add, select Project Output, and then select Primary Output. Click OK. This will add the exe and dependencies of your service.

> **Note**   If you are in the debug configuration, the output will be from the debug folder; if you are in the release, it will be from the release folder.

Now we need to create a custom action that will install the service.

Creating Custom Actions

Custom actions define how and what a setup program does. For our project, we need to install the service and the debug symbols. Your service may have other things to include, such as resource files, bitmaps, or configuration files.

Creating a Service Custom Action   First, we want to create the output that will build and install the service. Right-click the setup1 project again, and this time choose View and then choose Custom Actions. Click OK. Right-click Custom Actions. From the pop-up menu, select Add Custom Action. Select Application Folder and then click OK. Select Primary Output From Tutorials (Active) and click OK.

Creating a Debug Symbol Custom Action   Next, we want to add debug symbols. Right-click the setup1 project, select Add, and then select Project Output. Select Debug Symbols and click OK. Now the service and the debug symbols are ready to be installed.

Adding a Configuration File

Although Chapter 1 didn't have any configuration files, you should understand how to add them to your setup project in case you need them.

Right-click the setup1 project again, choose Add, and then choose File. Browse to where your configurations file is, select it, and click OK. You will notice that the file is now added to your project. Right-click the file and choose Properties, or double-click to open the file for editing. In the Properties window, you can change the output target name, location, and several other important attributes of the file when it is installed on the user or server computer.

Testing the Setup Project

To test the project, right-click the setup1 project and choose Build. By default, the setup project will not build each time you build the solution.

After you build the setup program, open Windows Explorer and browse to the generated setup1.msi file, right-click it, and select Install from the pop-up menu. The service will now be installed. You can verify installation by going to the Services window and verifying that you see the service listed. If you want to uninstall the service, you can use Add/Remove Programs or go back to your msi package, right-click it, and select Uninstall.

Note   If you need custom security settings or other things included with your project, review the MSDN documentation for creating setup projects.

Summary

- Determine whether you need to schedule the actions of your service, either through timing or monitored reactions.

- Service developers should be careful not to use too many resources on the server running the service by constantly running the service or monitoring it. If a service polls too often, it can cause heavy server resource usage, especially on the CPU.

- You have several choices for implementing how and when a service acts. In many cases, using multiple threads, events, or waits can help alleviate both CPU usage and wasted effort on the server running the service.

- There is no one way to use a data store to send or receive configuration data. Microsoft provides you with flexibility in the way you design and deploy your solutions and your configuration data. Remember that the decision to use dynamic configurations should be based on requirements and the overall number of changes that will be carried out. If your service change volume is very low and your service use is very low, simply scheduling a time to make the update and restart the service might be a better option than writing all the code required to make a useful, dynamically configurable service.

- Administrative UIs can be important to the administration of your service if the service requires many or frequent changes. The more complex your data configuration is, the more sensible it is to take the time to write a reusable administrative UI, whether it is a Windows client–based application or a Web-based UI.

- Creating setup projects for your service is fast and easy with Visual Studio 2008, and can be useful in making your service easy to administer and maintain on the servers that you need it installed on. Microsoft Visual Studio 2008 provides templates and wizards to make creating a setup project easy.

Chapter 13

Debugging and Troubleshooting Windows Services

When you write a Windows service, you'll want to be able to monitor that service and then, when necessary, debug that service. Microsoft makes it very easy to use the Microsoft Windows Debugging Tools or the Microsoft Visual Studio 2008 IDE to do just that. I'll demonstrate how to debug a Windows service in this chapter.

Debugging Services

Debugging Windows services is a little more difficult than debugging a standard application, because you cannot run a service directly from the debugger as you would a standard application. With a service, you have a couple of options, which I'll describe in the next sections.

Using the Visual Studio IDE

You can open the source code for the service and place breakpoints where required, start the service, and then attach to the service with Visual Studio 2008. To do this, follow these steps:

1. Make sure the service is running.

2. Open Visual Studio 2008.

3. Open the source files. (You can do this by opening the project.)

4. Select Tools from the Visual Studio 2008 menu bar.

5. Select Attach To Process.

6. Under Process, select the name of the service. In the Type column you will see it listed as Managedx86.

7. Select Attach.

When you are attached to the process, you can open any additional source files. You can then add breakpoints and step through the code as needed.

Writing Your Service as a Console Application

Another debugging option is to write all your code as a standard console application. Test and debug your application for major issues, such as memory leaks and application crashes. When you have completed debugging your code, you can create a service and add your code to the service application with minor changes.

> **Note** Be sure that any code you add to the service you also add to the stand-alone application so that you can debug it first.

However, this process can be tedious and it limits greatly the ability to accurately debug your service as it will be running in production. However, for functional or unit testing this can work very well.

Troubleshooting and Monitoring Services

A number of built-in and readily obtainable troubleshooting and monitoring utilities are available within Microsoft operating systems and the Visual Studio development environment to help determine whether your service is running as expected.

Task Manager

Task Manager, also known as System Monitor on some versions of Microsoft operating systems, is one of the best, most readily available, and yet underused utilities for monitoring and troubleshooting. Task Manager allows you to see all the running processes depending on your security privileges, and most of the resources currently being used. Task Manager is a quick and easy tool to view processor usage, memory usage (both virtual and physical), handles, threads, and much more. If you right-click on the Windows Toolbar of Windows 2000, Windows XP, or Windows Server 2003, you can select Task Manager from the pop-up menu and it will bring up the following window.

Using Task Manager will not only help troubleshoot your service, but also allow you to monitor a service to see how it performs. Suppose you write a service that requires a file in a specific directory, or a connection from an end user. You can start Task Manager, select your service, and then ask the service to perform the actions required. Even if the CPU, memory, handles, and threads all appear fine when the work is done, you may not like the amount of CPU or memory used while the work is being done. You may be able to find ways to lower the overall CPU usage. Imagine having 10 or more applications that use almost no CPU most of the time—but regularly spike to 50 or 60 percent of the total CPU availability. If they all did this at the same time, your system could grind to a halt.

Viewing Statistics in Task Manager

From the view in the following graphic, you can see the CPU and memory usage of the image name or process that is using those resources. If you select Options, you can select even more columns, such as handles and threads. Looking at these columns and statistical data provided by Task Manager is a very good idea when monitoring, troubleshooting, and debugging your services.

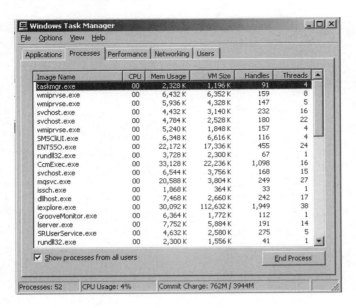

Understanding Task Manager Columns Usage

Reviewing the available columns in Task Manager can offer you a better view of how useful Task Manager can be for monitoring or troubleshooting your service.

CPU Utilization   Imagine that you have a service named TestServer. You are using this service's functionality and watching Task Manager. Imagine that the system starts to perform poorly or sluggishly. You look in Task Manager to see why. Under the CPU column, you notice that your service is running extremely high, between 50 and 100 percent. It continues to do so even after it should have finished the work it was meant to do. This tells you that, most likely, your code has an issue and you need to debug it. In this case, you need to attach a debugger to the service and step through your source code to find the reason behind the high CPU utilization.

Memory Utilization   In another example, your service might be running in the background, and you try to use some other applications on your server or workstation. You begin to receive Low Virtual Memory warnings or Out Of Memory errors. Look again in Task Manager. You can see that either Memory Usage or Virtual Memory is extremely high. And not only is it high, but it also continues to grow. You notice that after the service's work is completed, memory appears to stop increasing; however, it is also not going back down. The most likely explanation is that the service is not releasing the memory allocated to perform the work inside the service. You could again attach a debugger and walk through the code, using Task Manager to see when any memory spikes occur. For applications where you cannot attach a debugger directly, other utilities can also monitor for memory leaks. You can find them in the Microsoft Debugging Tools for Windows Toolkit at *http://www.microsoft.com*. Depending on the utility you decide to use, avoiding inaccurate debugging results can require an extensive knowledge of how memory allocation and caching works.

Handles   In another example, suppose you notice that your system is performing oddly, and when you look in Task Manager you see that Memory Usage and Virtual Memory are not extremely high, and neither is CPU. You can tell something is wrong—you are receiving Out Of Memory errors on your service and you do not know why. Using Task Manager, you see that you have an ever-growing number of handles and possibly even threads. Handles and threads can slowly eat away precious resources, and even though the amount of physical RAM may be large in your system, some types of memory—such as the desktop heap—can be depleted long before your physical RAM is used up.

Performance Monitor

Performance Monitor, or *Perfmon*, is another tool that has been included for a long time on most Windows platforms. Applications that are written for the Windows operating systems support *performance counters*, which are objects that represent information about an application. For example, let's say you developed an application that could open a TCP socket connection to a remote server or accept incoming socket connections. You want to know information such as current connections, total connections, failed connections, errors, and so on. You can code counters into your application and then provide that information through performance counters.

Performance Counter Consumers

Microsoft provides application programming interfaces (APIs) that you can use to expose performance counters to a *consumer*. Consumers are applications that can query an application for its performance counters and the current values of those performance counters. Performance Monitor is an advanced performance counter consumer that can monitor every application and every counter at the same time. Doing so, however, can cause resource issues or (depending on the quality of the code written to expose the counters) an issue with the application itself. Microsoft provides some built-in counters that are exposed for every application, which is very useful for troubleshooting and debugging applications.

Using Perfmon as a Performance Counter Consumer

As with Task Manager (which itself is a performance counter consumer), Perfmon is able to consume every counter that an application exposes. The other great thing that Perfmon can do is create a historical log that allows you to run tests—either automated or manual—against your application or service and record the results for later viewing. You can then use these results to determine issues such as leaks of memory handles and threads, as well as other possible errors.

Standard System Exposed Performance Counters

Standard exposed counters exist in Perfmon under the Process object. If, for example, you had 10 counters and 10 different processes, you would have 10 × 10 counters. Each process under the Process object is considered an instance because it is an instance of the set of 10 counters. Each process has its own 10 counters and they are not shared between processes.

Viewing Perfmon

Let's review Perfmon and its functionality. You can start Perfmon by clicking Start, clicking Run, typing **Perfmon**, and then pressing Enter.

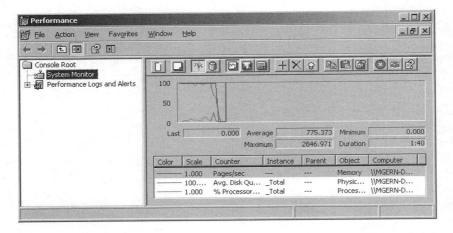

The preceding graphic shows an example of System Monitor, also known as Perfmon or Performance Monitor. It displays a graphical view of the counters that you have selected. For example, let's say you create a service called serviceexample.exe. You could run Perfmon, select the plus sign (+), and then select the Process object. Under the Process object, you will see the available counters on the left and the instances on the right. You select the process Foo.exe and then the counters to monitor, such as Threads, Private Bytes, Virtual Memory, or Handles. Viewing performance counters in System Monitor is a live viewing. Like Task Manager, you can run tests and view the results on the fly.

With many issues that require troubleshooting, or applications that need to be either monitored or debugged, symptoms, or the issue itself, may be random and cannot be easily reproduced. Perfmon allows you to create a Perfmon Counter Log that can be used to record data about a particular application's system-generated Process counters and custom internal application counters. Such logs can be crucial in discovering memory or handle leaks, high CPU spikes, and more.

Examples of Debugging and Monitoring Your Service

When monitoring your application, you need to understand what issues to look for and how to look for them. The following examples describe issues that many applications face, including what to look for and how to debug them.

In Listing 13-1, I have provided sample code from a Windows application I wrote to demonstrate using Task Manager and Visual Studio 2008 to create, debug, and validate both memory- and CPU-related performance and application issues.

Listing 13-1   Windows application CPU and memory sample code for debugging demonstration.

```
Imports System.Threading
Imports System.Net.Sockets

Public Class MemoryAndCPU
    Private m_CPUThread As Thread = Nothing
    Private m_ThreadsThread As Thread = Nothing
    Private m_MemThread As Thread = Nothing

    Private Sub Button1_Click(ByVal sender As System.Object,
ByVal e As System.EventArgs) Handles Button1.Click
        Try
            'this will demonstrate high CPU
            If Not m_HandlesThread Is Nothing Then
                m_HandlesThread.Abort()
                m_HandlesThread = Nothing
            End If

            If Not m_ThreadsThread Is Nothing Then
                m_ThreadsThread.Abort()
                m_ThreadsThread = Nothing
            End If

            If Not m_MemThread Is Nothing Then
                m_MemThread.Abort()
                m_MemThread = Nothing
            End If

            If m_CPUThread Is Nothing Then
                m_CPUThread = New Thread(AddressOf CPUThread)
                m_CPUThread.Name = "CPU Thread"
                m_CPUThread.Priority = ThreadPriority.Normal
                m_CPUThread.Start()
            Else
                m_CPUThread.Abort()
                m_CPUThread = Nothing
            End If
        Catch ex As Exception
        End Try
    End Sub

    Private Sub CPUThread()
        Try
```

```
            Do
                Dim iLoop As Integer

                For iLoop = 1 To 32000
                    Dim tmpStr As String

                    tmpStr = "My Test " + iLoop.ToString
                    Application.DoEvents()
                Next
            Loop
        Catch ex As Exception
        End Try
    End Sub

    Private Sub Button2_Click(ByVal sender As System.Object,
ByVal e As System.EventArgs) Handles Button2.Click
        Try
            If Not m_HandlesThread Is Nothing Then
                m_HandlesThread.Abort()
                m_HandlesThread = Nothing
            End If

            If Not m_ThreadsThread Is Nothing Then
                m_ThreadsThread.Abort()
                m_ThreadsThread = Nothing
            End If

            If Not m_CPUThread Is Nothing Then
                m_CPUThread.Abort()
                m_CPUThread = Nothing
            End If

            If m_MemThread Is Nothing Then
                m_MemThread = New Thread(AddressOf CPUThread)
                m_MemThread.Name = "Memory Thread"
                m_MemThread.Priority = ThreadPriority.Normal
                m_MemThread.Start()
            Else
                m_MemThread.Abort()
                m_MemThread = Nothing
            End If
        Catch ex As Exception
        End Try
    End Sub

    Private Sub MemThread()
        Try
            Do
                Application.DoEvents()
            Loop
        Catch ex As Exception
        End Try
    End Sub
```

```vb
    Private Sub Button3_Click(ByVal sender As System.Object,
ByVal e As System.EventArgs) Handles Button3.Click
        Try
            If Not m_MemThread Is Nothing Then
                m_MemThread.Abort()
                m_MemThread = Nothing
            End If

            If Not m_ThreadsThread Is Nothing Then
                m_ThreadsThread.Abort()
                m_ThreadsThread = Nothing
            End If

            If Not m_CPUThread Is Nothing Then
                m_CPUThread.Abort()
                m_CPUThread = Nothing
            End If

            If m_HandlesThread Is Nothing Then
                m_HandlesThread = New Thread(AddressOf CPUThread)
                m_HandlesThread.Name = "Handles Thread"
                m_HandlesThread.Priority = ThreadPriority.Normal
                m_HandlesThread.Start()
            Else
                m_HandlesThread.Abort()
                m_HandlesThread = Nothing
            End If
        Catch ex As Exception
        End Try
    End Sub
End Class
```

High CPU

Many application developers do not take into account what effect their application can have on the server that will run their application. In some cases this information can't be known in advance. Knowledge, experience with the language and the technologies you are using or integrating with, as well as the operating system you will be running on, can all be limited. Although during development, high CPU usage can be overlooked before releasing your code, you should always test for such an issue. Even with testing, however, many issues that can cause this situation can be overlooked: Variations in hardware, clustering, and differences in memory and Microsoft operating systems can all have an effect on CPU utilization. For this example I have created an application that will simulate this situation and how you would go about discovering it.

Run the test application MemoryAndCPU.exe, available on the companion Web site, and then open Task Manager. You'll see the following situation.

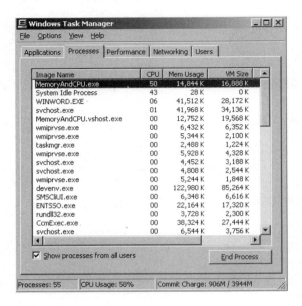

The MemoryAndCPU process is using 50 percent of the system CPU cycles on a dual-core server. On a single-processor server, the CPU processing time is closer to 100 percent. This could cause any server to perform poorly. We need to be able to determine why this is happening, so we need to run the application and then attach to it from the Visual Studio IDE.

Debugging the High CPU Problem

We see that the MemoryAndCPU.vshost.exe is using almost 100 percent of the system CPU cycles. Let's walk through the steps to determine what is going on in our application.

1. Open Visual Studio 2008, and then open the project for your application. In this case, it is MemoryAndCPU application.

2. Launch the MemoryAndCPU application.

3. Select Tools from the Microsoft Visual Studio IDE Menu.

4. Select Attach To Process.

5. Select the Process you want to debug. (In this case, MemoryAndCPU.)

When you are attached to the application, you can place breakpoints or view where the application is, assuming the source code matches the application we attached to. To find out exactly why the application is using 99 percent of CPU usage, follow these steps:

1. From the Microsoft Visual Studio 2008 IDE Menu, select Debug, and then select Break All.

2. From the Menu, select Debug, then select Windows, and then select Threads.

Viewing the Current Threads   Now you can see all the threads that are running under the debugger and application. In my case I named the worker threads that I created to recreate this situation. Looking at my thread window I see the following list of running threads.

Threads				
ID	Name	Location	Priority	Suspend
268				0
1512	<No Name>		Highest	0
484	<No Name>		Normal	0
2476	<No Name>		Normal	0
3096				0
3020	<No Name>		Normal	0
3184	<No Name>		Normal	0
780	.NET SystemEvents		Normal	0
3716	<No Name>		Normal	0
1164	CPU Thread	MemoryAndCPU.MemoryAndCPU.CPUThread	Normal	0

In the threads window, you can see the Name column, with a thread named CPU Thread. You can see it is running in normal priority and is currently in suspended mode. This by itself doesn't tell us much. It tells us which threads are running, but not what is going on with those threads. To find this information, double-click the CPU Thread line, or in your case your currently running thread, depending on whether you are using my example application or your own.

Viewing the Selected Threads Active Source Code   After double-clicking the thread, you will jump to the line of code that is being executed if the source code matches the application or service. When I do this I see the following code.

```
MemoryAndCPU                                    CPUThread
      Private Sub CPUThread()
          Try
              Do
                  Dim iLoop As Integer

                  For iLoop = 1 To 32000
                      Dim tmpStr As String

                      tmpStr = "My Test " + iLoop.ToString
                      Application.DoEvents()
                  Next
              Loop
          Catch ex As Exception
          End Try
      End Sub
```

You can see that the *Application.DoEvents()* is the currently highlighted line. More importantly, you can now step through the code to see what is going on. Quickly looking at this, I hope you can easily see the problem.

What I have done is created a loop in a loop that does absolutely nothing and never exits. It merely allocates memory, concatenating strings 32,000 times, then releases a small amount of time using *DoEvents*, which forces the thread to allow the system to process other commands, but only for a split second. After that, it starts the loop all over again. This constant looping forces the application to do nonstop work and uses up the entire scope of CPU cycles on the server. Although this may seem like an extreme example, I have personally seen this repeatedly in production environments.

You can debug issues, such as handle leaks and memory leaks, similarly. Microsoft provides many tools for debugging CPU, memory, handle, and many other resource issues for free in the Microsoft Debugging Tools for Windows, available in both x86 and 64-bit versions. Understanding how to use them can take time, but much information can be found about them on the Microsoft Web site and other locations on the Internet.

Summary

- Microsoft provides built-in utilities and diagnostic applications to help monitor, troubleshoot, and debug errant running applications or services.

- Task Manager and Perfmon (System Monitor) are extremely important in monitoring and troubleshooting applications that may have memory, CPU, or other resource-related issues.

- Microsoft Debugging Tools and Microsoft Visual Studio provide extensive, real-time debugging utilities and processes for debugging your application or service. Support for these tools can be found at *http://www.microsoft.com*, *http://support.microsoft.com*, and *http://msdn.microsoft.com*.

- Debugging applications or services at a low level requires practice and understanding of the technologies and utilities used for debugging.

Chapter 14
Adding Performance Counters

Performance counters are a way for services to provide information about their internal usage and statistics. Performance counters represent unlimited possibilities for developers and debuggers to coordinate issue resolution and issue detection. Using built-in system counters that are exposed by the operating system and custom counters that are exposed by a developer, we can use the resulting information to determine how well our service is working, how many customers we've had, and if and when we need to buy bigger and better hardware.

Types of Performance Counters

Performance counters can be both built in to the operating system and application-defined. Both types play an important role in determining the status of a service and the system itself. In many cases applications do not expose custom performance counters at all, and simply rely on the system to expose the standard set of counters. This works for many applications because their tasks do not require you to know the internal specifics or metrics. We are going to look at these different counter types and learn how to add them to a service.

Operating System-Exposed Counters

As I explained in Chapter 13, "Debugging and Troubleshooting Windows Services," built-in process counters are common to all applications that run on Microsoft Windows operating systems. They are not exposed by an application. Instead, the operating system gathers information that is then made available to the end user as performance counters.

The Process Category

The system-exposed counters are listed under several different objects. The primary set of counters exists for each application under the Process category. Let's take a look at a list of some of the counters available to us under the Process category. Keep in mind that this is not a comprehensive list.

Threads   The Threads counter represents the number of currently allocated threads in the selected process. The operating system keeps track of the number of actively created threads for each process.

Handles   The Handles counter represents the number of currently allocated handles in the selected process.

Private Bytes   The Private Bytes counter represents the amount of allocated physical memory for a given process. This counter is important when you are trying to debug or monitor for memory leaks in your service.

Virtual Memory   The Virtual Memory counter represents the amount of allocated virtual disk memory that is in use for your application. Virtual Memory is used when you do not have enough physical RAM for the system to allocate for your service or application. You can also use virtual memory to detect memory or other resource leaks.

CPU Usage   Central Processing Unit (CPU) usage is not actually a counter—it's a term used to describe how the application or service is affecting the overall CPU. Several different types of processor counters are available to help determine how much user time versus kernel time the process is using.

Elapsed Time   The Elapsed Time counter represents the amount of time an application has been running in memory since it started.

ID Process   The ID Process counter represents the PID that is assigned to each process when it is running in memory. As in Task Manager, you will see this as a unique number for each application and process that is running.

Administrators and developers can use many other counters—representing memory, disk, and CPU values—to monitor and debug their applications. The preceding list represents the primary counters used when debugging most applications. None of these counters requires any code from the developer and will be present on any Microsoft Windows operating system.

Application-Specific Counters

Microsoft operating systems and Microsoft developer products both expose and provide ways of creating custom counters specific to your application. These counters belong to your application (rather than the operating system) and require you to create the categories, counters, and instances, as well as to specify the values of those counters so that they can be exposed to consumers such as Perfmon.

Counters are coded into your application and then updated by your application. The values can then be monitored by administrators. Because counters are also a great way to gauge the scalability of your application, it is important that they accurately reflect the state of your application. Imagine trying to determine how many connections your application receives in a day, or at once, but the counters that you expose are improperly coded and are off by

50 percent or more. If the counters are inaccurate, they could be damaging to your application because they would provide improper metrics, and it will not be easy to determine the hardware requirements of your service.

Adding Counters to your Service

When you create counters, you have to decide exactly what information you want to expose. Because performance counters are merely numeric representations of internal metrics, you should expose whatever you think is important for an end user to know.

Creating Your Counters

After you define the information that you want to expose, you need to use that information to create a counter category and the appropriate counter objects you want to expose to the consumers.

In Perfmon, the category represents the Performance Object, which is the master object for all the exposed counters that exist within that category. Let's take a look at the system-exposed Processor category.

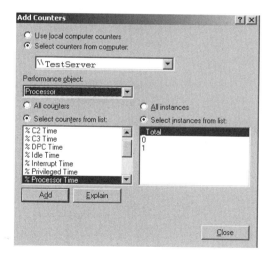

The category is called Processor. On the left are several available counters. On the right are the instances available for those counters. For each instance you will have a different set of values for the counters.

The *PerformanceCounterCategory* Class

To create our counters, we need to use the *PerformanceCounterCategory* class. This class will allow us to check whether our category already exists before we try to create it again. You should always ensure that your category exists before you attempt to create any counters. If you don't, you'll get an exception each time you try to access or create the counters associated with that category.

There are several different ways to use the *Create* method of the *PerformanceCounterCategory* class. You can create a single counter or a group of counters at once. In most cases you probably won't just have a single counter (although it happens), so I will demonstrate how to add multiple counters at the same time.

We are going to create a category called Sample PerfCounters and associate two counters with it. Then we will write the code to validate these counters and change their values. Finally, we will use Perfmon as the consumer to read these values.

Defining the Counters   I am going to define two counters and then associate them with our Sample PerfCounters. To define a counter, we use the *CounterCreationData* class. This class has three important properties:

- CounterName
- CounterHelp
- CounterType

CounterName represents the value that will be displayed on the left side of Perfmon when the category is selected. *CounterHelp* represents the help string that is displayed at the bottom of the Perfmon UI when the counter is selected. *CounterType* represents the numerical type that the data represents.

I'll create two counters: Loop Count and Counter Divided By 4. These counters do not really have any particular value and are only intended for demonstration purposes. Let's review the code shown in Listing 14-1 to define them.

Listing 14-1   Sample counter creation code.

```
Dim CounterOne As New CounterCreationData
Dim CounterTwo As New CounterCreationData

CounterOne.CounterHelp = "Number of Loops"
CounterOne.CounterName = "Loop Count"
CounterOne.CounterType = PerformanceCounterType.NumberOfItems64

CounterTwo.CounterHelp = "Number of Ticks / 4"
CounterTwo.CounterName = "Counter Divided by 4"
CounterTwo.CounterType = PerformanceCounterType.NumberOfItems64
```

For each counter, I have defined the three required properties of the *CounterCreationData* class. For *CounterType*, I have used a 64-bit integer to represent the data that I am storing. Next, we need to define the performance data counter collection used to create our counters.

Creating the *CounterCreationDataCollection* Class   We'll create a group of counters at the same time. To do this we need to define a *CounterCreationDataCollection* class that we'll use in the *PerformanceCounterCategory Create* method to instantiate our new counters. Because this is a collection, we need to add our counters to the collection. Let's review how to do this by looking at Listing 14-2.

Listing 14-2   Creating our performance counter data collection.

```
Dim pCounterCollection As New CounterCreationDataCollection
pCounterCollection.Add(CounterOne)
pCounterCollection.Add(CounterTwo)
```

As with any .NET collection, we use the *Add* method to add an instance of the counter to the collection. In our case we are adding two counters: CounterOne and CounterTwo. Then we are ready to create our performance counters.

Creating Counters with the *PerformanceCounterCategory* Class

As I mentioned, always ensure that you are really creating a new category before attempting to call *PerformanceCounterCategory.Create*; otherwise, you'll get an exception. Because we know the name of our category, let's review how to determine whether it already exists, as shown in Listing 14-3. If it does not exist, we want to create it and then initialize our counters.

Listing 14-3   Validating category existence.

```
If Not (PerformanceCounterCategory.Exists("Sample PerfCounters")) Then
    PerformanceCounterCategory.Create( _
                     "Sample PerfCounters", _
                     "Demo Counters from VB Service", _
                     PerformanceCounterCategoryType.SingleInstance, _
                     pCounterCollection _
                     )
End If
```

The *Create* method of *PerformanceCounterCategory* has many different overloads. In this case we are passing in the name of the category, the help message for the category, the instance type of the category, and the data collection of counters we created.

> **Note**   *PerformanceCounterCategoryType* tells the system how many separate instances of your counters it expects to expose. For example, if you have multiple processes in your service, you may expose multiple instances of your counters.

Multi-Instance Counters vs. Single Instance Counters

Performance counter categories can have two different types of counters—multi-instance and single instance. A multi-instance counter is used for category that covers multiple processes at the same time, while single instance counters are intended for services, applications, or processes.

If you look at the available system categories, you will see Process. The Process category uses multi-instance counters because all of the counters available to the Process category have their own value for each process running on the system. Take a look at the Thread Count counter under the Process category. If you were to select a given Process, the Thread Count value would be different for each. The operating system creates a separate instance of the Thread Count counter for each process. For a single instance counter you would only see one process associated to that counter or category.

> **Note**   System process counters also provide a Total counter that represents a total of all the instances of that given counter added together. If you use multi-instance counters, it is a good idea to also support this functionality.

It is important to validate whether the category already exists. You should check whether the category exists each time your service runs and create it if necessary. Now let's look at how we use the counters we just created.

Implementing Our Counters in Code

Although we have created the category and we have created the code to create the counters, we haven't yet created any code that will implement and use the counters in our code. If we don't do this, the counters will be useless to anyone who wants to view them. Let's review how to implement counters and expose their values to the consumers.

Creating Instances of Counters

We need to create an instance of each counter in the service so that we can modify the values of those counters as the service runs. To create instances of the counters, we use the *PerformanceCounter* class. Before we can create a usable instance of a counter, we have to know the counter name and the instance we wish to read or write to. In the case of a single instance category, the instance name is ignored.

Because we have two counters in our sample category, we need to create two counter instances. Let's review how to create the instances, shown in Listing 14-4.

Listing 14-4   Performance counter instance creation.

```
Dim LoopCounter As PerformanceCounter

Try
  LoopCounter = New PerformanceCounter("Sample PerfCounters", "Loop Count",
                                        "", False)
  LoopCounter.RawValue = 0
Catch ex As Exception
  LoopCounter = Nothing
End Try
```

First we define a PerformanceCounter instance, and then we attempt to create that instance. The *PerformanceCounter* class itself also has several overloads to choose from. We'll pass in the category name, the counter name, the instance name (which in our case is an empty string because we have a single instance), and then we set the read-only flag to false. Because other applications can create instances of our counters for read and write purposes, we want to make sure that we can modify the values. It is possible for another application to consume your counters directly. For those others who are using your counters in their own customer consumer applications, they should open the counters for read-only.

> **Note**   If you use a multi-instance counter, not only do you need to specify the process instance for this counter, but you also need a separate counter for that category.

Just after the counter creation, we set the RawValue equal to 0. The RawValue represents the value of the counter at its lowest level and is used to directly access and modify the counter value. You should only use the RawValue to set the initial value of the counter when you create the category itself for the first time. If you set the RawValue to 0 every time you create an instance of that counter, you will lose all of its accumulated values.

Updating Counter Values

After you've created a category and its counters, instantiated instances of those counters in your code, and set the initial value, you need to update their value appropriately.

You should only use the RawValue to initially set the counter value. The RawValue property provides the fastest access to the data but provides no thread access protection.

The *PerformanceCounter* class provides two methods for incrementing and decrementing the value of your counter.

Incrementing the Counter

To increment the value of the counter, you can either use the *Increment* or the *IncrementBy* methods of the *PerformanceCounter* class. Both methods are thread-safe, which gives us the ability to update the value of our counter. The *Increment* method simply updates the value of our counter by one, whereas *IncrementBy* takes a 64-bit integer as an argument and increments the counter with that value

With both methods, we are safe to update the counter on multiple threads and although we do have a performance hit, we are guaranteed to be thread-safe. In my case, I use *IncrementBy* because I want to be able to demonstrate the value changing dynamically. Let's review the code, shown in Listing 14-5.

Listing 14-5   Incrementing the counter value.

```
Do
    Try
        If Not LoopCounter Is Nothing Then
            LoopCounter.IncrementBy(INCREMENT_VALUE)
        End If
    Catch ex As Exception
```

```
    End Try

    Thread.Sleep(THREAD_SLEEP)
Loop
```

I have defined an INCREMENT_VALUE constant so that I can easily change the value by which the counter is updated. I pull this information from my configuration file so that every time I stop and restart the service the value can change, allowing me to be sure that it is updating as expected. Now let's look at how we decrement our counter.

Decrementing the Counter

Unlike the *IncrementBy* method, which allows you to increase the value of your counter by any value, there is no *DecrementBy*. The *PerformanceCounter* class only provides you with a *Decrement* method, which decreases the value of your counter by 1. If you wish to decrement your value by anything other than 1, you must set the RawValue. Let's review the code in Listing 14-6 to decrement our counter.

Listing 14-6 Decrementing the counter value.

```
Try
    If Not LoopCounter Is Nothing Then
        LoopCounter.Decrement
    End If
Catch ex As Exception
End Try
```

Let's say you're running a service that counts the number of active files to process in a folder. Each time a file is processed you could increment one counter to show successful processing and decrement another to show how many files are left to process.

Sample Service with Performance Counters

I have created a sample service which demonstrates the use of counters. The service, which is quite simple, demonstrates the use of counters from creation to instantiation to consuming. Let's take a look at the service, shown in Listing 14-7, and then use Perfmon to monitor the counter values.

Listing 14-7 A sample service with performance counter support.

```
Imports System.Diagnostics
Imports System.Threading

Public Class PerfCounters
    Private m_Thread As Thread = Nothing
    Private Const THREAD_SLEEP = 2500
    Private Const INCREMENT_VALUE = 5

    Protected Overrides Sub OnStart(ByVal args() As String)
        Try
            Dim StartLog As EventLog = New EventLog("Application")
            StartLog.Source = "PerfCounters"
```

```
            StartLog.WriteEntry("PerfCounters Starting",
                         EventLogEntryType.Information, 1000)
            StartLog.Dispose()

            m_Thread = New Thread(AddressOf PerfCounterThread)
            m_Thread.Priority = ThreadPriority.Normal
            m_Thread.Name = "Performance Counter Sample Thread"
            m_Thread.Start()

        Catch ex As Exception
            'do nothing
        End Try
    End Sub

    Protected Overrides Sub OnStop()
        Try
            Dim StopLog As EventLog = New EventLog("Application")
            StopLog.Source = "PerfCounters"
            StopLog.WriteEntry("PerfCounters Stopping",
                         EventLogEntryType.Information, 1001)
            StopLog.Dispose()
        Catch ex As Exception
        End Try
    End Sub

    Private Sub PerfCounterThread()
        Try
            Dim pCounterCollection As New CounterCreationDataCollection
            Dim CounterOne As New CounterCreationData
            Dim CounterTwo As New CounterCreationData

            CounterOne.CounterHelp = "Number of Loops"
            CounterOne.CounterName = "Loop Count"
            CounterOne.CounterType = PerformanceCounterType.NumberOfItems64

            CounterTwo.CounterHelp = "Number of Ticks / 4"
            CounterTwo.CounterName = "Counter Divided by 4"
            CounterTwo.CounterType = PerformanceCounterType.NumberOfItems64

            pCounterCollection.Add(CounterOne)
            pCounterCollection.Add(CounterTwo)

            Try
                If Not (PerformanceCounterCategory.Exists(
                                "Sample PerfCounters")) Then
                    PerformanceCounterCategory.Create( _
                    "Sample PerfCounters", _
                    "Demo Counters from VB Service", _
                    PerformanceCounterCategoryType.SingleInstance, _
                    pCounterCollection)
                End If
            Catch ex As Exception
            End Try

            Dim LoopCounter As PerformanceCounter
```

```
        Try
            LoopCounter = New PerformanceCounter("Sample PerfCounters",
                                       "Loop Count", "", False)
            LoopCounter.RawValue = 0
        Catch ex As Exception
            LoopCounter = Nothing
        End Try

        Do
            Try
                If Not LoopCounter Is Nothing Then
                    LoopCounter.IncrementBy(INCREMENT_VALUE)
                End If
            Catch ex As Exception
            End Try

            Thread.Sleep(THREAD_SLEEP)
        Loop
    Catch ex As Exception
        'Do Nothing
    End Try
    End Sub
End Class
```

The service allows us to see how to use counters in the code. The service supports our two counters and our single instance category. I have a single thread method, started by the *<Start>* method, that creates the category if it does not exist. Once the category is created, the thread creates an instance of the Loop Count counter and then goes into a loop where it increments the value of the counter by the INCREMENT_VALUE, which in this case is 5. The thread then sleeps for 2.5 seconds before incrementing the counter again.

Note   Each time the service is stopped and restarted, the RawValue of the Loop Count is set back to 0. This means that it will never have a cumulative total.

Service Validation

Once you create this service and run it for the first time, you need to validate that not only are the category and the counters being created but that the counters are also being incremented as expected.

Let's install the service and review the results. Once I have the service installed and run it for the first time, the category will be created. If you look in Perfmon and click the plus sign (+), you should see the following dialog box. If you don't, you should step through the code using the debugger and find out why your category was not created. If you previously had already created an instance of the category but with different counters, you will see the previous counters only, because the check to validate whether the category existed would have been successful and no attempt to recreate it would have occurred.

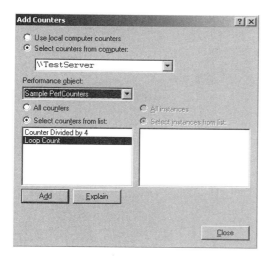

Note   To remove a category and its counters you must use the *PerformanceCounter-Category.Delete* method. Doing so will remove all performance data for your service or application.

Now let's select both counters, click Add, and then click Apply. If you have any other counters in your Perfmon instance, select them individually and press the Delete key. Once you have only the two Sample PerfCounters category counters added you should see their values, as shown in the following image.

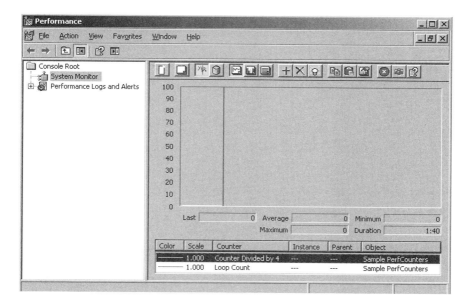

You can see that initially the counter values are at 0. To demonstrate the use of the counters and Perfmon we need to start the service. Once we start the service you should see the values of the Loop Count increase by 5 every 2.5 seconds.

Take care not to unintentionally reset your counters or to use the RawValue without providing some form of thread-safe locking.

Summary

- Performance counters come in two types: custom and system-defined.
- Custom counters are defined by an application and their values are controlled by that application.
- System-defined counters exist under the Process object and are useful for tracking down and monitoring issues in any application.
- Custom counters are nearly limitless in their use and are defined by the developer.
- Adding counters to a service is easy, but make sure that the values of the counters you expose are correct and useful. Also make sure that the code required to update these values is not so complex that it adds too much overhead to the service.
- Performance counters are read by consumers such as Task Manager and Perfmon.
- Perfmon is a generic performance counter consumer with a powerful ability to read, track, and store historical data about applications and their counters for later evaluation.

Part V
Appendices

Appendix A
Microsoft Internet Information Server (IIS)

The Microsoft IIS Service allows for HTTP and HTTPS protocol communication over TCP/IP. Microsoft IIS versions support HTTP 1.0 and 1.1 as well as ASP, ASP.NET, and many other Internet-based technologies and standards. The examples in previous chapters use Microsoft IIS Service. As long as you own a valid license for one of these products, you can install the Microsoft IIS Service by following the instructions in this appendix.

Installing Microsoft IIS

The following instructions are for installing Microsoft IIS on Windows Server 2003 and Windows Vista Ultimate.

To install Microsoft IIS on Windows Server 2003, follow these steps:

1. Click Start.
2. Click Control Panel.
3. Double-click Add/Remove Programs.
4. Double-click Add/Remove Windows Components.
5. Select Application Server. (This step varies with Windows XP and Windows 2000.)
6. Click Details.
7. Select ASP.NET, and then Enable Network COM+ Access.
8. Select Internet Information Services Manager, and then click Details.
9. Select Active Server Pages And World Wide Web Service.

You now need to configure IIS to allow usage of ASP pages as well as ASP.NET pages. To do so, follow these steps:

1. Click Start.
2. Click Run.
3. Type **Inetmgr**, and then press Enter or click OK.
4. Select Web Service Extension on the left, select Active Server Pages on the right, and then click Allow.

Installing IIS on Microsoft Vista Ultimate

On Microsoft Vista Ultimate, perform the following steps to install Microsoft IIS Services:

1. Click Start.
2. Click Control Panel.
3. Double-click Programs And Features.
4. Click Turn Windows Features On Or Off.
5. Expand Internet Information Services.
6. Select the World Wide Web Services check box.

   You now need to configure IIS to allow usage of ASP pages as well as ASP.NET pages. To do so, follow these steps:

7. Expand World Wide Web Services.
8. Expand Application Development Features.
9. Select the ASP and ASP.NET check boxes.

Installing IIS on Windows XP

On Windows XP, perform the following steps to install Microsoft IIS Services:

1. Click Start.
2. Click Control Panel.
3. Double-click Add/Remove Programs.
4. Click Add/Remove Windows Component.
5. Click Internet Information Services (IIS).
6. Click Details.
7. Select Common Files.
8. Select World Wide Web Service.
9. Click Apply.

You now need to configure IIS to allow usage of ASP pages as well as ASP.NET pages. To do so, follow these steps:

1. Click Start.
2. Click Run.

3. Type **Inetmgr**, and then press Enter or click OK.

4. Select Web Service Extension on the left, select Active Server Pages on the right, and then click Allow.

After you install the Microsoft IIS Service, you can create directories that IIS can use to allow transfer of both incoming and outgoing files. You can post and upload files and run scripts, CGI applications, ASP and ASP.NET Web applications, and download an unlimited number of HTML pages.

Appendix B

Microsoft File Transfer Protocol Service

The Microsoft FTP Service is a file transport server that allows for sharing and distributing files. Microsoft FTP Service is available on Windows XP, Windows Vista, Windows 2000, and Windows Server 2003 as used in this book for demonstration purposes. As long as you own a valid license for one of these products, you can install the Microsoft FTP Service by following the instructions in this appendix.

Installing Microsoft FTP Service

The following instructions are for installing the Microsoft FTP Service on both Windows Server 2003 and Windows Vista Ultimate.

Installing the FTP Service on Windows Server 2003

For Windows Server 2003, follow these steps to install the Microsoft FTP Service:

1. Click Start.
2. Click Control Panel.
3. Double-click Add/Remove Programs.
4. Double-click Add/Remove Windows Components.
5. Select Application Server. (This step will vary in Windows XP and Windows 2000.)
6. Click Details.
7. Double-click Internet Information Services (IIS).
8. Select Microsoft File Transfer Protocol.

Installing the FTP Service on Windows Vista Ultimate

On Windows Vista Ultimate, perform the following steps to install Microsoft FTP Services:

1. Click Start.
2. Click Control Panel.
3. Click Programs.
4. Under Program and Features, click Turn Windows features on or off.

5. Expand Internet Information Services.

6. Select the FTP Publishing Services check box.

7. Click Apply.

Installing FTP Services on Windows XP

On Windows XP, perform the following steps to install Microsoft FTP Services:

1. Click Start.

2. Click Control Panel.

3. Double-click Add/Remove Programs.

4. Click Add/Remove Windows Component.

5. Click Internet Information Services (IIS).

6. Click Details.

7. Select Common Files.

8. Select File Transfer Protocol.

9. Click Apply.

After you install Microsoft FTP Service you can create directories that FTP can use to allow transfer of both incoming and outgoing files. Normally you want to avoid having a catch-all directory to do both kinds of file transfer. In previous chapters, we needed to create both upload and download directories.

Appendix C
Microsoft SMTP Service

The Microsoft SMTP Service is an e-mail transport server that allows you to send e-mail over the SMTP protocol. Microsoft SMTP Service is available on Windows XP, Windows 2000, and Windows Server 2003 as used in this book for demonstration purposes. As long as you own a valid license for one of these products, you can install the Microsoft SMTP Service by following the instructions in this appendix.

For Windows Server 2003, follow these steps to install the Microsoft SMTP Service:

Note Windows Vista does not come with an SMTP Service, so you will need to use either Windows Server 2003 or Windows XP.

1. Click Start.
2. Click Control Panel.
3. Double-click Add/Remove Programs.
4. Double-click Add/Remove Windows Components.
5. Select Application Server. (This step will vary in Windows XP and Windows 2000.)
6. Select Internet Information Services (IIS) and press Details.
7. Select Microsoft SMTP Service.

Installing SMTP Services on Windows XP

On Windows XP, perform the following steps to install Microsoft SMTP Services.

1. Click Start.
2. Click Control Panel.
3. Double-click Add/Remove Programs.
4. Click Add/Remove Windows Component.
5. Click Internet Information Services (IIS).
6. Click Details.
7. Check Common Files.

   8.   Check SMTP Service.

   9.   Click Apply.

After you install Microsoft SMTP Service, you can set up incoming and outgoing mail directories, as well as set up relaying to other e-mail servers. We have used SMTP a great deal in our chapters for notification. You can also set up the POP3 service if you want to send and receive e-mails on Microsoft Windows operating systems for free.

Index

About the Author

Michael Gernaey is a Senior Enterprise Solution Consultant at Microsoft, with a focus on corporate solutions using BizTalk, Microsoft SQL Server, and Visual Studio. He has more than a decade of experience at Microsoft, during which time he has designed and written many large-scale application solutions for customers. This close contact with the enterprise has made him aware of the need to provide guidance for Visual Basic programmers on how to create robust, modern, service-oriented applications.

What do you think of this book?

We want to hear from you!

Do you have a few minutes to participate in a brief online survey?

Microsoft is interested in hearing your feedback so we can continually improve our books and learning resources for you.

To participate in our survey, please visit:

www.microsoft.com/learning/booksurvey/

...and enter this book's ISBN-10 or ISBN-13 number (located above barcode on back cover*). As a thank-you to survey participants in the United States and Canada, each month we'll randomly select five respondents to win one of five $100 gift certificates from a leading online merchant. At the conclusion of the survey, you can enter the drawing by providing your e-mail address, which will be used for prize notification only.

Thanks in advance for your input. Your opinion counts!

*Where to find the ISBN on back cover

ISBN-13: 000-0-0000-0000-0
ISBN-10: 0-0000-0000-0

00000

0 000000 000000

Example only. Each book has unique ISBN.

Microsoft®
Press

No purchase necessary. Void where prohibited. Open only to residents of the 50 United States (includes District of Columbia) and Canada (void in Quebec). For official rules and entry dates see:

www.microsoft.com/learning/booksurvey/